FROM
THE
GROUND
UP

SPIEGEL & GRAU

NEW YORK

FROM
THE
GROUND
UP

*A Food Grower's
Education in Life, Love,
and the Movement That's
Changing the Nation*

JEANNE NOLAN

From the Ground Up is a work of nonfiction.
Some names and identifying details have been changed.

Published in the United States by Spiegel & Grau, an imprint of
The Random House Publishing Group, a division of Random House, Inc., New York.

SPIEGEL & GRAU and design is a registered trademark of Random House, Inc.

LIBRARY OF CONGRESS CATALOGING-IN-PUBLICATION DATA
Nolan, Jeanne.
From the ground up: a food grower's education in life, love,
and the movement that's changing the nation / Jeanne Nolan.
p. cm.
ISBN 978-0-8129-9299-1
eBook ISBN 978-0-679-64447-7
1. Nolan, Jeanne, 1968– 2. Organic farmers—United States—
Biography. 3. Organic farming—United States.
4. Organic gardening—United States. I. Title.
S605.5.N65 2013
635.092—dc23
2013001393

PHOTO CREDITS: Courtesy of the author, 1, 73; Justine Kurland, 61;
Verd Nolan, 208; Donna Pinsof, 9, 28, 29, 87, 89; Hallie Pinsof, 54; Les Pinsof, 68,
123; Steve Rosenblatt, 109; Susan Ryan Photography, 166; Lawrence Siskind, 46;
Susan Paddor Varick, xiii, 155, 169, 193, 217; Jennifer Wood, 226

Printed in the United States of America on acid-free paper

www.spiegelandgrau.com

2 4 6 8 9 7 5 3 1

FIRST EDITION

Art on title page © istock
Book design by Barbara M. Bachman

This book is dedicated to my parents,
Les and Donna Pinsof,
with my respect, love, and appreciation

Though I do not believe that a plant will spring up
where no seed has been, I have great faith in a seed.
Convince me that you have a seed there,
and I am prepared to expect wonders.

—HENRY DAVID THOREAU

We shall not cease from exploration,
And the end of all our exploring
Will be to arrive where we started
And know the place for the first time.

—T. S. ELIOT

Alice Waters

I FIRST MET JEANNE NOLAN IN 2007 ON A WARM OCTOBER MORNING AT the Lincoln Park Zoo in downtown Chicago. I had come to give a talk at Green City Market next to the zoo, and my friend Abby Mandel, who had founded the market, brought me over to see the five-thousand-square-foot organic garden Jeanne had planted. It was everything you'd want an edible garden to be: towering heirloom tomato plants with fruit still heavy on the vine, lush stands of Brussels sprouts, broccoli, eggplant, Red Russian kale, Bright Lights chard. Where a patch of sweet corn had been harvested weeks earlier, the dried stalks served as a natural trellis for climbing tricolor beans. There were Moulin Rouge and Mammoth sunflowers, whose huge heads drooped under the weight of their seeds, and the split-rail cedar fence that bordered the garden was barely visible beneath the Mexican flame vine and morning glories blooming in periwinkle, indigo, and cream.

It would have been beautiful anywhere, but here in the heart of the city, set against a backdrop of skyscrapers and highways, it was particularly moving. I watched Jeanne, with her loose braid and her wide smile, engage with visitors, and I was struck by her power as an educator. As dozens of visitors streamed into her garden—

where, I later learned, some twenty-five thousand people visit in a year, most of them children, teachers, and parents—I watched them take part in a rich sensory experience, learning about the value of good food through touch, taste, smell, and sight.

This book, like an extension of Jeanne's gardens, is wonderfully approachable. It does not get bogged down in complex instructions or arcane horticultural details, but it bears facts and insights that will educate even the seasoned farmer. In clear, lively, deeply personal prose, Jeanne tells her story of following her passion for growing organic food. She is unafraid to reveal how she stumbled and struggled, and shows, beautifully, how she found her way through.

Similarly, my own life's path has been rooted in gardens. My mother tended a victory garden, and one Fourth of July, for a costume contest, she actually dressed me up as the Queen of the Garden! I was only three or four years old, but I vividly remember my outfit: a skirt made from big lacy stalks of asparagus gone to seed; a lettuce-leaf top; bracelets and necklaces made out of peppers and radishes; and a wreath of strawberries on my head. Much later, after I had opened Chez Panisse, I scavenged herbs and flowers from the gardens of my neighbors to take to the restaurant, and soon I had a large lettuce garden in my own backyard; every morning we would pick baskets full of lettuce—rocket, chervil, frisée, young romaine—for the salads we would serve. Edible gardens like this—the sorts of edible gardens that Jeanne is committed to building—connect us to the earth and to the changing seasons, to our friends and to our communities. They ground us, quite literally, and give us a deeper connection with nature.

Perhaps what moves me most about Jeanne's story is the fundamental truth that growing your own organic food has a kind of healing power. When we first started the Edible Schoolyard at Martin Luther King, Jr., Middle School in Berkeley, it was inspired by the Garden Project, a program for ex-convicts and parolees from the San Francisco County Jail who grew vegetables for homeless shelters. The Garden Project was so successful—so rewarding for its participants—that I wanted to try to replicate it in a public school (if it could do that much to enrich the lives of ex-convicts, I reasoned, think what it could do for schoolchildren!). With the Edible Schoolyard Project, gardens and kitchens become interactive classrooms for academic subjects. Children are counting beans instead of buttons, measuring the vegetable beds for their math classes, and learning about the history of civilization when they're harvesting corn. The program shows what a profoundly transformative exercise gardening can be—helping children learn the values of stewardship, nourishment, perseverance, and cooperation. Every year, the Edible Schoolyard Project is made stronger and better by the growing community of like-minded garden programs around this country, and the world.

What Jeanne shows so effectively is that virtually anyone, anywhere, can grow his or her own food—not just on rural farmland, but in settled suburban neighborhoods, in public parks, on highrise rooftops, and in abandoned inner-city lots. "After all my travels," Jeanne writes, "I had learned that the meaning and purpose

I'd sought in extremity—an authentic way of relating to self, to others, and to the earth—is, in fact, available to us all in our own neighborhoods and yards, in our own suburbs and cities." By turns a memoir, a manifesto, and a how-to, *From the Ground Up* lures the reader into this beautiful experience—the textures, scents, and the quiet, patient pleasure—of growing your own food.

INTRODUCTION

Faith in a Seed

I DON'T KNOW IF I CAN DO THIS. THAT THOUGHT CROWDED OUT ALL others as I stood in front of a five-thousand-square-foot plot of land on the southern edge of Chicago's Lincoln Park Zoo. It was a cold, gray April morning, and I was focused on the raised rows of carrots, beets, and peas that I'd planted ten days earlier. But instead of bare earth punctuated by newly germinated seedlings, what I saw before me was weeds—so spindly and numerous that when I squinted for a better look they appeared to merge together into a thick green carpet of grass. And it was my fault; I knew exactly what had happened. I'd been so excited at the chance to plant a new garden in the city that before adding a six-inch layer of compost I'd tilled and retilled the neglected soil with a vengeance. In the process, I'd driven the relentlessly persistent seeds of many previous decades of weeds to the surface. I had no choice but to kneel into the muddy soil and start yanking up the thin stalks as fast as I could without snapping off the roots, which would only spark more growth. It seemed like a hopeless task.

A tall, barrel-chested passerby stopped to watch, his hands on his hips. "That there's nut grass," he said. "That's the worst thing you can get!"

With each handful of weeds I pulled out, it felt like another would immediately jump up. My jacket, with its faux-sheepskin lining, made me too hot and too cold at the same time; after a few minutes, my jeans were soaked through with a chill at the knees, and I could feel a crust of mud forming at the center of my forehead where I'd wiped away my sweat. The heavyset stranger who'd identified the nut grass (a uniquely prolific weed that I had, in fact, encountered before, on a farm near Austin, but that extends beyond Texas to most of the fifty states including, as I experienced on that day, Illinois) sympathetically offered one last piece of advice before walking away: "Using your hands won't do it. You need a couple big bottles of Roundup!" In organic gardening—defined in *Taylor's Dictionary for Gardeners* as "growing plants without using synthetic fertilizers and pesticides"—Roundup, a glyphosate-based herbicide, was not an option.

By that moment in the spring of 2007, I'd discovered enough about myself and the local and national zeitgeist to be aware that the garden at the edge of Lincoln Park Zoo had the chance to become something big, a turning point in my own life and career and beyond that. In fact, less than six months later, Alice Waters, a pioneer of the burgeoning organic food movement, would visit the garden, and other leaders would follow. But I'd experienced so many low points before then that I knew that absolutely nothing was guaranteed.

I HAD EXPERIENCED ONE of those low points three years earlier, at the age of thirty-five, a breakdown of sorts that had brought me back to my hometown of Chicago. Standing at the baggage claim in Chicago's O'Hare International Airport, I spotted my father steadily making his way down the escalator, square-shouldered and unmistakable in his tweed overcoat, olive fedora, and polished brown shoes. His immaculate poise, which had once seemed to me oppressively rigid, now struck me as measured and dignified, the sure posture of a man who knew who he was. It triggered an emotion in me so wholly unexpected that my knees buckled from an overwhelming feeling of relief. He must have been anything but relieved at the sight of me. I was underweight, visibly distraught, and carrying a wild-haired child, his granddaughter, who was wearing dirt-stained overalls. But he smiled broadly, gathering me and two-year-old Thea in his arms, and said, "Welcome home, my beauties." We'd flown in after an abrupt departure—an escape—from a working commune in rural North Carolina.

I'd spent the previous seventeen years away from home, trying to find myself. Instead I'd gotten progressively more lost. After I returned with my father that day in 2004 to my hometown of Winnetka, Illinois, I would describe my years away in conversations and job interviews as a period of research and discovery on three large organic farms in California, Texas, and North Carolina. What I omitted was that those farms were part of an experiment in group living whose leaders viewed outsiders with suspicion and referred to the world beyond their property's boundaries as a "death culture." It was for all intents and purposes a cult.

At the age of eighteen I'd left home in what felt like a dead sprint to join that commune with the naïve and grand ambition of saving myself and the world at the same time. Inspired by Thoreau's motto from *Walden,* "Simplify, simplify," I'd lived with the commune's three dozen members in remote locations across the country, rising through the ranks from performing basic gardening tasks like composting and harvesting to eventually managing the seventy-five- to three-hundred-acre organic farms that housed and fed our community.

But instead of achieving the lofty ambitions that had led me to commune life, I'd wound up discovering, collapsed on the floor of a remote Appalachian farmhouse, that I had trapped myself and my young daughter in a place and vision I did not believe in. I had deeply wounded my parents, my sister, the rest of my family, and my friends. I had harmed everything I would once have recognized as myself; and I had found and then lost a great love. And rather than freeing myself from what I had harshly judged to be the illusions of a materialistic upbringing, I had unwittingly subscribed to another, much more damaging set of illusions. I had nowhere to go but back to my parents' house in Winnetka, a suburb of Chicago that, when I'd left, had seemed to me to be the epitome of everything wrong with American life and society.

I didn't know then, in that Appalachian farmhouse, that I was about to embark on another, much more intense journey that would change me and my understanding of the world in a more profound way than all of my wide-ranging seeking had. Strangely—or perhaps not so—I would begin to find the life purpose I'd been searching for: not in the would-be bucolic seclusion of a utopian commune, but in my own backyard, in the settled suburban neighborhoods I'd biked through as a child, and in the public parks, narrow high-rise rooftops, and abandoned urban lots of my home city of Chicago.

Ultimately, my re-immersion in these places would connect me to a movement that is gaining momentum, relevance, and popularity throughout the world. I would figure out how to use the one talent I had (or the only one I thought I had)—organic farming—to start a business, create a nationally acclaimed educational and family attraction, and work alongside mentors and friends, both new and old, to raise awareness and understanding about the transformative potential of fresh food and the impact of our choices in growing, distributing, and eating it. In the years to follow I would help to plant hundreds of gardens for families, schools, churches, synagogues, restaurants, nonprofits, and corporations; for suburbanites and city dwellers; for the wealthy and the less fortunate. I would plant them on sprawling estates, rooftops, and asphalt playgrounds, as well as in backyards and even in Chicago's Lincoln Park Zoo.

None of this seemed possible when I returned home in 2004. All I knew then was that I had wandered off my own personal path, and that the rest of my life, and my daughter's life, depended on my reorienting myself and finding a way back. I had to dig in. And I did.

Breaking Ground

Chapter 1

WHEN MY FATHER PICKED ME UP AT THE AIRPORT IN 2004, THE SUM total of my personal belongings was a faded dark green duffel bag containing most of Thea's and my clothing; an oversize backpack containing a decade's worth of journals; and a suitcase filled with a few of Thea's favorite toys, along with photographs, letters, and other odds and ends. My father insisted on carrying all of the luggage while I carried Thea on my hip, her arms clasped around my neck. She'd picked up on my anxious mood and was withdrawn, surveying the strange surroundings as she had all day but not asking her usual piping round of "Why?" questions in response to my ongoing monologue about airplanes and airports.

"This is your Papa Les, remember him?" I said as we trailed my father on the moving sidewalk through the glittering corridor toward the main parking garage. "We're going to his house."

As soon as I strapped Thea into the toddler's car seat that my parents—in the day and a half since I'd called to say I was coming—had already purchased and prepared, she began to drift off. She was fast asleep by the time my father slid the car into gear.

"We have food," he said, keeping his voice hushed as we drove through the day's gray drizzle. "Your mother stopped at Whole Foods. Milk, eggs, bananas, vegetables." He meant the organic versions; my parents never bothered with organic for themselves, but

since I'd joined the commune I'd been vocal about eating only organically. "We can stop on the way, though, if there's anything else
you need." I shook my head; my parents lived just thirty minutes
north of the airport, and after my hectic departure from Asheville,
North Carolina, that morning and the numbing buzz of travel, I
was eager for someplace, anyplace, to sit still.

"We have a crib set up for Thea," he continued. "We can put it
in whichever room you want. And your mom got a head start on
making dinner." I was relieved that he wasn't asking any of the
questions I knew were on his mind—why had I left the commune
after all this time, why hadn't I given them more notice—until I
realized, from his quick sidelong glances, that he was determined
not to say anything that might upset me and prompt me to leave
again. What he didn't know—what he had no way of knowing—
was that I had no intention of leaving, because I had nowhere else
to go.

We'd lapsed into silence by the time we turned into my parents'
neighborhood, a narrow, curving stretch of widely spaced Colonials, Georgians, and Tudors sheltered by just-budding maple, dog-
wood, and cherry trees. I reflexively pulled down the visor to check
myself in the lighted overhead mirror, suddenly self-conscious at
the thought of greeting my waiting mother. My hair was frizzy,
unevenly flattened on one side from the airplane headrest; my fingers got tangled in my bangs when I tried to smooth them out. My
clothes hung too loosely; I'd shed almost fifteen pounds in the past
few months. My eyes had dark circles under them—circles so pro-
nounced they startled me—and my face was angular, gaunt. A
stranger's face.

The final turn on the way to my parents' house took us alongside the Indian Hill golf course—one of the most upscale areas in
Winnetka—a vast, rolling expanse of green dotted with the occasional beige of sand traps. Up ahead, through the half acre of trees
that provided calm and privacy, I glimpsed the high Jeffersonian
brick front of the house. My father slowed the car and glanced

across at me, stopping a moment as though giving me a chance to collect myself before turning into the driveway. The tires crunched on the wide stretch of pebbles that served as my parents' front yard. Other than the woods in front, there was no grass or landscaping, just those small stones, making the house itself, with its oversize entrance door and wide portico, appear even more imposing.

Since I'd left home in 1987, I'd visited numerous times, but on those trips I'd always felt myself to be at a remove, sealed inside the protective bubble of the "real" life I believed lay back at the commune. There, I'd lived in cabins and in shared rooms in old rehabbed farmhouses surrounded by acres of fields and wilderness. I'd viewed everything at that time in terms of stark opposition: real versus phony, authentic versus false and materialistic; I'd dismissed the relatively grand scale of the materialism of my parents' lifestyle out of hand. Now that I had nowhere else to go, I found this house—and everything about their way of life—newly overwhelming.

My mother appeared so quickly on the front steps that I knew she must have been watching by the door. She was trim and elegant as always, in a pair of loafers, pressed khakis, a button-down blouse, and cream-colored cardigan. Her welcoming smile froze for just a moment too long as I stepped out of the car—I wondered if I looked even worse than I'd thought—but she hugged me tightly, enveloping me with a whiff of the perfume I'd known all my life, then turned toward Thea.

"Maybe we should let her sleep. . . ." I started to say. But my mom was already unbuckling her, picking her up with a fluid, practiced motion, kissing the top of her head, smoothing out her hair, and quietly hushing Thea's vaguely murmured protests as she carried her inside.

Thea's mouth gaped when my mom gently set her down in the entrance hall—as she took in the vaulted ceilings, the elegant wallpaper, the gleaming polished floors, and the thickly carpeted stairs.

She had been off the commune only rarely since her birth, and had never experienced anything like these lavish surroundings. Rather than finding this environment claustrophobic, as I had when I'd left home, I now found its orderliness and deep-pile softness comforting. I'd left civilization in 1987 feeling betrayed by suburbia, but now I was returning feeling betrayed by wilderness. I tried to fill in the gaps between these two extremes for Thea. "This is Grandma Dino, remember her?" She stared up at my mother. Though it had been some time since she'd seen my parents, on their last visit to the commune, I'd shown her pictures as I packed up, in an effort to ease the transition. "This is the dining room where we're going to eat," I said as I took Thea's hand and led her through the house, which was filling with the smell of the cottage-fried potatoes my mom was making on the stove, a childhood favorite of mine. "This is the kitchen where we're going to cook, that's the backyard where you can play. . . ."

"This is home. For now," I finished as we entered the upstairs bedroom where we were staying. Though I managed to keep my tone bright, I was thinking, *How can I possibly make this work?* On my own, I would have curled up in a fetal position on the bed, shell-shocked and disoriented, but Thea was watching me, looking for cues. I also could not bear to disappoint my parents after the obvious care they had taken to make Thea and me feel comfortable and cared for.

There was enough time for me to give Thea a bath before dinner. Though she looked around wide-eyed at the gleaming white bathroom, she relaxed in the tub. We'd had running water on the commune, but we were also sticklers for conservation and would share bathwater. By the time it was your turn to bathe, the water was generally somewhere between lukewarm and cool, depending on where in the order of things your bath fell. Thea looked in wonder at the clouds of steam rising around her, and when I splashed her, she giggled—the first smile I'd seen from her all day.

I struggled to find an outfit for her in the bags my father had carried upstairs. Every six months or so, my mother had mailed large care packages of Gap Kids clothing for Thea, who would insist on trying on everything at once, layering three shirts, two pairs of pants, two pairs of socks (she was a tomboy, and my mother knew enough not to try sending skirts or dresses). But the last round of clothes had gotten stained and torn from the largely outdoor life we lived at the farm, where the dirt constantly blew in from the fields. I settled on the least stained pair of jeans I could find and a long-sleeved top with two buttons at the front. I told Thea, as I rubbed her blond shoulder-length hair dry with the towel, "Grandma Dino's made a special dinner for you." I'd asked my mom, before we came upstairs, to make Thea's favorite comfort food, poached eggs and brown rice—normally a breakfast food, but I wanted her to experience at least one familiar thing today.

As she followed me through the downstairs hall to the kitchen, Thea looked around inquisitively. "Hi, Thea!" my mother said. Thea looked past her toward the kitchen and then at the empty den, summing up all the questions that must have been running through her mind all day with one so focused and observant it stunned me: "Where are all the people?"

After dinner, I worried that Thea might have trouble falling asleep in the new place, but she dropped off almost instantly when I turned out the light. I pulled the white quilt up to her chin and settled quietly into the bed beside her. I was exhausted, too, but my mind was racing. The question that kept recurring, what I couldn't understand, was how the hell I had reached this point in time— how I'd fallen so far from my initial, idealistic hopes for a better life.

IN SEPTEMBER 1987, in a moment that was in almost every way the opposite of my homecoming experience, my father had walked me to the gate at O'Hare for my departure to California and the commune, known at that time as Zendik Farm Arts Cooperative. I'd worn a tank top, a long cotton Indian-print skirt, and Birkenstocks with two different-colored kneesocks, and I had winnowed the contents of my life down to the bare essentials (*Simplify!*): my cat, Louie; sixteen books, including Thoreau's *Walden*, Carlos Castaneda's *The Teachings of Don Juan: A Yaqui Way of Knowledge*, and J. D. Salinger's *The Catcher in the Rye*; a toothbrush; and a backpack full of clothes. My dad had hugged me at O'Hare with tears in his eyes—my mom had been too upset to go to the airport—and I knew he was scared for me. But as I'd walked through the departure gate I wasn't scared: I was breaking from everything I knew, parting with the past, exhilarated by what I thought lay ahead. It wasn't until I got to Zendik Farm that I felt some trepidation.

Looking out the window of the cab from the airport as I'd first approached the farm in the high desert seventy miles east of San Diego—Louie, travel-weary and disgruntled, perched in my lap—I scanned the arid landscape uneasily: Surely nothing could grow here, least of all organically. The surroundings were starkly beautiful—high boulders, sparse scrub, the looming shape of the aptly named Rattlesnake Mountain rising in the near distance (rattlesnakes, I would soon learn, had infested the farmhouse before it was rehabbed). The landscape looked like a scene from a John Ford Western. But then I spotted the acres of cultivated vegetable gardens at the edge of the property—lushly, lavishly green with late-summer and early-fall crops: tomatoes, peppers, eggplant, broccoli, cabbage, cauliflower, lettuce, spinach, kale, and chard, most of them growing in three-foot-wide rows.

Soon after I arrived, when I'd finished settling my bags in the brightly painted Quonset hut that I'd be sharing with three other women, I was handed a dog-eared copy of *Rodale's Encyclopedia of Organic Gardening*. I'd mentioned my interest in learning to grow organic food when I'd first called after reading the commune's ad in a local Chicago newspaper—this was, in fact, one of the main reasons I'd wanted to join—and I was almost immediately led out into the fields for a tour and to harvest sugar snap peas. "We like to learn by doing here," Arol, the fit, charismatic cofounder and leader of the commune told me, fixing me with her intense blue eyes. (*Exactly the kind of person I've been looking for,* was my first impression as I noted her handmade ankle-length denim skirt and fossilized shark tooth necklace. *Exactly the kind of person I want to be.*)

This was, I thought, exactly what I'd been searching for in life and had started doubting I'd find. A short distance away from where I stood with Arol, down the drive that led to the farmhouse, I could glimpse the arched entrance gate where a hand-painted sign contained a play on the motto inscribed on the entrance to Dante's *Inferno:* YE WHO LEAVE HERE, ABANDON ALL HOPE.

ON OUR FIRST MORNING at my parents' house, Thea woke just before sunrise, startling me with a warm hand placed on my cheek. I reflexively reached to smooth her hair and swung my legs over the edge of the bed, murmuring a string of words that I hoped would help her locate herself and adjust. "We're in Dino and Papa's house,

MY THIRTIETH BIRTHDAY, ZENDIK FARM, 1998

remember? We flew here in an airplane yesterday. You took a hot hot bath. . . ."

Downstairs, I sat at the kitchen table and pulled Thea into my lap, looking out across the terrace to the tree-enclosed backyard. I was comforted to see a few pressed grooves in the newly growing grass where several deer had spent the night, and pointed this out to Thea. Though my parents lived in a decidedly suburban, culti-vated area, there was still enough wildlife around—deer, birds, rabbits, even an occasional coyote (sheltered in part by the nearby golf course)—for me to hope that Thea would feel some connection and kinship to the rural landscape in which she'd spent all of her nearly three years. I pulled a blanket I had grabbed from the den over her shoulders and carried her out into the yard so that she could hear the birds just waking—robins, cardinals, redwing black-birds, and a few mourning doves clumsily hop-stepping around the overflow of seed from my mother's standing feeder.

All throughout that first morning and afternoon—in between meals and getting dressed—I kept returning to the backyard with Thea, wanting something familiar for her and for me. My mother noted this and over lunch—grilled cheese for Thea—she asked if I might like her to find a jogging stroller so that I could take Thea for walks along the golf course and in the nearby area parks where, before Thea was born, I'd walked alone for hours. I told her yes and thanked her for the suggestion.

Our exchanges that day consisted mainly of carefully worded, tentative questions from my mother—about food, about whether we had enough blankets, about the temperature of the house—and my own brief answers. I knew from her hesitant tone that my mom, like my dad, was in some ways scared of upsetting me. Before I'd left for the commune, and in a series of harsh letters written while I was there, I'd been very explicit in my criticism of my parents for living the "wrong" (read: non-Zendik) way. *What's the point of your big house?* I'd said. *What's the point of all the things you buy? It's all a waste; it's nothing. It's obvious it doesn't make you happy.*

Though we'd seen one another at least twice a year since I'd left, we'd never healed the breach I'd caused between us and I had no idea how to begin doing so.

Later that afternoon, as Thea was napping upstairs and I sat with my mother staring at but not managing to actually read the *Chicago Tribune,* the phone rang. My mom answered, and then said, with her hand cupped over the receiver, "Verd." Verd, a man with whom I had been romantically involved on the commune before my relationship with Thea's father, and who had been forced out by the commune's leadership, must have heard somehow of my departure. I pictured his face—straight nose, square chin, ruddy cheeks, and vivid blue eyes. I'd believed for years that he was the love of my life.

I signaled my mom with a quick motion across my neck to say I couldn't talk to him. I felt a terrible weight of guilt for the way I'd treated Verd—letting him go, years before, without any explanation or even saying good-bye. But I was too depleted and overwhelmed at the moment to open the gateway on more raw emotions, other than those I was already struggling to address with Thea, my parents, and myself.

My mom pressed her lips tightly together, but after she hung up—telling Verd I wasn't able to talk—she refrained from asking about him. I was relieved by her silence. She'd met Verd several times on her visits to the commune, but I wasn't sure if she'd remember who he was, as she'd never been aware of my relationship with him. She did pick up on my distress, though; she walked over and put her hand on my shoulder.

Thea called out for me from the bedroom. She didn't want to let me out of her sight, and I realized, as I rushed upstairs, that I didn't want to let my mother out of *my* sight. Over the next few days, an aerial view of the house's interior would have shown a kind of comedy (if only it hadn't been so painful) of Thea constantly calling out and wandering to find me, and me constantly wandering with her in tow to find my own mother.

I wasn't sleeping—or rather, wasn't sleeping well, jerking awake from strange, fragmented dreams that slipped away the moment I tried to make sense of them. I'd always tried to find meaning in dreams: One of the beliefs at the commune was that vivid dreams gave valid information about the world around you; they signaled that you were "in tune" with yourself. A dream I'd had not long before I left, in fact, had comforted me in my leaving: Thea, or rather a wishful, imagined future version of Thea at age twelve or thirteen, tall and serenely confident in a white dress, had led me through a maze of carefully set tables in a green, hilly setting that I'd only gradually recognized as the lawn at Lake Shore, a country club my parents belonged to in Glencoe.

My current dreams, by contrast, were jagged and disturbing. As I tried to calm myself each night by listening to the rasp of Thea's steady breathing beside me, I couldn't shake the feeling that I'd left something behind at the farm—that I'd made a terrible mistake by leaving. The dreams were just collages, I told myself; they meant nothing other than my sleeping mind trying to make sense of the jumble of places and people my conscious mind hadn't yet been able to. They told me nothing that I didn't already know. I hadn't been able to live out my ideals of an "authentic" life in the wilderness, and I doubted whether I could do so in the opposite extreme of these hypermanicured surroundings. Every morning, the unavoidable mirror over the bathroom sink told me that the circles under my eyes were getting larger. And despite my parents' careful efforts with food, I still wasn't gaining back the weight I'd lost.

"You *have* to get some rest," my dad announced as I picked at dinner one night. My mom's expectant look told me that this conversation was something they'd rehearsed. "Let yourself off the hook. Let us take care of Thea for a day or two."

"That's not it," I said. I knew I'd spoken in a harsher tone than I'd intended to when he sat back and my mom got up to start clearing plates. But I was convinced that lack of rest was not the problem. Since I'd been home I'd done little but sit beside piles of books and newspapers I had no interest in reading or go for walks with Thea in her stroller through scenery that, however lovely, couldn't pull me out of my own thoughts: *You're a failure. You've hurt everyone you've ever been close to. You have nothing. You've done nothing with your life.* "I don't need rest," I said quietly as I helped Thea down from her booster chair. "I need to *do* something."

My mom was rinsing plates in the kitchen and couldn't have heard me. But the next morning, as I helped her dry the breakfast dishes, she said, "You could plant a garden."

I looked at her. *What?*

"In the backyard." I followed her gaze out the window. The large yard was enclosed on one side by the house and terrace and on the other three sides by stands of tall pines, oaks, and maples that separated it from the yards of the neighboring houses. "A vegetable garden. Like what you grew on the farm." I must have frowned because she quickly added, "If you want to."

My only experience growing vegetables had been in open fields on large farms. And my only area of expertise was working organically. My parents' backyard was chemically treated, and it was heavily landscaped: a professional crew had visited twice in the past week to perform the work of "spring cleanup" with leaf blowers, tree trimmers, and lawn mowers. Other landscaping crews had been working in the yards of houses up and down my parents' street and on the adjoining golf course, creating a constant background din I was unaccustomed to. Even if I *were* interested in planting a garden in my parents' yard, I didn't know if what my mom suggested was even possible.

Chapter 2

THE WINNETKA I KNEW AS A CHILD AND TEENAGER WAS ONE EM-
bodiment of the American Dream of the 1970s and '80s—it was a
key inspiration, in fact, for John Hughes's classic teen comedies
The Breakfast Club, Sixteen Candles, and *Ferris Bueller's Day Off.*
Stodgy, conservative, and on the affluent side of the mainstream, it
was home to roughly four thousand households, headed largely by
doctors, investment bankers, lawyers, and Realtors. Sixteen miles
north of Chicago, Winnetka is one of several well-heeled suburbs—
including, among others, Glencoe, Evanston, Wilmette, Lake Forest, and Highland Park—that are together known as the "North
Shore" and that stretch up toward Milwaukee from Chicago along
the western bank of Lake Michigan. It wasn't just Winnetka but all
of those towns—the only world I'd known—that I'd turned my
back on.

Though the cars and clothes I saw around me when I came back
had changed since 1987—from Volvos and Fair Isle sweaters to
BMWs and zip-front fleeces—I assumed it was still largely the same
place. The houses—perfectly maintained and tended—looked almost exactly the same, mostly Georgians and Colonials with long
front walkways and imposing façades, acres of grass, and endlessly
churning sprinklers. Before I returned, it was the last place I could
have imagined myself living.

I decided to attempt the backyard garden. As we began work, a landscaper from my parents' yard crew offered to help and carted in the wooden timbers that would form the edges of the garden bed. My mother led me to the garage to show me the sparse assortment of gardening tools she kept to plant annual flowers—petunias, impatiens, and geraniums—in small pots on the back terrace. I picked out some old trowels and a set of pruners, but I knew I'd need more.

I borrowed my mom's car and some money and drove with Thea to the local hardware store. The tools I'd used on the farm had seemed ancient, classic, and ageless, either purchased second-hand from local farmers or handed down from the previous tenants on the land. I was pleasantly surprised to find many of the same tools in this gleaming modern space, displayed on racks amid cartons of Miracle-Gro and chemical fertilizers: a round-nose shovel, a strange-looking hoe with a diamond-shaped head that I knew would be good for making furrows, and a hard rake for shaping raised rows. Despite differences of theory and opinion, gardening, I realized then, was just gardening.

At Zendik Farm, we'd always planted our crops in raised rows— long, deep mounds of soil roughly three feet wide, aerated to a depth of twelve to eighteen inches. Plants grow best, I'd learned, in loose, well-aerated, nutrient dense soil: The thin, filament-like roots of most plants can extend at least this far, and every extra inch of root extension in an air-rich soil allows a plant to take in more nutrients. In my parents' garden, I planned to fill the entire raised bed with twelve inches of fresh, loose soil, with rows spanning the three-foot width I was accustomed to: This would give plant roots plenty of room to grow (horizontally as well as vertically), but also allow me to easily reach across the row from either side without stepping on the soil around the roots. (Walking can exert up to ten pounds of pressure per square inch of earth, which compresses the soil.) Making clear walking paths alongside the rows would help ensure that the soil around the plants would stay loose and aerated.

Back home, I pulled out a yellow legal pad and drew a crude rectangle representing the garden plot, intending to map out what I should plant and when I should plant it. But I stopped after just a few minutes, realizing in frustration that I had no idea what vegetables would grow well in Illinois, and even less of an idea of when to plant them. On the commune, I'd lived and farmed in three very different climates, and with each new move, I'd talked to local farmers at length about their preferred crops, the native growing season, and area pests (I'd encountered everything from drought to floods, grasshoppers to fire ants). But there were, of course, no farmers in Winnetka's carefully gridded 3.9 square miles—or anywhere, for that matter, on the North Shore.

I bundled Thea up in her coat and strapped her into the car seat yet again, this time for a trip to the bookstore in town where as a teenager I'd spent hours exploring books about Eastern philosophy and Native American spirituality. I picked out some children's books to keep Thea occupied while I ran my fingers across the spines in the narrow gardening section. I was thrilled to find a copy of my first and favorite gardening book, *Rodale's Encyclopedia of Organic Gardening*. Paging through the words I'd memorized at the farm about planting depth and soil aeration, I felt like an old friend was talking to me.

But there weren't any books about the Illinois gardening season—not with the kind of hands-on information I needed, such as what specific varieties of lettuce and tomatoes would do best in the area, and what week in April or May would be the optimum time to start planting. (In California and Texas, I'd planted as early as February.)

When we got back home I stayed outside, wandering the yard for a long time. The landscaper had torn up the plot of grass where the garden would be, but he hadn't yet finished screwing together the timbers for the raised bed. Staring at what was, essentially, a dark gaping hole in the middle of my parents' manicured property, I felt another wave of doubt. I'd planted and tended acres of crops

in my life, and every kind of vegetable ranging from allium to zucchini, but this was going to be different, and not only because of
the limited space. On the farm I'd generally worked in small groups,
alongside other women who tended the fields on a regular basis,
and, during all-out planting and harvesting frenzies, with as many
as two dozen other people who'd pitch in. We would often yell
advice on planting depth and spacing to one another across the
rows. Here, I was on my own.

And after having spent years separating myself as best I could
from all things industrial and chemical, I had a hard time not thinking about the toxins already in the ground here. Lawns in general
are heavily treated with chemicals. More than eighty million pounds
of pesticides (including both weed and insect killers) are applied
each year to the roughly forty million acres of lawn grass in the
United States—pesticides that include as key ingredients chemicals
categorized by the Environmental Protection Agency as possible
carcinogens, such as carbaryl, pendimethalin, and malathion.
While lawns evolved relatively late in American history—the first
suburban neighborhoods emerged after the Civil War—80 percent
of households in the United States now have them. In the growing
season, roughly 238 gallons of water per person per day are poured
onto lawns, in addition to the two pounds of chemicals spread per
acre per year. My parents' lawn had already been chemically treated
at least once in the time I'd been home.

But ultimately, whatever the difficulties and whatever was in the
dirt, I felt fortunate to have a place to live and work. And the next
day, when the landscaper completed construction on the raised bed
and offered to fill it with a mix of sand, topsoil, and compost, I
took him up on his offer, even though I was sure none of the mix
was organic. Any forward movement on the garden felt like progress.

The few encounters I'd had with friends and neighbors in my
brief trips to town had only made me more self-conscious about
my life. Carol, a sixtyish acquaintance of my mother's, called out

my name as I tried to slink past unseen on my way back to my mom's car from the bookstore with my newly purchased *Rodale's*. She gave me an appraising glance from head to toe (baggy clothes, unkempt hair). "How are you *doing?*" she asked, her heightened emphasis on that last word making me acutely aware that everyone in town, even strangers, likely knew my story: *High school superstar goes AWOL, lives on commune for seventeen years, comes home a shell-shocked single mom.* It was a story of extremes—I hadn't just rebelled, I had repudiated; I hadn't just run away, I'd vanished off the face of the earth. And here I was back in town, chastened, if not defeated.

Carol and others seemed—in my imagination at least—to regard me with the smug satisfaction of having their own lives validated. I'd come back, hadn't I? And I didn't have much in the way of marketable skills. I'd left home in 1987; I'd missed the beginning of the rise of the digital economy and the nineties real estate boom. *What exactly,* I could almost hear these people asking, *did you accomplish?*

I ASKED MY MOTHER to pick out a fence to border the raised bed. I wanted the garden's exterior as much as possible to complement her carefully planned aesthetic. In the past, this would have seemed a petty concern to me, but I wanted badly for her to like every part of this project. After a few days of searching, she found a white picket-style fence she liked at a store in the nearby town of Niles. She insisted, however, that I go look at it first. "I'm sure it's fine," I said. She shook her head, saying, "I want it to be what *you* want." We could have gone back and forth all day—"You choose," "No, you"—because it wasn't actually a fence we were talking about but the distance and uncertainty I'd created between us over all these years.

In finalizing plans for the garden space, sourcing seeds and seed-

lings was my last challenge. Knowing little about which specific
varieties of vegetables would thrive, I'd decided simply to plant
crops I knew and see what did well and what didn't, adjusting as
the season progressed. But I had no idea if I'd be able to find seeds
that were certified organic. I looked up gardening stores in the
phone book and started driving from one to another in my mom's
car, with Thea in her car seat asking questions, which, after her
relative quiet of the first few days, I took to be a reassuring sign:
"Where are we going?" "Why are there so many cars?" "When can
we play outside?"

I hit pay dirt at a Smith and Hawken store in Highland Park
(ecologically aware enterprises such as Smith and Hawken hadn't
been prominent when I left) and loaded up my cart with seeds for
organic butternut squash, sugar snap peas, green beans, watermelon, pumpkins, several kinds of lettuce, spinach, and cucumbers,
as well as sunflowers, cosmos, and zinnias. But they had no seedlings. I was used to transplanting seedlings for warm-weather-
loving crops such as tomatoes, eggplants, and peppers; on the farm,
we'd started many of our own seeds from the previous year's crops
in greenhouses we'd built ourselves from recycled discarded glass. I
drove around to two more stores before finally finding seedlings at
a nursery in Highland Park, picking out tomatoes, sweet and jalapeño peppers, eggplants, and herbs. The plants were all yellowish
and sickly, but I thought I had no other options.

It wasn't until I'd hauled the first load of seedlings from the car
out to the garden and focused on their unhealthy yellow-green hue
that I realized I just couldn't do it. Much of gardening has to do
with understanding the possible: knowing what can and can't be
done based on climate conditions and the plants themselves. I'd
gotten carried away at the second Highland Park store by my desire
for a quick solution, but there wasn't anything I could do to save
those plants. I got back in the car and returned them. My parents'
landscaper had recommended a place called Chalet Nursery in the

town of Wilmette, and I drove there and picked out the first seedlings I saw that were sturdy and green. They were not organic but,
more important, they were not on the brink of death.

I worked hard over the next few days to prepare the garden bed
for planting. I planned a walking path straight down the center as
well as two paths along the sides. I shaped my three-foot-wide rows
with a hard rake, lined up north to south as I'd done on the farm,
which helps to prevent the taller plants from shading out others in
the sun's transit from east to west. Using a recipe adapted from
Rodale's Encyclopedia, I mixed my own fertilizer in a five-gallon
bucket in the backyard, combining ingredients from five-pound
bags of kelp meal, blood meal, bone meal, greensand (a substance
consisting in part of mineral deposits that originate on the ocean
floor), and dehydrated manure that I bought on a return trip to
Chalet.

I loosely raked the fertilizer into the top few inches of soil. On
the farm, we'd always used fertilizer (also called soil amendments)
to improve the structure of the soil and add nutrients, and it seemed
all the more important to use it here, given that I wasn't sure of the
underlying health of either my parents' soil or the newly imported
compost. The kelp meal in the mix I prepared was rich in trace
minerals and potassium (potash); the blood meal was rich in nitrogen; the bone meal was rich in phosphate; and the dried manure
was rich in nitrogen, phosphorous, potassium, and various healthy
bacteria and micronutrients—all of them essential to plant growth.

Thea worked with me as I planted in the first week of May—just
over a month after we'd straggled into O'Hare to meet my dad. She
carefully placed the seeds into the furrows made with my hoe, using
the "pat-pat" motion I'd taught her on the farm to smooth the soil
back over the seeds without pressing down too hard. She remembered the big gardens we'd had at the farm where she'd loved to
walk the rows and announce the names of plants ("Peas! Bwoccoli!
Bok choi!"), and was excited for this, her *own* garden. Every morning after we ate breakfast, Thea led the way out to the garden, run-

ning across the terrace and taking a special delight in unlatching the gate and holding it open for me.

Things seemed to be coming together. Thea was for the most part happily adapting to our suburban life, but there were some adjustments that she struggled with—in particular the societal expectation that she wear clothes. On the farm, whenever the weather allowed it, Thea and the other young children played naked both indoors and out. The farm's perspective was that this was completely natural, and we didn't want kids to think of nudity as "dirty" or "wrong." I loved it that Thea was unself-conscious in her bare skin, but after discussions with my mom I agreed that it wouldn't be safe for her to be exposed to the public in our yard, and that she should be dressed in front of my parents and visitors inside the house. We settled on the compromise that Thea could roam naked on the second floor. In our first weeks back, Thea was baffled by my insistence that she wear clothes, but over time she began to adapt to the concept of privacy.

JUST OVER TWO WEEKS after we'd planted, the thin stalks of plants in one-half of the garden started to emerge. But the other half remained a wide stretch of bare earth. I'd been so excited about the garden that maybe I had gotten ahead of myself. As I walked around the plot with Thea it became clear what had happened. My cold-weather-loving crops had all come up. It was the warm-weather crops—melons, pumpkins, squash, and cucumbers—that I wasn't seeing. Even after my research, I'd still planted too early. The first week of May would have been a perfectly fine window of time to plant in California, Texas, or North Carolina, but in Illinois, it was clearly too early; the soil temperature had been too cold.

I replanted the warm-weather crops later that morning, using the leftover seed in the packets from my first planting, with Thea again happily "pat-patting" the soil alongside me. It felt good to have solved the problem, and to work quietly alongside my child to fix it. After I'd washed my hands in the spigot alongside the house, I tried to tell my mother, who'd been on the terrace working on her potted annuals, how much this meant to me—not just the garden itself but the fact that, after all this time and distance, she still knew me well enough to have suggested it. But she was distracted, helping Thea brush the garden dirt from her knees because it was time to head in for lunch. And I couldn't find the words I'd hoped to find. I could, however, see the circles closing, and more important, I could feel it—a layer of angst lifting, giving way to the first sensations of hope.

Chapter 3

SHORTLY BEFORE I LEFT THE FARM FOR GOOD—WHEN I WAS AT ONE
of the lowest of my low points there—my mother had sent me a
letter that brought me to tears. *I'm sorry,* she'd written, *for not
listening to you more when you were in high school.* My mother—
even after everything I'd done, in my mind, to hurt her—was actually apologizing to me, going over mistakes she felt she'd made
extending back into my childhood, mistakes she felt might have
harmed me and contributed to my estrangement from my family.
*I'm sorry for not paying closer attention to what you tried to tell
me before you left.*

I was stunned by her words. We'd never talked directly about
these matters—we'd never, in my family, been very good at talking
when it came to painful, emotionally loaded issues—but more than
that, I was stunned because in my mind, *I* was the one who'd hurt
my parents. They had been, if anything, too attentive, more loving
and more concerned than any other parents I knew, and they'd remained loyal to me while I was on the farm, visiting me there, my
dad abandoning his khakis and button-downs for blue jeans and
T-shirts to try to fit in; my mom going out into the field and getting
her Tretorn sneakers dirty while harvesting beets with me. They
were sticklers for table manners, but when they came to visit they
joined our communal meals in which food was served on cracked

plates or in scuffed stainless steel bowls, everyone sitting on a couch or standing in the living room, using one fork or spoon or occasionally bare hands. Even at my angriest, it was my parents' way of life and what I saw as their narrow worldview that I'd criticized, not their personal actions.

But I understood the impulse behind my mother's letter, and I thought about it often as I waited for the garden in the backyard to germinate, going for long walks with Thea in her jogging stroller. It was an impulse to try to understand the mystery of what had happened to my life—more specific, how I (*of all people*, I was sure the town gossip went, meaning that I had no excuse) had reached this point: thirty-five, broke, and a single mom with no plans for the future.

The only way I could begin to understand it was that it was as though I'd had two entirely separate lives, parallel and often overlapping. In the first life—the life I consciously believed was mine until the age of fifteen—I was the perfect daughter and all-around good girl. In the second life—full of half-formed feelings and impulses of which I wasn't wholly conscious, hungering for more knowledge of the world, a purpose, and a wider range of human experience—I was angry, irresponsible, and at times even brutal. The bridge between the two worlds—when the first one began to collapse entirely—was Mark Peterson, a handsome, troubled, brooding fifteen-year-old. I met Mark in the late spring of 1984; he introduced me to Thoreau, and it was his influence that led me to turn my back on my parents and their values. *I deeply regret,* my mom wrote in her letter, *not trying to understand and get along better with Mark.*

But something more than Mark had set the change in motion. Looking back, the seams of the eventual break had been there all along. One of my strongest childhood memories was of playing hide-and-seek with the neighborhood kids on a warm July evening when I was nine years old. I'd slipped into a neighbor's backyard, where I'd found a garden with tall plants growing. I dove inside, feeling suddenly like I was in a domed jungle, incredibly lush and silent. I saw a cucumber dangling on the vine, and I grabbed it and bit into it. The juiciness of it was shocking, and the crunch seemed thunderously loud. I lay on my back in the rich black soil looking at the clouds through the fragrant leaves, feeling indescribably safe and still. It felt like hours later when I became aware of the other kids calling my name. In a way, I could say I'd spent a lifetime trying to rediscover that paradise, the stillness, sweetness, and safety of it, the aliveness of the senses.

I have no idea where that feeling came from: There were no gardeners in my family, past or present. My mother had never counted the few flowers she planted as gardening, and her one attempt at growing vegetables—beefsteak tomatoes, sometime in the late seventies when I was ten or eleven—had been a drooping, yellow-leafed failure. But that feeling was strong and persistent, and it had come to me again on my first day at Zendik Farm, standing in the fields.

MY CHILDHOOD HOME WAS a short drive across town from my parents' current house. It was a midsize Georgian with a tree-filled backyard on a quiet block of similar houses. My mother had been a schoolteacher before I was born and was then a stay-at-home mom until I was fifteen, when she returned to school for a degree in social work. My father worked for a company that had been founded by his grandfather, SiPi Metals Corporation, a refinery that makes metal alloys used in everything from construction materials and tires to plumbing fixtures, electronics, and metal sculpture (including the bronze used in the Oklahoma City National Memorial and Museum and the Harry Caray statue at Wrigley Field).

My dad was home every night by six o'clock, and our family—my parents and my younger sister, Hallie, and I—would sit down to dinner that my mom had cooked from scratch. Afterward, Hallie and I would finish our homework and then watch TV in the den, alternately jostling each other for a better position on the leather couch and braiding each other's hair. Hallie was (and still is) funny and ebullient. We were close growing up. She's just under three years younger than me, and in elementary school we often chose to dress like twins.

On many nights, from the time I was a child all the way into my teens, I would climb into my parents' bed while they were reading and tell them in detail about my day—whom I'd played with and whom I'd sat with at lunch, what book we'd talked about in English class, and what scores I'd gotten on my recent tests. I'd listen to them as they talked about their neighbors and friends in town— who was "insecure," who was having their kitchen redone, who was getting a new car, who was hosting a big dinner party, who was getting a d-i-v-o-r-c-e. Their talk was never mean-spirited, but their awareness of and attentiveness to these matters reflected the prevailing social mores of a community in which people generally dressed a certain way, acted a certain way, and kept their houses to a certain standard, and where any deviations from these norms were strictly noted.

Growing up, I was aware that there were some tensions in my extended family: Both sets of my grandparents were the children of Eastern European Jewish immigrants who pulled themselves up by their own bootstraps in America, but the hardships they'd endured had left shadows and scars on their families. My paternal great-grandfather had started out in the rough-and-tumble Chicago of the 1900s as a scrap metal dealer and metal alloy producer, incorporating in 1905 and only gradually building the business into SiPi. My maternal grandmother was the seventh child in a family of limited means who was forced to drop out of school during the Great Depression to take care of the household and her siblings; her favorite sibling, an outgoing younger sister, died of rheumatic fever.

My grandparents, in particular my mother's mother, Grandma

Rose, had always been warm and doting with me. Grandma Rose, as well as my father's parents, Grandma Blanche and Papa Phil, even traveled to visit me while I was on the farm (Grandma Rose, who walked with a cane, hobbled around the farm in Texas with her pants legs rolled up to the knees declaring, *"It sure is hot here!"*). But as with many in their generation, the lack of emotional intimacy and intellectual stimulation they'd experienced in their own childhoods had affected their actions as parents. They'd done everything in their power to make sure that my parents had ample opportunities to succeed in life. But they'd had a hard time communicating their emotions, believing that children should be seen and not heard.

None of that carried over into my childhood—if anything, my parents erred in the opposite direction, determined not to repeat what they felt were the mistakes of their own childhoods. My mom later told me that she remembered very clearly holding me as a baby and promising to be the "perfect mother." She threw herself into the role—cooking, cleaning, decorating the house, always willing to play board and card games with me, and letting me play dress-up in her clothes. She was energetic, pretty, petite, and had a dazzling smile. I loved watching her set out her clothes before going to a party, and I loved trying on her jewelry. There's a picture of us taken when I was four years old, of my mom asleep on the couch with me asleep beside her, spooned into her chest; the photo captures the general feeling of physical and emotional closeness we had before I turned fifteen.

My father, like my mother, was warm and caring. On trips to visit Grandma Rose and Papa Bob in Florida, my dad would arrange a day just for me and him to go deep-sea fishing together, leaving the house when it was still dark out and picking up sweet rolls on the way. He taught me how to stand on the fishing boat with my legs spaced and bent at the knees, rolling with the waves. There were never many other children on board, and I loved that my dad saw me as grown-up and capable. At the age of seven, when I actually caught a fat red grouper, I felt wildly proud.

DEEP-SEA FISHING WITH MY DAD, FLORIDA, 1974

I regret, my mom wrote in her letter, *not taking what you said when you came home from Red Pine more seriously.* When I was ten, I went to summer camp for the first time, to an all-girls sleep-away camp in Wisconsin's Northwoods. The campers slept in rustic cabins, had meals together in the large dining hall, and had no access to TV or radio. We participated in outdoor sports—swimming, canoeing, sailing, archery—and helped to clean the cabins and serve our own food. I loved it and threw myself into every aspect of life there—so much so that I received the award for best camper. But I started feeling a vague dread when it was time to return home, and on my first night back, as my mother tucked me into bed, I started crying, telling her, "It isn't right, the way we live, with television and telephones. There's a better way to be." Despite whatever intuition or longing had led me to say that, I had no memory of it until my mother brought it up years later, and I don't remember thinking anything along those lines again until I was fifteen.

When I received my mother's letter, I was living in relative isolation with Thea apart from the commune's other members in a small cabin set a short distance away from the main living quarters on the 116-acre North Carolina property. I'd been sent to live there for an indefinite period of time as punishment for a number of real and imagined rule infractions. The commune, for all its promises of personal and collective freedom, did have rules—about conversation, work, sex and relationships (with more rules about sex and relationships than almost anything else), and parenting, and I didn't fully understand the implications of these rules until I wound up on the wrong side of them, first because of my too-close relationship

SWINGING WITH THEA, ZENDIK FARM,
ASHEVILLE, NORTH CAROLINA, 2003

with the man I loved, then because I became too close to my daughter.

Every morning during this semi-isolating period in the cabin, I would wake with Thea, bathe, feed, and clothe her, then pass part of the day reading to and playing with her. I joined the larger group of forty people for lunch and dinner, but I could feel the leadership's disapproving eyes on me, and I knew that even my good friends who shot me sympathetic looks—women I'd worked beside for well over a decade, gardening, tending the goats we kept for milk, and butchering chickens; women who'd cared for me with home-brewed herbal teas whenever I was sick—would be condemned if they got too close or showed too much interest in me. Worst of all was being stripped of most of my responsibilities in the garden and kitchen, leaving me with hours (particularly during Thea's long nap times) with nothing but my own thoughts to occupy me.

Reading my mom's letter at the small table in the cabin's central room and realizing that she had struggled for the past seventeen years to figure out what had gone wrong with my life, I finally understood the gravity of my situation. What kind of life could I hope to provide for Thea in this place? What kind of mother, I wondered, was I? How exactly, given the good, caring parents I was starting to realize that I had, had I wound up in the Carolina mountains, away from those who truly cared about me?

BEFORE THE AGE of fifteen, the only unusual fact about my life was that I was Jewish in a predominantly WASP town. But aside from one incident in elementary school when a girl who was a known troublemaker called me a kike, it wasn't an issue. My parents considered themselves agnostics, and they had both WASP and Jewish close friends.

At New Trier High School, I excelled as a student. I joined the Social Service Club, got nearly straight As, and became an Illinois

State Scholar. I was elected student body vice president, and many mornings I'd set my alarm for five o'clock so that I could arrive at school an hour early to prepare for student government duties that included setting up a new communication system, with one student per homeroom designated to act as a liaison who could voice student concerns at faculty and school board meetings. On school nights, I went to great lengths planning my outfit for the next day—choosing from a selection of cable-knit or monogrammed sweaters with button-down shirts, turtlenecks, pleated corduroys, and Top-Siders—standard *Sixteen Candles* preppy fare. Before the night I met Mark, I was well on my way to acquiring a life checklist in keeping with the preppy-yuppie aesthetic and values signaled by those clothes: good high school, good college, good graduate school, and job as a lawyer or doctor—all things that I would, just three years later, be dismissing as hallmarks of the "death culture" of mainstream American society.

I didn't normally go to. parties in high school because I disapproved of my friends' smoking and drinking (years later, my mom would laugh when recalling that she had worried I was too much of a prude), but in the spring of my sophomore year, I went with friends to a party at a classmate's house celebrating the end of final exams. I immediately noticed a sandy-haired guy sprawled across a couch in the living room: Mark. He was at once morose and deeply charismatic, interior and intense, unlike anyone I'd ever met. He claimed to be bored by the party—bored by everything about Winnetka, in fact.

While I'd always been a good student, I'd never before thought about literature as relevant to *life*—the way Mark, with his passionate quotations from Thoreau and Hermann Hesse, made it sound—and I started reading some of the books he mentioned in our first long conversation. Thoreau's *Walden* was one of his favorites: "Rather than love, than money, than fame, give me truth. I sat at a table where were rich food and wine in abundance, and obsequious attendance, but sincerity and truth were not." Flipping through the book and finding passages like this, I was hooked. Friends told me Mark was a druggie, a stoner, but nothing deterred my interest. I started spending all my free time with him, pushing the limits of the curfew my tolerant parents had never before felt the need to set. I knew they didn't like Mark—my mother pointedly remarked, after meeting him for the first time, that he wouldn't look her in the eye when he shook her hand and that this was a sign of "bad manners"—but they didn't forbid me to see him.

Mark was a lover of the outdoors, and he took me to area parks that I'd driven past all my life but had never before explored. The topography of the North Shore is less flat and more widely varied than I'd realized, pressed out and layered by the same thick sheets of glaciers that formed the Great Lakes. Mark showed me a series of forest preserves around Winnetka—the Skokie Lagoons, Somme Prairie Grove, Allison Woods—that revealed something close to the landscape's pristine, undeveloped form. There were rocky paths, boulders, hidden streams, and hundred-year-old pine and deciduous trees. Mark loved to wander golf courses as well—the North Shore contains dozens of them—at night in particular, when their hypermanicured perfection dissolved into a spectral expanse on all sides that eroded the boundaries between earth and sky. It was on one such night, after hours of kissing in a park near Lake Michigan, that I had sex for the first time, and I connected the physical excitement I felt in the act with my sense of discovery in everything else I was reading, seeing, and experiencing at the time.

Sex with Mark could be exhilarating—he was patient and gentle but also unafraid and intense. At the same time, it sometimes left me, after a quick flush of pleasure—hurrying to get dressed in his bedroom during school lunch breaks—with a nagging feeling of incompleteness. But because I had no other knowledge of sex, and nobody to discuss it with, it felt like a secret that Mark and I were inventing together, and I wanted to learn and experience more and more with him. *I love you,* he'd whisper as we lay on a deserted golf course under a star-drenched sky. *Eternally.*

The flip side of Mark's passionate intensity was a tendency toward depression that could be overwhelming. Not long after we started dating, he confessed that he'd had thoughts about killing himself going back to the age of nine. He told me that he wanted to live "truly" or not at all. I took his depression as a further mark of his authenticity.

One day in a local forest preserve, Mark and I found ourselves almost face-to-face with a doe that clearly wanted to cross over into an area that was sealed off by a tall chain-link fence—I was close enough to see every flutter of its panting chest and the drops of spittle trailing down from its mouth. The tableau summed up Mark's general philosophy, that the natural world, along with "authentic" ways of living, were being ever more encroached upon by modern civilization. He wasn't politicized and felt no call to action—very few people in Winnetka in the 1970s and '80s were aware of larger environmental issues—only a deep anger and depression. He often said he'd been born in the wrong time in history.

Mark always dressed simply, in jeans and T-shirts, and I started dressing differently, too, abandoning my preppy gear for mismatched hippie-ish clothing that my parents hated: two-different-colored socks, beaded macramé choker necklaces, a wool hat in warm weather. Before meeting Mark, I used to love walking down the wide central hallway of New Trier, smiling and waving at all the students and teachers I knew, feeling recognized and important, part of a community. But now I found myself feeling distanced, distracted, and dismissive of their cares and concerns about grades, meetings, sports, and clothes. "Our life is frittered away by detail," Thoreau wrote. "Simplify, simplify."

I asked my father, one night around that time, what he lived for, and he answered, "To make money, so that I can take care of my girls." I was disgusted by his response. I'd started seeing things in terms of either/or: Either you lived in the materialistic world or you lived an ascetic, spiritual life; either Winnetka was all good or it was all bad. Money, big houses, cars, vacations, and clothes had nothing at all to do with the real, authentic life I was starting to become determined to find.

In November of my senior year, with the feeling that I was about to jump off a high cliff, I called my parents into the den to talk. My dad was still dressed in his business clothes, and my mom wore a red plaid skirt that she kept smoothing nervously. The brown leather cushion beneath me groaned as I leaned toward them. "I don't want to go to college," I announced. "I'm dropping out of school." I let this settle. "And I'm moving in with Mark." Mark had dropped out of school eight months earlier. His parents, who were in the middle of a divorce, had tried to get help for what they recognized as clinical depression and did their best to discipline him, but he shut himself off from them and came and went as he pleased, and we spent uninterrupted hours alone in his bedroom. Before the shock even registered on my parents' faces, I walked out of the room, headed upstairs, and locked myself in my room.

I tried to ignore the sound of my parents' voices downstairs and then moving up into their bedroom as they engaged in a heated discussion until late into the night. They arrived, finally, at a consensus; the plan presented to me the next evening (after either my mother or my father must have spent a considerable portion of the day on the phone to New Trier) was that I could stop going to classes if I wanted. I'd taken a number of AP courses and had almost enough credits to graduate. They would arrange for a tutor to come to the house a few times a week to help me complete my remaining credits. But moving in with Mark and his family was out of the question.

I went along with their plan—I was still just seventeen, a minor, and felt I had no choice—but I resolved to move in with Mark as soon as possible after I graduated. I was angry with them, angrier than I could ever remember being. They were blocking me from what I saw as my "real" life, and I punished them by barely speaking to them for the remainder of the school year. I rarely ate meals with them and spent all my time when I wasn't with Mark in my room, which I'd made into a kind of bunker, the walls draped in tapestry, my mattress dragged onto the floor. I would sometimes hear my father or mother lingering outside my door, looking through the keyhole to make sure I was still alive. At their insistence, we went together to see a family therapist. But nothing would have made a difference. Less than two months after I graduated, I moved with Mark into a small apartment in Wilmette.

I got a job at a hot-dog stand and then another doing minor sewing repairs at a dry cleaner's. Mark worked at a local shop fixing outdoor lawn furniture. We were saving up money for the grand plan we'd dreamed up together: to buy a camper van and journey out to New Mexico or Arizona so that we could experience the beauty of that landscape and find a different way of life.

After several months during which I barely spoke to my parents, answering them in clipped monotones whenever they called, Mark and I had saved up enough to buy a dark brown 1969 VW camper with a pop-up top that we nicknamed "the Buggy." A week or so before we headed west, my dad called and asked to see me. One evening, I went with him to Tower Road Beach at Lake Michigan in Winnetka. I told him we'd be leaving soon. He said he had known that the day was coming; he'd felt it was inevitable. There wasn't much else to say, but I could feel how hurt he was. The night we left town, he met me as we were driving away and handed me an envelope with three hundred dollars of "emergency cash." I accepted the gift, again aware of the hurt I was causing, but also aware that I had to go.

The southwestern landscape was indeed beautiful; we camped in state parks in the mountains of New Mexico for two months before heading to Arizona. One afternoon, a state trooper pulled us over on a winding wooded road within the Gila National Forest. After checking our licenses, he said, "Jeanne, your parents are worried about you. Please give them a call." I hadn't spoken to my parents in well over a month; my father had given our license plate number to the New Mexico State Police and requested a search for the van.

Mark and I eventually settled in Flagstaff, where I found another part-time job to support us. But Mark's depression was growing steadily worse, and sometimes he'd drink himself sick. He was dismissive, as he'd always been, of my suggestions that he get counseling or help. We argued about this, and by the time we cut short our hegira and headed back to Illinois that July, our sexual and romantic relationship was effectively over.

Mark did make one more attempt the following year to find the better way of life we'd imagined, working for a time on a ranch in Texas. But he returned again to Illinois, and his depression spiraled further out of control. The last time I saw him, on a summer evening after our trip in the camper, we walked through one of the forest preserves we'd explored in high school and reminisced about the time we'd spent together. He told me with conviction that he was sure I'd find the place and the people I was looking for someday. I didn't realize then that he was saying good-bye.

I wasn't surprised, a few months later, at Zendik Farm in the high desert of Southern California, to receive a phone call from my dad telling me that Mark had committed suicide. I set down the phone and sat for a few moments in silence. Mark was my first love, and so much a part of me in so many ways that it was hard to imagine a world without him in it. But in a strange sense, I also understood his suicide. When my tears finally came, I even saw what had happened as inevitable. He did not, he'd always insisted, belong in the world as it was. He had been unable to find a truer, more naturally rhythmic way of life or a way to believe it was possible to make the wider world a better place.

BY THAT TIME, I believed that I had found the life that I wanted to live. Though our experience in New Mexico and Arizona hadn't been what we'd imagined, I had gained something of lasting value from the trip. At a small store in Flagstaff where Mark and I had stopped to buy groceries, I'd seen a sign advertising "organic" produce—a term I'd never heard applied to food before. A customer who came in just after me, a fit, pretty blond woman in hippie clothes riding a bike with a big basket in front, talked at length with the shopkeeper about the organic vegetables he was selling. She was excited, enraptured, passionate about this food, and after she left I asked the shopkeeper what, exactly, *organic* meant.

It was 1987, and I was blown away when he told me that most food was grown with chemicals. I knew a little bit about how the pollutants from industry affected air and water quality—and the crying Iron Eyes Cody "Keep America Beautiful" commercial against littering and pollution was omnipresent in my childhood. But I had no idea that most of the food in the United States, the food I'd been eating my entire life, had been grown with chemicals.

Most food produced prior to the 1940s would have been what we now call *organic*—grown on small to midsize family farms, with soil fertilized largely by the waste of local farm animals. But that changed when a wealth of chemicals became widely available in the postwar industrial boom, most notably for agricultural purposes anhydrous ammonia and DDT. Anhydrous ammonia became a cheap, quick way to boost nitrogen content and productivity, but it and other industrial fertilizers damaged the underlying balance and biodiversity of the soil, creating a vicious cycle as more and more chemicals were added to increase the food-growing capacity of the less and less inherently productive soil.

The damage to the health of the underlying soil, coupled with the rise in the number of large industrial single-crop farms beginning in the 1950s, also made food crops more vulnerable to insects and disease, and this contributed to multiple applications of pesticides. Between the mid-1940s and 1960, more than two hundred new chemicals were developed for use as pesticides; synthetic pesticide use increased from 124,259,000 pounds in 1947 to 637,666,000 pounds in 1960. By the early 1990s, according to the EPA, roughly 60 percent of all food consumed in the United States contained detectable levels of pesticides.

When I returned home from Arizona, moving back in with my parents with little in the way of explanation or apology, I resolved to find a life that was connected to farming and organic food. My discontent with mainstream society and my desire to find what I viewed as a better, "truer" way to live had coalesced around this one issue. But I had no idea what I could actually do.

It was my mom who found an ad for Zendik Farm. She was a private person and she'd kept much of her confusion and sadness about my odd, drawn-out rebellion to herself. But she had recently started working, and one day she voiced some of her concerns to a sympathetic colleague. She was relieved that her colleague had a word for me—"Oh, so she's *earthy.*" The colleague mentioned an ad that she'd just seen in the Chicago *Reader,* a free local paper, for "a kind of artsy place that does gardening and all that." She brought the ad in for my mother the next day.

I knew this was exactly what I'd been looking for the moment I set eyes on it: *"Apprentice on Farm/Arts Cooperative outside of San Diego. Learn organic farming, animal husbandry, carpentry, dance. Must be hardworking."*

Chapter 4

I CALLED ZENDIK FARM WITHIN MINUTES OF READING THE AD. THE FIRST question I asked of the upbeat-sounding man who answered was about food and farming. I was standing in a guest bedroom that doubled as my dad's home office. "I was wondering," I said, wrapping the phone cord tight around my fingers, "what you mean by 'organic farming.' I mean . . . why organic food is important to you. To the cooperative."

"You know what's happening to the earth, right?" He was both patient and urgent. Before I could shape the thoughts and impulses I'd had over the past few years into a coherent answer, he continued. "The planet is dying. There are chemicals in our air and water, chemicals in our food. The earth is being destroyed and we're trying to do something about it."

I was floored by this: In the almost three years since I'd become aware of these issues, this was the first time I'd had a conversation with anyone who'd captured my fears and concerns in such direct language. "How?" I managed to ask.

"Showing the way," he said. "Providing a model for the world of better ways to live, ways that are respectful, not destructive. We try to live in balance with the earth. We conserve our resources. We rehab and build our own houses from recycled materials; we compost our food and farm waste. Growing food is a big part of it—

living off the land, leaving the soil better than we found it. All of us here cooperate, we help each other by communicating honestly, being real with each other. Have you read *The Catcher in the Rye*?"

I was shocked by this reference to one of my favorite books from someone who'd already put into words so much of what I'd been feeling. I saw Holden Caulfield as a hero in his stance against everything "phony," conformist, and materialistic, and I kept a copy of the book beside my bed.

"We're trying to be the catchers," the man said, to "preserve innocence and idealism. That's the only way forward."

I was hooked, so wildly excited that at the end of the call I rushed into my parents' room looking for my mom. I could hear the swish of water in her bathroom—she had said she'd be taking a bath—and though we weren't any more comfortable with nakedness in my family than we were discussing sex or difficult emotions, I couldn't contain my excitement. I knocked, and she called me in; she drew up her knees as I sat on the edge of the tub. It's a testimony to the nurture and care that she'd given me that even as I was rejecting everything about her way of life, I wanted her help and approval in doing so.

"I'm so glad," she said when I'd finished my breathless narrative about shared philosophies and *The Catcher in the Rye*. But after a brief pause, she followed with some practical questions that I'd known she would ask and that I'd managed to address before hanging up the phone: Where exactly was the farm located? (In the town of Boulevard, roughly seventy miles east of San Diego.) What exactly were the terms of the apprenticeship mentioned in the ad? (The apprenticeship lasted six weeks, for a cost of two hundred dollars for room and board.) But then she added a few other questions I hadn't anticipated. "He said 'commune'?" she asked. *Communal* was the word he'd used in describing the living arrangements, but he hadn't contradicted me when I'd asked if by that he meant a *commune*. I'd heard the term several times growing up, most notably in the eighth grade during a workshop on creativity that had culminated in a student performance in which we all wore 1960s-inspired hippie clothing and played a recording of the Beatles' song "Baby, You're a Rich Man," with its critique of materialism, to an assembly of well-coiffed, well-to-do parents, many of whom complained to the school board afterward. The word *commune* referred, I'd thought, to something from the past, a history lesson, a vanished way of life.

"'Commune,'" my mother continued, "not 'cult'?" This was 1987, less than ten years after the mass suicide and murder of more than nine hundred men, women, and children in Jim Jones's Peoples Temple cult. My memories of the news stories about that horrific event were graphic enough that I realized I should, in fact, try to gather more information about Zendik before leaping into a potential abyss.

I ran to grab a blank legal pad from my father's office and again perched on the edge of the tub, pen in hand. I scribbled down questions as my mother and I thought of them: *Was* Zendik Farm a cult? Would I be free to leave any time I wanted to? Would I be free to make phone calls any time I wanted to? Would my family be able to visit me? How far away were the nearest farms or houses? Some of these questions, we decided, I should look into myself, and some I should ask directly of someone at the farm. I headed off first to do research at the Winnetka public library, but I couldn't find anything about Zendik Farm Arts Cooperative specifically in any card catalog or microfilm database. I did find what seemed to be useful information about communes in general. The dictionary definition appealed to me immediately—*a group of people not all of one family sharing living accommodation and goods.* This was what I most wanted—the possibility of finding a group with whom I could share everything, people who would understand my views and make me feel not as isolated and purposeless as I had often felt in Winnetka.

Communes in the United States, I read, actually dated back long before the 1960s: the Harmony Society founded a chapter in Penn-

sylvania in 1805; Brook Farm, a transcendentalist group in Massachusetts chronicled in Nathaniel Hawthorne's *The Blithedale
Romance*, was launched in the 1840s; the Oneida Community in
upstate New York, well known today for the silverware its members
handcrafted, was founded in 1848. Though the social, economic,
and religious beliefs of these groups varied, they shared in common
the desire to build a utopia—a concept that dates much further back
in time, to Plato's *Republic*, written between 380 and 360 BCE, and
Thomas More's *Utopia* (the first actual use of that term), written in
the sixteenth century. I thumbed through the dictionary to *utopian*
and found what the man on the phone at Zendik Farm had described, what I'd been searching for ever since reading *Walden* and
Siddhartha: *advocating or constituting an ideally perfect state.* One
of the books I'd found contained a photo of a commune from the
1960s: a group of men and women in a desert-like setting dressed in
clothes that had a vaguely Wild West, outlaw, pioneer look. Some of
the men wore Davy Crockett raccoon caps, and the women all had
long, flowing hair. They were young, tanned, and good-looking, all
of them grinning with an air of ease and confidence that I craved for
myself.

WHEN I MADE my second call to the farm, right after returning home
from the library, I asked my mom to sit next to me—both to reas-
sure her and to make certain for myself that I addressed all of our
remaining questions. I was relieved that the same man from before
answered—it hadn't occurred to me that someone else might until
I sat waiting while the phone rang for what seemed a long time. He
responded patiently to my questions. Yes, I could leave any time I
wanted; yes, I could use the shared phone in the main house any
time; there were no close neighbors but there was a bus stop just a
few miles away; family and friends were welcome to visit any time.
"Look," he said with a trace of humor as I reached the end of my
list. "You sound like an intelligent young woman. It's simple—if

you come here and you don't like it, you can leave. If you come here and you do like it, you can stay." My mom squeezed my hand and nodded *okay* to indicate that she didn't have any other questions.

Over the next few weeks, I felt a newfound sense of purpose as I made arrangements to go—packing up my neo-hippie clothes, picking out which books to take with me, buying the plane tickets my father insisted on making round-trip. My mother and I came up with an escape plan "just in case": If I arrived and didn't like it—if I had any reason to think that it was, in fact, a cult—I'd call my parents and start speaking French. Though none of us knew more than the basics, they'd know I was signaling trouble, and they'd arrange for some close friends of theirs who lived in San Diego to drive out immediately (with the police if necessary) to get me.

But from the moment I set foot on the farm, I felt certain our precautions weren't needed. Just as I'd hoped, the thirty or so Zendik members—most of them, like myself, in their late teens and early to midtwenties—shared my concerns about the environment. We discussed these concerns at length in impassioned conversations over shared dinners of fresh-grown organic vegetables and farm-raised meats in the high-ceilinged dining room. "Jacques Cousteau says the oceans are dying," someone would say, "and American culture responds with *The Love Boat.*" "One hundred unique species of life are being lost a *day*," someone would say, "and nobody's even paying attention."

I felt a new kind of closeness not only to the group, but also to the natural world as I immersed myself in the hands-on work of gardening. Zendik Farm's property encompassed seventy-five acres that were located less than ten miles from the Mexican border to the south and from the Anza-Borrego Desert State Park to the northeast. Much of the property was wilderness, marked only by narrow hiking and riding trails with stunning views of desert washes, wildflowers, rock formations, and boulder-strewn mountains and canyons, as well as fleeting glimpses of wildlife, including rattlesnakes, turkey vultures, coyotes, mule deer, and red-tailed hawks.

The farm was accessed by a narrow dirt road that led up from the entrance off a main road. The first part of the property visible on the two minutes' drive in were the vegetable gardens where I spent most of my days—two acres of wide, raised rows and stand-alone patches for asparagus and berries, all of it interplanted with colorful sunflowers, tithonia, marigolds, and cosmos. Beyond that was the arched entrance gate with the Dante quote, and past that, large flower beds bordered by rock walls, then the living quarters—four Quonset huts painted with bright murals, and an old rehabbed farmhouse with a glass addition made from recycled materials. Beyond the farmhouse there were several barns, enclosed paddocks, and pastures for the Alpine and Nubian goats we bred and kept for dairy, draft horses, donkeys that had been airlift-rescued from Death Valley, chickens, and turkeys. The donkeys had not been native to Death Valley; they were brought there by miners and prospectors seeking their fortunes in the early 1870s. Over the years, burros escaped or were turned loose. They adapted well—too well—to the environment. As their numbers increased, burros impacted the springs, vegetation, and the landscape through their proliferation of trails. They were airlifted out by the Fund for Animals, which was founded in 1967 by prominent author and animal advocate Cleveland Amory. The donkeys had a good life on the farm, amid other rescued and domesticated animals. Dogs and cats roamed freely, along with several geese and assertive peacocks. Louie fit right in until she disappeared after we were at the farm for about a year. We assumed she'd been eaten by coyotes. We often heard coyotes howling at night, and cats had died that way.

There were two outhouses (the house had running water and a bathroom, but we generally used the outhouses as they were more environmentally friendly), and a materials storage area (a junkyard, really) where old machinery and recycled materials such as bricks, boards, and glass from tear-downs were kept until they could be used in other projects.

The leaders of Zendik Farm liked to change locations roughly every five to ten years for reasons that I never clearly understood. They said they were seeking out a more comfortable climate and more fertile farmland; there was also the practical economic consideration of selling a property that had grown in value and buying more affordable land elsewhere, as well as the loftier stated goal of spreading the Zendik way across the country. With every move, it was hard to leave the land we'd come to know so well, and the buildings we had rehabbed and constructed by hand, but the new locations were always beautiful.

We moved from California to Texas in 1991, in a rickety caravan of dozens of trailers filled with animals and farm equipment. The new property was located in Bastrop, thirty miles outside Austin. Its three hundred acres afforded a beauty no less stunning in its way than that of the California farm. It was bounded on two sides by a U-shaped bend in a river that we often swam in to escape the intense heat; the shade trees and coolness of this spot had, in earlier centuries, made it a watering hole for buffalo and a favorite hunting ground for Native Americans. The surrounding rural countryside was lush and green, with rolling hills, woods, and lovely fields of bluebells and other wildflowers. We expanded the farming operation in Texas to include several different types of grain—field corn, oats, triticale, spelt, and millet—for a total of roughly two hundred cultivated acres. We also expanded the barn area and added more goats, bringing the total to sixty, plus a few dairy cows and pigs. The uncultivated parts of the property were rich with sprawling centuries-old pecan trees, and in the fall all of us would gather overflowing buckets of the ripened nuts.

The North Carolina property, where we moved for the milder climate in 1999, was a 116-acre farm that had been in the same family since the 1800s. It was located about forty-five miles outside

HANGING OUT AT THE FARM IN TEXAS

Asheville in the town of Mill Spring. The farm's specialty had been sweet potatoes—a crop, like blueberries, that thrived in the high acidity of the native soil—and in addition to an old barn and a nineteenth-century Appalachian farmhouse with a porch built on piles of craggy rocks, there were two potato-curing houses (sweet potatoes need to sit in a well-ventilated space at 85 to 90 degrees for two weeks after the harvest), all of it tucked into a lush valley with a creek running through it. We built several new structures, including a large cob kitchen and dining hall and a free-form log cabin with enormous windows. From the gardens where I worked I had an unobstructed view of a cluster of mountains that were part of the Great Smokies.

In my seventeen years at Zendik Farm, I learned more about growing organic food than I ever could have hoped to. Starting with my initial experience tentatively harvesting snap peas on my first day in California, I learned every step of the farming process through hands-on daily work: hauling huge piles of barn muck to the compost pile to preparing large barrels of "compost tea"; enriching the soil with kelp meal, gypsum, colloidal rock phosphate, and other amendments; planting wide varieties of vegetables and discovering which combinations of plants worked best together (basil planted among tomato plants attracts beneficial insects that prey on hornworms, for example; dill or fennel planted with members of the brassica or cabbage family repels cabbage worms and loopers; castor bean plants repel gophers; tomatoes and potatoes should not be planted next to each other as they're both in the nightshade family and become more vulnerable to pests in close proximity); tending; and finally harvesting.

I learned the value of "green manure"—of planting cover crops such as alfalfa, clover, hairy vetch, and winter rye, which are then worked into the soil, to enrich it with nitrogen, improve its texture, and discourage weeds. I learned how to build cold frames, also called low tunnels, to add five to ten degrees of frost protection and extend the growing season for vegetables such as spinach, lettuce, kale, and chard, attaining year-round growth for those crops in California.

I learned other, broader lessons about organic farming as well. My friend Kare was in charge of animal husbandry, and I learned from her how to make herbal poultices and mixtures of carrot juice and molasses to help tend to sick goats. I spread feed for the chickens and held them for butchering, learning the hard way to hold *very* tight in order to keep them still and prevent their running around after Kare delivered the death blow to their necks. I also learned how to defeather and gut the birds. I helped rehabilitate animals that had been injured. I learned how to milk goats and how to make the kefir that was one of our main sources of dairy. And I learned the most basic and sweat-inducing of farm tasks: how to muck out a barn without throwing out your back. We grew grapes, strawberries, raspberries, and blackberries, and I learned the names of fruits I'd never heard of before—cherimoya, sapote, and guavas—and the best ways to harvest them. In California, we drove out to the orchards and organic farms around San Diego to gather those fruits, as well as figs, pomegranates, persimmons, apricots, and other fresh-picked, sun-ripened delicacies that astonished me with the depth and intensity of their flavors.

Though our ideal was to be entirely self-sustaining, we weren't able to grow all of the organic grains, beans, and herbs we needed ourselves, so we sourced those products as locally as we could— for the cost savings as much as for environmental reasons, researching to find the local and regional suppliers for the nearest Whole Foods or other health food stores and making arrangements to order in bulk. Our diet included some goat meat, from the young male goats butchered on the farm (that was one task I chose to sit out); some red meat we ordered in bulk; the chickens that we raised and butchered; and some fish we ordered whole from area suppliers. We kept bees, and sweetened fresh-baked goods with our own honey. Overall, in the height of the gardening season, our diet consisted of roughly two-thirds foods we grew or raised ourselves, though in the winter that number might fall to as low as one-third.

The shared task of cooking was one of my favorite parts of communal life, with different individuals and small groups rotating through a loose schedule. I often made chicken soup from scratch with my friend Kare, boiling the bones to make a rich broth, and huge stir-fries out of onions, carrots, broccoli, greens, tofu, and ghee, as well as big heaping bowls of tossed salad. By the time we moved to Texas, I was in charge of one or two dinners a week, working closely with two other people who'd help with the prep. Though the meals themselves eventually became a source of great pain and friction—they developed into a forum for group criticism of members, like me, who violated the commune's often unspoken rules—in my first days, months, and even years at Zendik Farm, throwing myself into the work and shared rhythms of daily life, I felt that I'd finally found my true home. I clung to that feeling far longer than I should have, long after my doubts and frustrations had started to outweigh it.

———

TWO MONTHS AFTER MY RETURN to Winnetka, the garden I had planted in my parents' backyard was finally coming to life. After days of waiting and miles of walks with Thea in her stroller, I finally spotted sprouts from the second round of seeds we'd planted when the first had failed. Thea marveled at the arrival of the new green shoots, which gave way over time to thicker stalks and spreading leaves, bright splashes of flowers, gradually swelling fruit, and ultimately an abundance of plant life in that enclosed space that I hadn't anticipated. I was used to the farm's more spread-out growth, but here everything was condensed—it was a veritable mutiny of peas, cucumbers, melons, eggplants, berries, green beans, sweet and jalapeño peppers, squash, pumpkins, red onions, lettuce, spinach, kale, and chard, bordered by mammoth sunflowers, cosmos, and zinnias.

Thea and I began tending the growing plants. I applied "side dressing," gently raking in additional fertilizer from the mix of kelp meal, bone meal, blood meal, greensand, and dehydrated manure that I'd prepared before planting to help boost nutrients and growth. I did this in particular for the eggplants, tomatoes, and peppers, which tend to have longer growing periods and therefore a higher likelihood of depleting soil nutrients. I also practiced foliar feeding—spraying liquid organic fertilizer directly onto the leaves (plants can absorb nutrients not just through their roots but also through their leaf pores) roughly every two weeks, always spraying in the early morning or late evening, when the pores were more receptive and the leaves less vulnerable to scorching from direct sun.

At the farm, the use of foliar feeding and side dressing to boost soil nutrients had been so effective that in California, in what were essentially desert conditions, we'd grown a field of corn so tall it might well have been in Iowa. There, I'd mixed up batches of "compost tea" and "manure tea"—water in which I steeped giant bags of compost or manure. To make the tea, I would fill fifty-five-gallon barrels with water and add fresh compost or manure in burlap sacks that functioned as huge tea bags, using a ratio of roughly two parts water to one part compost or manure. I would remove the burlap sacks after three to five days and then spray entire rows of leaves with the "tea" from a five-gallon sprayer strapped to my back. I didn't need as much fertilizer for my parents' small garden, and the mixing process itself would have been too messy, so instead I used a store-bought concentrate of fish emulsion and seaweed that I diluted and sprayed on the plants.

The work in my parents' garden was energizing. It wasn't just the physical labor that invigorated me. I was also glad to have something with tangible results to focus on, something outside of my mind's swirl of anxieties. And I loved watching Thea enjoy the garden as it grew. In the beginning she walked and crawled around the "baby" plants; eventually she was looking up to observe the vining plants and flowers as they grew taller than she was, stretching her arms up high toward the tops of the green stalks as they unfurled beyond her reach.

The spinach and lettuces—green and red oak-leaf, freckles romaine, and butterhead lettuce—were the first foods ready to be harvested, and in early June, right before dinner one evening as my mom finished setting the table on the terrace, I pulled off enough leaves to fill a large bowl. I hurried inside to soak them in cold water, "hydro-cooling" them, a technique I'd learned to keep lettuce crisp and fresh. I mixed a simple dressing I'd learned to make on the farm—apple cider vinegar, nutritional yeast, tamari, and olive oil—and after drying the leaves, I tossed it all together in a bowl. My father in particular loved it, and I felt gratified when he went back for seconds.

The air was starting to cool as we finished eating; my mother had brought out a jacket for Thea, who sat in my lap. Feeling Thea resting against my chest and looking at my parents as they sat relaxed in their chairs, breathing in the air that carried the heavy scent of earth and vegetation from the garden, I felt something close to happiness for the first time since I'd been home. "I can't believe I'm actually here," I said. "With you . . ." My voice caught. "I can't, either," my father said. "We never imagined this." My mom nodded, smiling back at me, and I felt in that moment that she understood—they both understood—that I was talking about more than just this moment: that I meant the ways they had supported me all along, and how the path I'd followed when I'd left was the one that had ultimately brought me back home.

AS THE BACKYARD GARDEN yielded more and more food, I started to regain some of the weight I'd lost, feasting on fresh tomato and cucumber salads, grilled eggplant slices, and berry smoothies. I was sleeping somewhat better, too, and finally felt strong and rested enough to answer some of the phone messages left by childhood friends who were still in Chicago, including Pammy Swartchild and Mollie Karger, friends since nursery school who'd heard of my return through the inevitable small-town information network. My relationships with my friends from Winnetka had become strained over the previous seventeen years. Some of them had tried to stay in touch, writing letters and occasionally calling. Mollie had even visited me once in Texas. My sister, Hallie, had been the most persistent in staying in touch, calling regularly and visiting whenever she could at all three locations. But the commune's leaders implicitly discouraged too-close contact with anyone who didn't live there.

Family and friends were always "welcome" to visit at the commune, but the leaders—Arol, a former actress in her forties, and Wulf, a failed sometime beat poet and novelist in his sixties—insisted on passing the final judgment on everyone and everything. Visits from friends and family would often be followed by Arol and Wulf's "honest," supposedly definitive commentary. My father was dismissed as "Daddy Warbucks"; my mother as a "typical guilt-inducing mother." Outsiders who didn't share the commune's bohemian aesthetic were labeled "uptight" and (the commune's ultimate insult) "square." These comments pained me, but I didn't voice my objections because there was so much I loved about my life there, and I understood from early on that if I directly crossed the leadership, I would be forced to leave.

Even minor disagreements could cost you. Arol played favorites among the group's members, giving and pointedly withholding her approval. For my first year or so, after Arol had welcomed me on my first day, I had very few one-on-one interactions with her. But on the night I received my dad's phone call telling me that Mark had killed himself, Arol, who had heard the news, invited me upstairs to the suite that she and Wulf shared in the main farmhouse.

Their space had the feeling of a private zone or sanctuary: People entered only by invitation. I walked upstairs with a sense of occasion. Arol and Wulf each had their own bedroom, next door to each other just past a small seating area at the top of the stairs. Beyond that, there was another bedroom and a small kitchen with a wall of windows looking out on the breathtaking high desert scenery. The décor was more bohemian than hippie—dark-toned couches with bright, multicolored throw pillows covered in Indian prints. On the kitchen walls was a collage of pictures, including multiple photos of Arol when she was an actress in her twenties in Hollywood (she'd had a minor role on the 1960s TV show *Petticoat Junction*)— dramatic, beautiful images capturing the full force of her charisma, which, I thought, had only grown since then. There was a photo of a beatnik Wulf from the late 1950s, working at his old-fashioned typewriter while living on the Left Bank in Paris. There were other pictures from the early days of Zendik Farm, which had been started outside Los Angeles in 1969 as a commune for young artists, primarily musicians, who wanted to "drop out" of mainstream society. The photos showed people with long hair and dresses, large floppy hats, hand-carved instruments, and a classic sixties school bus painted dark purple. Drugs had been a big part of early farm life, and during the first decade of Zendik Farm, its members were "raw fooders," eating only vegetarian, uncooked foods. By the time I arrived in 1987, the drug use was waning and the group had incorporated cooked foods and occasional meat. A few months after my arrival, the group decided en masse to collectively quit smoking both marijuana and tobacco and to wean themselves off caffeine and alcohol in order to be healthier and more productive.

Arol's room was long and narrow, with a wall of windows looking out toward the rocky outcropping of Rattlesnake Mountain. Its most unusual feature was a claw-footed bathtub set along the opposite wall from the queen-size bed. There was no bathroom upstairs, but there was running water both to the kitchen and that tub; on later occasions, I'd talk to Arol as she bathed, with an ease and comfort with her body that was quite different from how I'd been raised. That night, Arol wore a handmade lightweight poncho-type top with loose-fitting pants; Wulf wore the patchwork bathrobe he often wore even during daylight hours (because of his emphysema and chronically bad health, he rarely left their living suite). We didn't talk directly about Mark's suicide, but I knew that was why they'd invited me upstairs. Their invitation meant a great deal to me. It was a mark of acceptance and approval, a sign that they were drawing me closer. They talked about the weather and the harvesting tasks to be done the next day (it was September, and there was a large amount of work ahead) and about their dogs (they always kept at least half a dozen, unleashed and forever jostling around the farm and their suite). They spoke with a kind of familiarity that made me feel at home. Arol and Wulf seemed to share my belief that the wider world was false, materialistic, destructive to the earth, and inauthentic. The word *zendik*, I'd learned shortly after my arrival, was Sanskrit for someone who was a heretic or outlaw, someone who did not follow the established order. These people were doing the very thing I believed had to be done to make the world a place where creative people like Mark would choose to live.

I don't remember what I said in our conversation that night, but

AROL AND WULF'S "TREEHOUSE," ZENDIK FARM,
AUSTIN, TEXAS, 1995

soon afterward Arol drew me closer and began giving me more responsibility—not only in the garden but also on the business and activist side of the farm's operation. I was proud that she had seen something in me, but I was also aware that there was a dark side to her praise. Of all of Zendik Farm's unwritten codes, one of the most pervasive was eschewing privacy. The only phone we could use for personal calls was located in the living room, the farm's central social gathering place. We were almost never alone when talking to friends and family, and we felt constantly monitored: Any excess of warmth we showed to an outsider was taken as proof that we valued the wider world too much and weren't fully committed. There was always bound to be someone listening who would pass on news of any questionable behavior to Arol, whose playing favorites encouraged competition and a certain amount of backbiting. I was criticized so sharply for the particular warmth I showed Hallie in phone calls ("Maybe you'd be more comfortable back *home* in Illinois with her") that over time I called Hallie less often, and toned down my enthusiasm in conversations with her and other outsiders. Eventually, my friends stopped calling.

I WAS SORRY FOR the distance I'd allowed to grow between us, but when I called Mollie Karger back not long after my return home, she dismissed my concerns and invited Thea and me to a gathering of friends and their children at her home in Chicago. Pammy and her children would be there, as would Joanne, a friend of ours since fifth grade who was visiting from New York.

Mollie lived in a contemporary house she'd designed in the city's Lakeview neighborhood. The forty-five-minute drive from Winnetka took us down Sheridan Road and then to Lake Shore Drive, past the glittering sweep of high-rise apartments and office buildings overlooking Lake Michigan. After so many years of living in rural locations, I felt uncomfortable in that steel and glass landscape, which made me all the more nervous about facing my old friends. My mother, whom I'd asked to come at the last moment, pointed out the lake and bright-colored sailboats to Thea with determined cheerfulness.

If Mollie and the others were surprised to see my mom with me, they didn't show it. Mollie smiled excitedly when we arrived, and Pammy and Joanne jumped up from the couch to hug us. Thea shyly clung to my legs as they greeted her, and clung still tighter when Mollie rounded up the children to introduce them. "She just needs some time to warm up," I said apologetically.

I pulled Thea into my lap as I sat down on the couch. Mollie led the conversation as Pammy and Joanne joined in, trying to include me as though I'd never left. No one asked me any intrusive questions or spoke to me in a tone that implied there was anything unusual about my life or current situation. There was no way they didn't know that I was back home living with my parents, and that my once vaunted ambitions hadn't turned out as planned. But everything about their ease of manner and light, casual tone was intended to show me that I wasn't judged by them for any of it—that I was accepted.

Their good intentions left me feeling almost worse than if they had been appraising or skeptical. They weren't judging me, but I'd been judgmental of them during all my years away; I'd viewed myself as superior, a "warrior for the cause" of saving the world. And while my own life had been unraveling, they'd been accomplishing tangible things: They all had careers, husbands, houses, and resources, as well as an air of confidence about their choices and in themselves that I lacked.

After we'd been there a short while, Mollie rounded up the kids to head downstairs to a playroom. They were all happy to leave the adults, barely bothering to look back at their mothers—except for Thea, who shook her head fiercely.

"It'll be fun, sweetie," I assured her.

"No!" she cried out.

"It's okay," I said. "Look, the other kids are all going."

She shook her head again, clinging to my leg and repeating, "No!"

"Mommy will be right here."

She started crying loudly, angrily, and I scooped her up, giving an apologetic smile to my friends as I headed down to the basement playroom with her. She quieted when she saw I wouldn't leave, gradually letting herself be drawn by one of the older children into playing with a set of blocks.

I found myself upset, not by Thea's behavior in itself—she'd rarely let me out of her sight since we'd been back—but by what I was worried my friends thought of me as a mother. *A bad mother*— that had been one of the sharpest criticisms I'd faced at Zendik Farm, a phrase that still echoed in my mind. On the farm, parents were sharply criticized when their children acted out. It was considered a reflection of the parents' own emotional dysfunction. Children were expected, as soon as they could, to work alongside adults, doing everything from tending the gardens and animals to cleaning and cooking. Anthropologically, the theory went, this was how early humans developed; only in modern civilization did children come to be spoiled and coddled away from their natural state.

Most crucially, parents were discouraged from having "too close" bonds with their children. It was for my bond with Thea that I'd received the harshest criticism. Although parents were always held accountable for their kids' behavior, children were seen as the children of everyone in the group; close parent-child bonds were believed to interfere with the child's bonding with the community as a whole. In retrospect, after reading about the attitudes toward child rearing both of early experiments in group living like the Oneida community and later arrangements such as kibbutzim, I've come to understand that these beliefs are not unusual for such groups. But at the time, I took very personally the criticism and punishment I received for the close connection I'd formed with Thea, including my "exile" to the cabin with her. And whatever the logic of or justification for the punishment, it just did not work for me. Nothing changed my behavior. From the moment of Thea's birth, I felt an intense love for her and couldn't hide my strong desire to hold her or the fact that my eyes went first to her in any group or room. She was mine, and no well-intentioned or wrong-headed theory could or would change that.

Even before she could talk, Thea had also resisted efforts by commune members to interfere with our bond. Each set of parents had a small cadre of about six people on the farm, mostly younger women, who would regularly help take care of a baby or toddler. By the time she was about ten months old, Thea could identify our group caretakers and, when she saw them approach, would thrust out her hand in rejection while uttering a defiant shrieking sound. She often refused to quiet down until I'd carried her away.

My mother sought me out in Mollie's basement playroom. Reading my mood, she gave me a reassuring squeeze on the shoulder. "Thea's just moved halfway across the country," she said calmly. "She just needs time." For all the progress I felt I'd made since coming home, I realized that I needed time, too.

Chapter 5

As I HEALED SLOWLY, DAY BY DAY, IN THE REFUGE OF MY PARENTS' guest room and in the garden, the good memories of my time at Zendik Farm still mingled with regret. I often lay awake at night thinking about Arol's relentless criticism of my inability to be a good member of the group, of my inability to correctly mother Thea, and—the next strongest area of criticism after my parenting—of my too-close relationship with a man I'd come to love, "Verd" Nolan. Sifting and putting to rest those negative aspects of what had happened during my time at the farm was a large part of my unfinished business.

Verd's real name was Philip. Everyone on the commune took on new names to symbolize their new identities. I chose Shey, a riff on the name of the title character of the Western novel *Shane,* which had made a lasting impression on me when I'd read it in the eighth grade. He picked Verdant, a word he had loved ever since he'd first learned it in a fifth-grade English class—"*verdant*: green with life"—and inserted it into sentences whenever he could. I shortened his *Verdant* to *Verd*. A high school dropout ten years younger than me, Verd joined the commune a few years after our move to Texas. He had a pale Irish complexion, blue eyes, and strawberry-blond hair down to his waist. He'd grown up in Oak Park, a Chicago suburb just twenty miles from Winnetka, on a quiet street in a shingled two-story house with a small vegetable garden, a crab apple tree in the backyard, and a porch where the neighborhood kids loved to congregate. He was gregarious and warm, and after being surrounded on the farm largely by people from the East and West coasts, I loved sitting around and listening to him speak in the flat Midwestern intonations I'd known all my life.

In high school he'd been a bright but restless student, more interested in graffiti, break dancing, and bongs than in attending classes. He'd spiraled into a depression when his girlfriend dumped him for another guy, and started skipping full days of school to work at a kennel where he cleaned cages for $6.50 an hour. One evening at a party, in February of his junior year, he saw a Zendik magazine a friend had picked up at Lollapalooza with an advertisement for the farm's apprenticeship program similar to the one I'd seen.

Verd's father, also named Philip, had a master's in public health and was a community organizer on Chicago's West Side and a public mental health administrator. His mother, Annette, a kind and honey-voiced woman from Oklahoma, was the head psychiatric nurse at Edward Hines, Jr., VA Hospital and later at Michael Reese Hospital in Chicago. They were hardworking and devoted parents who, like mine, trusted their kids and gave them a lot of freedom. Verd's older sister, Kisten, was athletic and popular, an accomplished dancer and a strong student who rarely got into trouble. When Verd first started skipping school at fifteen and then experimenting with drugs, they'd sent him to a child psychiatrist who determined that there was nothing clinically wrong with him except mild ADD. The doctor prescribed Ritalin, but Verd hated the way it made him feel and threw away the pills. He had begun to express a serious interest in farming, and when he described the ad for Zendik to them, his parents thought the farm could be a healthy, drug-free environment where he could follow his ambitions. They called both the local police and the FBI to do a background check on Zendik Farm, and, satisfied that it wasn't a cult and wasn't completely cut off in the wilderness, they put Verd on a train to Austin, Texas.

THOUGH MY FIRST and most lasting impression of Zendik Farm was of wilderness—in its proximity to unspoiled nature and our separation from the wider world—life there was, in fact, an eclectic mix of wilderness and contemporary society. The farm was always connected to the "grid," with running water and electricity. There were several cars available for use by members, as well as computers, stereos, and a television in the main living room, where kids—in spite of the strict codes about raising children—would sometimes be left to watch cartoons. There was a Zendik band that included a keyboard, acoustic bass, electric guitar, and electric bass; the band played jazz/blues–inflected music for which Wulf wrote many of the lyrics, and every year or so we'd advertise for a concert and host other bands (primarily alternative rock) and as many as a few hundred fans. Though we did not, as individuals, receive a wage or use money to purchase goods or services from one another on the farm itself, Zendik's operations—its property taxes, supplemental food, and utilities—were largely financed by a series of trips undertaken by its members (including me) to sell Zendik magazines, CDs, T-shirts, and bumper stickers (the most popular featured the slogan STOP BITCHING, START A REVOLUTION) on hip street corners in cities across the country and at concerts and festivals such as Lollapalooza, Ozzfest, the Chicago Blues Festival, and Mardi Gras. We were, in that sense, financially dependent on the society we were critiquing.

The farm attracted people from all walks of life. They included a Juilliard-trained classical musician, former marines, high school dropouts like Verd and near-dropouts like me, brilliant MIT and Harvard grads who were otherwise social misfits, and a tattooed ex-con seeking to kick his drug habit. Some came from as far away as Canada, Japan, Colombia, England, and Australia. I formed

ZENDIK FARM, ASHEVILLE, NORTH CAROLINA, 2002.
THEA AND I ARE SEATED AT THE CENTER.

close friendships with people I would never otherwise have met and developed a much fuller understanding of American society in my partial removal from it than I would have in the relatively narrow world I'd known on the North Shore. The members' varied backgrounds led them to pursue a variety of interests on the farm—everything from gourmet cheese making to electronica music, beekeeping, metalworking, tattooing, painting, mechanical repair, and farming with draft horses.

Verd's first job at the farm was to work with me in the garden, learning basic skills—starting with weeding. I watched him that first day in our large onion patch as he tackled a sprawling mass of thistle, curly dock, and bull nettle. He worked without stopping for half the day, red-faced and dripping sweat. Though he'd never gardened seriously before, he had an affinity for it—and for most jobs on the farm, in fact. He was a quick study in everything from cooking and animal husbandry to masonry, carpentry, and welding. But his passion was dancing, and when he wasn't working he spent most of his time in the farm's dance studio, practicing everything from ballet and jazz to modern and hip-hop, often for hours at a time.

I began to crave his presence—his warmth and kindness, his confidence and optimism. His only flaw was that he seemed to view clothing as an integral form of self-expression and was at times the single worst dresser I had ever seen, which was saying something on a commune full of people who were consciously rejecting the status quo. We dressed in a number of different styles—from combat fatigues and T-shirts with stenciled Zendik slogans to Daisy Duke–style cutoffs and tank tops. We tended toward simplicity and earth tones; on a working farm this was the most practical. Verd, on the other hand, had multiple piercings and an affinity for bling. Typical outfits would consist of a black silk shirt and vintage black leather bell bottoms one day, huge overalls the next with chunky rings on every finger. His look—equal parts hippie and hip-hop— would have turned heads in Times Square. Set against the rolling farmland of rural Texas, he was an especially peculiar sight. But he was, for all that, *Verd,* and even when his outfits made me cringe, I loved his bravado. I loved that he managed to be himself, distinctively, even among a group of iconoclasts. I felt good when I was around him, more carefree, relaxed, and alive than I could ever recall feeling.

ON THE COMMUNE, the rules about sex and romantic love paralleled those about parenting: Exclusive pair bonds implied a threat to the greater whole. This was again essentially a corrupted application of anthropological research—of the idea that much of what was wrong with the modern world derived from the fact that humans had strayed from their natural, "true" states of being. The argument went that human beings had evolved in groups rather than in nuclear family settings, sharing equally the duties and pleasures of life ranging from the gathering and preparing of food to child care, finding shelter, and sexual partners. Returning to these prehistoric patterns of behavior in work and daily life was, in this view, recovering a state of nature, reclaiming something akin to innocence.

Arol and Wulf's stated belief about sexuality was that it should be celebrated as the highest form of human and social communication, and as such it was regarded as a talent, a skill to be practiced and deepened. They stressed communication—touching, talking, discovering what you liked and didn't, and being carefully honest with your partner about those likes and dislikes. The specific rules about sex on the commune revolved around a notion of "dates." A *date* meant sex. Typically, people used a third party to help arrange dates. So, for instance, if someone was interested in a date with me, a friend would ask me on his behalf, thus avoiding the uncomfortable prospect that anyone would have to turn down anyone else face-to-face. Certain cabins (or "fornicatoriums," we occasionally joked) were set aside for these rendezvous. At the farm in Texas, there was a sign-up board on which any couple could request a location for a date—and through which everyone always knew whom everyone else was "dating." After a date, it was the norm to discuss explicit details of the encounter with others, and to openly voice any lingering feelings.

Arol and Wulf alone were exempt from the sign-up board; they had their own private quarters in Texas as they had in California and had been together as a couple since the 1960s—when Wulf (taken from his last name, Wulfing) was forty-two and Arol (adapted from Carol) was twenty-four—and they were, in their own way, committed to each other. Arol, by all accounts, had been an ardent believer in Wulf's vision and talent since she had first read his work, when he was trying to make it as a novelist; though his literary ambitions weren't realized, she continued to believe in his vision of the world. He was a kind of organizing cause for her, giving her the focus to design and run the day-to-day operations of the farm. Her belief, in turn, helped to prop up and sustain him in spite of his poor health and lack of acknowledgment from the world at large.

But their relationship was far from exclusive. They each had a series of (always younger) lovers on the farm, and they each always knew who the other was sleeping with—usually right next door. They sang the virtues of such openness in relationships, and described themselves as superior and sexually enlightened, but they struggled over the years with an off-and-on jealousy. At times they'd return to a monogamous relationship, only to break off from it again. Their own complicated union, however, did not stop Arol from wanting to guide and direct the sexual relationships of others at Zendik Farm, monitoring, criticizing, and punishing people whenever she felt that too strong a bond had formed.

In the beginning, the general transparency about sex at the farm appealed to me. I'd become so frustrated with the repression of the subject of sex that it felt like a welcome change. It made sense to me that sex, if approached safely and with compassion, could be a particularly meaningful way to connect with and understand others while at the same time exploring and understanding oneself. Sometimes on the farm a sexual encounter would be awkward and fizzle, and other times it would lead to powerful and unexpected chemistry and a breaking open of boundaries. Either way it was a learning experience. And it seemed to work. Things could go quietly, even smoothly, for months. But the system could become a source of enormous conflict if you came to desire one person and only that person, to the exclusion of others. I started to feel that way about Verd—intensely and completely connected. For the first two years we tried to avoid the inevitable, continuing to have dates with other commune members. But eventually it became impossible for either of us to be with anyone else.

Verd and I started seeing each other exclusively, leaving our encounters undocumented. We flouted periods of imposed celibacy (commune members were encouraged to be celibate for various periods during the year, supposedly to create space for introspection). Eventually Arol, who was aware of our growing romance—or, as she saw it, our splitting off from the group—started in with a campaign of humiliation. Since I was ten years older than Verd, she described the relationship as a power play on my part, saying that Verd was my "dildo" and that I was using him solely for my own physical pleasure. She criticized me for slacking off in my work because I was consumed with this scheme, and said I was causing Verd to slack off as well. I was, she said again and again, threatening the "survival" of the group.

At the time, I couldn't imagine any kind of life outside Zendik Farm. I basically equated leaving with committing suicide. When we were finally presented with an ultimatum to end the exclusive relationship or leave the farm, I'd lived with the group for almost thirteen years. I wasn't sure if I even *had* a self beyond the commune—my identity had become submerged in the notion that I was a key member of a self-sustaining community creating a model that would somehow (the mechanics of which were always vague) save the world. I believed at my core that we had noble goals—of cooperation, of honesty, of simplicity, of living responsibly and respecting the earth—and even as we fell short of those goals, giving up on them was not an option.

I ended my relationship with Verd. There was no explicit breakup; I just turned my back on him. I ignored his longing glances. I moved to the other side of the garden when he arrived, and across the dining hall when he entered. I have often thought about the pain I caused him, and have been humbled and grateful for his ability, years later, to forgive it. But at that time, it cost me in ways I couldn't understand. In moments alone I dissolved into shrieks and sobs, thinking it couldn't be possible to hurt as much as I did and continue to live. At night I cried silently so my roommates wouldn't hear. I couldn't admit, though, that I was wrong, because admitting that I wanted Verd above all meant facing that I needed to change my entire life. I craved privacy and quiet and space to think, but I shared a room with eight other women. And there wasn't much tolerance in our community for anguish. Not long after our breakup, on a cold fall morning, without saying a word to me beforehand, Verd left.

IN THE AFTERMATH of that relationship, one longtime friend helped me more than any other. Bryan (farm name Chen, taken from the *I Ching*, an ancient Chinese text that functions as an oracle) was the first person I'd ever spoken to at Zendik Farm—it was he who'd answered the phone during my initial call and talked to me at length about *The Catcher in the Rye*. Bryan had been a long-term member and true believer in the commune's environmentalist and anti-consumerist stance—in all the things we'd discussed in that first call. I related to his background as well: He'd been a student body president and star quarterback before leaving home. He was smart, intense, good-looking, and serious; he'd read widely in philosophy, psychology, religion, and anthropology. He was older, in his early thirties when I joined the group, and had quickly become a friend and mentor, alternately teaching me the basics of ecology and commune philosophy and teasing me affectionately. I admired and trusted him, and he showed enormous kindness and strength of character as he helped me regain my footing.

We would spend hours walking in the woods and talking. *What do you want in your life—what do you really want?* In my personal life, I'd most wanted two things: deep romantic love, and to become a mother. It was starkly clear to me that I couldn't have my vision of romance at Zendik Farm. But I still wanted a child. I was almost thirty-two, and the more I thought about it the more I realized that this was something I was afraid of missing—a profound human experience that I worried I might already have missed. Admitting that to myself was like opening a door. I talked with Bryan, the person at the farm whom I most respected and had grown to love as a friend, about having a child together, and we decided after significant discussion to try.

Whether to have a child on the farm was generally left up to the individuals involved. Arol discouraged certain people from having children if she felt they weren't ready. But there was never any pressure to have kids, and, in fact, only seven children were born in all the years I was there. We used natural methods of birth control, practicing fertility awareness techniques that we learned from a women's clinic in San Diego. We women used thermometers to take our basal body temperatures each morning (an indicator of ovulation) and we kept detailed charts of our menstrual cycles. Dates were always arranged in advance, so each evening after dinner the women would gather for "spec checks," *spec* being short for speculum. Each of us had our own speculum, and we would help each other with vaginal exams, looking for additional visual signs of ovulation (such as the consistency of cervical mucus and the size of the cervical opening). We could then make an informed choice about whether to go through with a date; if the woman might be fertile, the couple could opt for a date without intercourse. The "spec check" practice added to the sense of community and kinship among the women and was largely successful. Unplanned pregnancies were few and far between.

Like the other women who gave birth in my time there, I had regular appointments throughout my pregnancy with a local midwife in the neighboring city of Asheville. Walking up and down the farm's long dirt road with Bryan for exercise in my ninth month, I imagined what the baby would look like—whose eyes, whose hair and smile. I was ravenously hungry from the start to the end of the pregnancy; that and the baby's size (just under nine pounds) made me certain it was a boy. Both Bryan and I were pleasantly surprised when, as we'd secretly hoped, the baby turned out to be a girl.

Bryan was an attentive and extremely dedicated father to Thea—though, like me, he was eventually criticized for the intensity of his bond with her—pushing her on a swing for what seemed like hours, walking through the woods with her perched on his shoulders, and pointing out trees, insects, flowers, and wildlife. Thea's first full sentence was "I love you, Daddy." Over time, he voiced his differences with the leadership, for reasons I would only later come to realize were valid—in large part, defending me from Arol's harsh criticism. He was forced to leave just a few months before I finally did. He was crushed, later describing this as the low point of his life, but he was barred from the property and had no choice.

Arol demonized Bryan after he left, calling him "selfish," "egotistical," "irresponsible," and a "sellout." Even though I knew on some level that this wasn't true, that he'd always been good to Thea and to me, I'd been too weak to argue. In the years since, I've thought a great deal about my failure to stand up to Arol. The closest I can come to understanding it is to admit I was indoctrinated. From the age of eighteen, my sense of right and wrong was heavily

AROL, MY MOM, AND BRYAN, 1998

influenced by my desire to please her and live up to the ideals of the commune.

My departure from Zendik Farm, after all that had happened there, was, in the end, anticlimactic, more of a reprieve than an escape. My depression and sense of alienation only deepened after Bryan left, when it hit me, truly for the first time, that I was alone with Thea in a place where there was no other real advocate for her. My uncertainty about the future turned to apprehension, and I felt like I was sleepwalking through my days. I wasn't able to contribute to the life of the farm in any of the ways I had done before. And the farm itself was changing. After a long decline, Wulf had died from emphysema in 1999 in North Carolina. Soon after his death, Arol was diagnosed with the cancer she would later die of, and without her longtime partner she became more and more volatile and hot-tempered. She started alienating and then systematically ousting the members of the commune who had been there the longest and who had their own ideas about how the farm should evolve. Then Arol started planning yet another big move, to West Virginia, and I simply could not fathom moving. I couldn't bring myself to participate in the preparations to once again uproot our community. When Arol suggested that I think about leaving—not permanently, just for a short break—I knew that if I left I wouldn't be coming back.

On a warm morning at the end of March, I called my parents from a phone in one of the commune's shared offices. My father answered and I immediately said, "I need to come home." He asked me when. I said, "As soon as possible."

There was a pause as he registered what I was saying and the urgency in my tone. "Do you need me to come get you?" he asked. I said I thought I could get home on my own. We agreed that he'd book us a flight for the next day.

That afternoon, I stood in my bedroom on the second story of the rehabbed old Appalachian farmhouse, packing up our belongings—clothes; Thea's picture books, most of them mailed to her by my mother; photographs, including pictures of me pregnant with Thea. Every once in a while I'd stop and look out the huge window by my bed overlooking the old barn and the mountains. People were walking back and forth—from the kitchen and the main house to the mechanic's shop, the barn, the fields, and the goats and horses in the pastures—in the steady rhythms of the farm's life that for years had meant everything to me. The following morning, sitting beside Thea in the backseat of one of the farm's cars, an old Subaru station wagon, as a friend drove us to the airport, I watched the mountains and the road to the farm recede behind me and recognized that an entire way of life was ending. I had no thought of a new beginning.

AT MY PARENTS' HOUSE, two months after my return, the backyard garden was growing by leaps and bounds—so much so that I realized, as the sprawling plants gradually obliterated the paths I'd planned, that I'd planted too abundantly. The sunflowers eventually grew twelve feet tall; the heirloom tomatoes became almost insultingly red, plump, and heavy on the vine; the pumpkins swelled to an enormous girth beneath massively broad leaves; the butternut squash grew so wildly that by the end of the summer it threatened to jump the fence and invade my parents' manicured lawn. My mom was so impressed with the beauty of this riotous growth in what had previously been a flat, unremarkable stretch of grass that she became determined to get a picture that would "do it justice." She pulled out her camera and experimented with perspectives from across the lawn and from the terrace, even climbing a chair before deciding that a ladder was the only possible way to capture the effect of the whole. We carried a stepladder from the garage, and she stood at the top, leaning this way and that, and snapped several shots.

Though my parents had always loved to have parties, they'd put their social lives largely on hold since I'd been back. A few weeks into June, my mother asked me if I'd be up to having some old family friends over for Sunday brunch. Jean and John Berghoff, a striking couple I'd known my whole life, had a grandson who was close in age to Thea, and my mother thought he'd be a good playmate.

Jean and John were kind and encouraging to me. Jean was one of my mother's close confidantes, and I was sure she knew as much as anyone about what I'd been through and what I'd put my parents through over the years. But I didn't feel self-conscious or accused by them. When Jean asked "How are you doing?" I knew she didn't have anything but the best hopes for me; when she asked if I had any plans yet for the future, I felt comfortable enough to answer honestly that I'd been trying to get by one day at a time. We sat on the terrace looking out toward the garden, chatting about my interest in growing food among other things. John was on the board of Green City Market, a farmers market in Chicago that focused on local and sustainably grown foods.

Later, when they said good-bye, John told my dad that Abby Mandel, the founder and director of the market, had said in passing that she was looking for an assistant. John asked my dad if I might be interested in applying for the job.

It was news to me that there was a farmers market of any kind in the city of Chicago. But after months at home, I now felt strong enough—physically, at least—to start thinking about work. Though my parents had been more than generous, I didn't want to be dependent on them forever. I quickly called John and told him that yes, I was definitely interested.

11.

PLANTING

Chapter 6

WHILE I WAITED TO HEAR BACK ABOUT AN INTERVIEW WITH Abby Mandel and Green City Market, I worked with my mom to prepare for Thea's upcoming third birthday in July. We'd decided to invite over a small group of close family and friends—Grandma Rose, who now lived in an assisted-living apartment in Chicago; my uncle Bill and his wife, Suzan; and Mollie Karger and Pammy Swartchild and their families, including their parents, who were longtime friends of my parents. We also invited Bryan.

Our relationship had been strained after his departure from the farm, but he had come for a visit in early May. When Thea saw him at the door, she jumped from my arms into Bryan's. They held each other for a long time, and when she finally let go, all three of us were crying. He told me that he wanted to move from North Carolina to the North Shore to be close to her and involved in her life. Seeing them together, there was no way I could say that his move to Chicago would be anything less than good.

Bryan and I both knew, without having to discuss it, that we weren't going to get together as a couple. Bryan had a tendency at times toward pessimism and gloom (the flip side of his passion for building a better world) that didn't work well with my own penchant for worrying and brooding. As friends, we'd been able for years to bring out the best in each other—teasing, encouraging, supporting. As a romantic couple interacting daily, however, our faults had tended to magnify each other's. But we both wanted to rebuild the close friendship we'd had for Thea's sake, and Bryan eventually found an apartment less than fifteen minutes away in Evanston.

ON THE MORNING OF Thea's birthday party, I held her up to the bathroom mirror so that she could admire the new clothes she'd picked out while shopping with my mom. I hadn't been sure, given her bouts of shyness since the move to Winnetka, how she would respond to being the center of attention, but she seemed happy during the party, and tore open her presents with abandon. Her favorite was a ladybug tent with an attached tunnel that G.G., her great-grandma Rose, had given her. As she peeled off the wrapping, I smiled when I overheard Bryan mentioning to my parents how much she'd always loved opening the boxes of Gap clothes they'd mailed to the farm. Bryan, with his goatee, faded denim jacket, and jeans, represented a worldview entirely different from theirs. Yet, even so, we all felt that we were on common ground, united around Thea.

A few days after the party, my friend Pammy came by the house with her younger sister Amy. It was a comfortably warm day, and I led them out to sit on the terrace. "Wow," Amy said, staring at the garden. Amy and Pammy both wanted to walk through it, so I led them down the narrow path I'd managed to clear at the center as they volleyed exclamations back and forth. "This is incredible!" "Look at those crazy tomatoes!" "And those cucumbers and gorgeous flowers!" "Jeanne, do you realize how amazing this is?"

When we walked back up to sit on the terrace, Pammy looked at me and announced, "Other people are going to want this, and they won't know how to do it. You should start a business!"

I was flattered that she saw me as capable of running a company, and amazed that she thought any kind of hands-in-the-dirt food-growing enterprise could succeed on the North Shore. Sensing my skepticism, she added, "This isn't the Winnetka you used to live in. People are now more environmentally aware." Her perspective fascinated me, but after three months home I was still just barely finding my feet. As I lay in bed that night trying to think through the practicalities that would be involved in building a business of my own, from the tools and the truck to the seeds and the compost, I felt a kind of paralysis. I was still waiting to hear back from Abby Mandel, and it seemed better to start out with a simple, focused job like that, as someone else's assistant—*if* I did, in fact, get the job (and as the days passed without hearing back from her, it seemed like an ever bigger *if*). I was worried about the substantial holes in the résumé I'd mailed to Abby (I'd omitted the word *commune*, but working on farms was hardly adequate qualification for an office job), so I was startled when I answered the phone while puttering around the kitchen one afternoon and heard, "Jeanne Edith Pinsof, please."

"Yes?"

"This is Abby Mandel."

"Ms. Mandel!" I exclaimed, my enthusiasm colliding with her brisk, efficient tone.

She invited me to her home for an interview. Then she asked, "Have you been to Green City Market?"

I answered quietly, "No."

She replied that I should go before we met.

Early the next Wednesday, after a fifteen-mile drive down the lake from Winnetka to the Chicago neighborhood of Lincoln Park, Thea and I walked for the first time into Green City Market. I now remember it as one of those moments in life when you can feel things changing for you. I could not have imagined such a place. The outdoor market itself looked like nothing so much as a scene from a European village: under the looming Chicago skyline were dozens of booths and tables strewn with green-and-white check-ered gingham cloths selling organic vegetables, meats, and other produce. Each booth had a placard stating the farmer's profile and proximity to the city. Other vendors sold local comb honey, gluten-free baked goods, and artisanal cheeses, homemade salsas, and flowering plants. All of this was drenched in sunshine, with hundreds of people milling about and enjoying themselves, many of them families with young children. I registered the scene in fragments: live music, running dogs, Frisbees, smoothies, bare feet in grass. It was almost as if the future I'd worked toward at the farm—a piece of that dream—had come vividly to life.

I'd experienced farmers markets before—at one point, in Texas, the commune had even experimented with selling tomatoes and other excess produce at a local farmers market—but never in a major city. On the drive down I had imagined that Green City Market, in the heart of Chicago, would be a small, quaint, and limited affair because no one I knew in Winnetka growing up in the 1970s and '80s—or anywhere else in or around Chicago, for that matter—would have gone out of their way to buy local and/or organic food. Most people I knew at that time had shopped at big chain supermarkets, which had been invented only two generations earlier, in the 1930s. Before then, most Americans would have grown their own food or purchased their fresh meats and produce from local farms or a butcher, supplementing with dry and canned goods they'd either preserved themselves or bought from small specialty stores. As people moved increasingly from rural areas to cities and suburbs throughout the twentieth century, and as industrial-scale farms began to swallow up small and midsize farms, the number of supermarkets swelled. Improvements in refrigeration and all forms of transportation made it easier and cheaper to store and ship food over long distances—from increasingly far-flung suppliers to big supermarket chains. I was aware that in recent years there had been some growing interest in healthy and organic food on the North Shore. In 1995, a Whole Foods Market had opened in Evanston, but that was a college town with more of a progressive, bohemian edge than Winnetka. But here was

Green City Market, one of the most successful strictly local farmers markets in America, and Abby had built it over a period of six years, starting in 1998 with nine farmers.

That first day, Thea and I wandered the market for hours. Much of the time I followed her lead as she ambled from booth to booth munching samples. I talked shop with some of the farmers—*What's the earliest I can plant corn here? What's the best cover crop to use in this region?* They were quick and generous with their feedback. Growing food is one of the most humbling human endeavors, and farmers are forced to be perpetual students. Most of them are happy to share what they've learned with those who show a sincere interest, and I love to gather new theories, techniques, and ideas, and to toss whatever I've picked up into the discussion. Our easy camaraderie felt like a comfort and a relief, another circle closing.

But what struck me most was the chatty ease and enthusiasm among the market's customers. It felt like an open-air party as the people around me laughed and talked while eating fresh crepes, sipping their juices, and trading information. *Did you know that bagged carrot sticks are treated with chlorine? Try pickling your cucumbers in apple cider vinegar.* They spoke a common language, a version of which I'd been speaking for the previous eighteen years. Listening to them reminded me of the best moments at Zendik Farm, and I started to think that maybe my life hadn't been such a strange journey after all. Here was a community working to realize aspects of the vision that had been so urgent to me when I'd left Chicago, when I'd wanted out at all costs. Now I was back in the city, almost two decades later, with the sudden feeling of wanting in.

ABBY MANDEL LIVED IN GLENCOE, the next town over from Winnetka. When she met me at her door she looked impeccably chic—red manicured nails, perfectly coiffed hair with honey highlights, an Hermès watch, and a delicate gold necklace. At seventy, she looked fifty-five. Her handshake was formal and polite. She led me to her kitchen, a large, beautiful space with hanging copper pots and French ceramic tiles, where she taught cooking classes and tested recipes for her weekly syndicated column in the *Chicago Tribune*. A *boeuf bourguignon* bubbled on the stove, tended by a smart, serious young chef named Sarah Stegner, who was collaborating with Abby on a cookbook.

"So?" Abby said, "What did you think of the market?" Abby had unmistakable gravitas, but she was enough like the women I'd grown up around that I felt at ease. I told her that the experience had been unexpectedly moving for me—that what I'd seen was more than just great food and produce and an impressive network of local farmers. With its focus on sustainability, it was a model for social change.

Abby nodded almost imperceptibly. She began to quiz me on my knowledge of organic farming techniques, and I left her home an hour later thinking that things had gone well. So it stung when I followed up with her a couple of days later and she said flatly: "I can't offer you the job." I had thought little of it when she'd asked offhandedly toward the end of our interview about my computer skills and I had casually replied that I'd used a computer at the farm to keep track of finances, but that it had a dial-up connection and I didn't know much about the Internet or email. "I'd love to hire you," she said, "but this position requires computer skills."

I said the first thing that came into my head: "I'll *get* computer skills." Minutes later I was Googling "North Shore computer tutor" and found someone who taught basic skills from his home. I signed up for a four-session tutorial in "Internet, email, and Word document skills," and called back to report this development to Abby. She agreed, conditionally, to hire me when I finished.

Slogging through those four computer sessions was a challenge. They threw into stark relief how much of the recent world had passed me by. I'd left home in 1987, when monitors were the size of televisions and the only one I'd ever seen belonged to an Apple IIe.

Now, in 2004, monitors (and televisions) were as thin as blackboards, there were millions of websites, wireless was almost everywhere, and I didn't even own a cellphone. The world had leaped into the digital age while I'd been pulling weeds. As I futzed with tables in Microsoft Word I became infuriated with myself. *This is absurd. I'm a thirty-five-year-old unemployed single mom who at one point was on track to go to an Ivy League school. Now I'm not qualified for an entry-level clerical job.* But I quickly remembered that my circumstances could have been—and *had* been— dramatically worse. I felt grateful for my opportunities and intent on moving ahead.

ON MY FIRST DAY of working for Abby, I typed a letter to the mayor of Chicago in which I spelled Abby's name A-b-b-e-y. On day two, I created a paper jam in the printer that took Abby's other assistant, my patient colleague Chris Djuric, and me a couple of hours to fix. On email after painfully wrought email, I failed to attach the essential documents. It was becoming clear to everyone that I did not have the disposition to excel at a desk job, and I inevitably found myself staring out the window, transfixed by a huge garden I could see through a gate across the street. Spanning a tenth of an acre and bordered by an old stone wall, the garden clearly hadn't been thoroughly tended in years, with overgrown masses of plants I imagined to be sweet peppers and snap peas and vines of melons gone rogue.

For all my clerical failings, I did well at any task that involved dealing with people, including planning for and coordinating the vendors at the market and helping to organize Green City's regular schedule of readings, lectures, guest chefs, and cooking demos. I became familiar with the network of local and organic farmers, as well as with the beekeepers, cheese makers, bread and pastry bakers, flower growers, crepe makers, and the like who sold their products at the market. I was getting to know chefs and entrepreneurs

who were at the forefront of the city's booming trend in green restaurants. A world was opening, and I was realizing that I fit in.

I think Abby sensed that I wanted to get more deeply involved
with the market's activities (though it's also possible that she
wanted to get me out of the office so she could hire a more efficient
assistant), and one afternoon we drove downtown to Lincoln Park
Zoo, located across from the market, where she took me on a tour
of a scraggly thousand-square-foot plot of land. Years earlier it had
been part of an exhibit, but now it was just a forgotten garden with
stumps of dead and dying plants. The zoo had offered the site as a
possible location for a demonstration garden connected to the
farmers market. A stone's throw from the plot was a garden space
four times its size that was already in use, dedicated exclusively, per
an agreement with one of the zoo's sponsors, John Deere, to indus-
trially farmed crops such as corn, wheat, alfalfa, and soybeans.

Abby leaned on the picket fence surrounding the smaller plot,
smiled with a sly light in her eyes, and said, "Can you do here what
you did on your farms?" She'd been thinking about a project of
Alice Waters's, the Edible Schoolyard, which had been designed to
teach children how food grows and then travels from farm to fork.
Abby envisioned something of a live theater—a garden happening
in real time, a place where families could participate in whatever
care the growing plants needed, from turning the compost to pulling up weeds to participating in the harvest. Her vision was exciting, and I jumped at the chance to get out of the office and back
into the dirt. For the first time in a long while I did not hesitate and
wonder whether I was up to the task.

I went into research mode—first exploring online resources such
as Edibleschoolyard.org. The original Edible Schoolyard is an acre
of land that serves as an interactive outdoor classroom for the Martin Luther King, Jr., Middle School in Berkeley, California. The
kids grow crops such as potatoes, corn, garlic, grains (quinoa,
buckwheat, wheat), and leafy greens (kale, collards, and chard in
particular), learn to prepare the food, and get hands-on lessons on

the connections between food, health, and the environment. The program has succeeded in improving children's diets and has inspired spin-off projects around the country.

I also began to investigate the urban food-growing efforts in Chicago. I hit the pavement in search of people such as Jaime Zaplatosch of the environmental group Openlands, who was working with inner-city public schools to build vegetable gardens for their students—smaller scale versions of the Edible Schoolyard project with less funding and infrastructure. Jamie explained that Chicago was on the front lines of a broader movement known as "urban agriculture." In dozens of cities, from Seattle to Baltimore, local gardeners and farmers were growing food in and around city centers in response to a number of pressures—rising fuel prices, unemployment, a worsening obesity crisis, concerns about the environmental and moral costs of industrial agriculture, and a desire to reconnect with the sources of their food.

I sought out a number of urban growers in Chicago who were happy to share their knowledge. Ken Dunn, who had a graduate degree in philosophy from the University of Chicago, had run the nonprofit Resource Center in Chicago for more than thirty years. His organization was promoting a sustainable society by practicing different ways of recycling materials, including turning a portion of Chicago's waste into huge quantities of compost each year. Ken told me that urban agriculture can actually be *three to five times* more productive per acre than traditional large-scale farming. Ken's City Farm, the best-known of the Resource Center's projects, encompassed a number of organic gardens spread throughout the city's vacant lots. The biggest obstacle to growing food within city limits is finding affordable space amid sky-high real estate prices, but Dunn had been savvy about navigating Chicago's legendary bureaucracy and convincing city officials to donate empty lots where he could grow fresh produce and train city residents to become farmers.

Visiting City Farm's main location, near the site of the former

Cabrini-Green housing project at the intersection of Division Street and Clybourn Avenue, I was amazed by the lushness and productivity Dunn had achieved with his signature method of growing in compost. He lined the soil of sites with an impermeable layer of clay to seal off toxins, then added a thick layer of at least eighteen inches of fresh compost. On a handful of lots in impoverished areas that otherwise appeared desolate, City Farm grew no less than twenty-five thousand pounds of vegetables and herbs each year (including famously flavorful tomatoes that were sold to some of Chicago's top restaurants).

I met with Harry Rhodes of the organization Growing Home, another Chicago program that demonstrated the vast potential of urban farming. Rhodes worked with people who had been homeless and struggled with substance abuse and trained them in the basics of gardening and soil science. Rhodes believed that when people take responsibility for caring for something, it helps them build self-esteem and a sense of purpose. On a relatively small site of two-thirds of an acre at the Wood Street Urban Farm on Chicago's South Side, Growing Home was training dozens of men and women and growing thousands of pounds of certified organic produce each year.

The best-known urban farming program in the region was the Milwaukee-based Growing Power, originally founded in 1993 by Will Allen (who would win a MacArthur "genius grant" for his visionary work there). Growing Power had expanded to Chicago, where Will's daughter, Erika, oversaw the development of multiple farm sites throughout the city. These sites focused on both food production and job training for people who had trouble finding traditional employment, such as the formerly incarcerated. Growing Power defined itself as a "living museum" or "idea factory" to encourage the spread of urban agriculture, and offered many workshops in gardening techniques to the public on every aspect of organic gardening, from the basics of planting and weeding to innovative concepts, including using compost as a source of renewable energy. Growing Power's Milwaukee-area programs alone produced more than one hundred thousand pounds of fresh food.

A Chicago master gardener I'd met through Green City Market, Bill Shores, gave me the chance to observe firsthand a number of new techniques for maximizing crop yield in limited urban spaces at the garden he maintained for the restaurants of celebrity chef Rick Bayless. His garden was a visual masterpiece with unique varieties of vegetables and herbs, and had become a model for urban efficiency over the previous few years. It showcased methods such as succession planting (growing many crops of lettuces and greens back-to-back throughout the season); using insulated containers for year-round vermicompost (compost made with the help of worms) to create a high-potency fertilizer; cultivating microgreens, small-leafed vegetables grown from broccoli, cabbage, and other seeds that require little growing space and are harvested when young, producing multiple yields per season; and covering raised garden rows with bent-wire hoops that support floating row covers made of fabric (as opposed to the traditional plastic, which can become overheated on sunny days) to extend the growing season into the fall and even winter months. It made me incredibly hopeful to see the pioneering work of Chicago's urban farmers. I was amazed to realize that the garden Abby had proposed at the zoo complemented the work they were already doing and could perhaps even contribute to moving it forward.

My next step was to map the gardening season, which began with studying the patterns of weather and temperature in Illinois. I drew up lists and charts of what I'd plant and when I'd plant it, what resources I would need, and what kinds of activities I'd do with the kids and families who visited. All these considerations would factor into a budget proposal that I would present for the zoo's approval in January. Through the fall and into the winter, as the project took shape on paper, I began to see the dried-up thousand-square-foot plot of land at the edge of the zoo as a kind of emotional and professional life raft.

One night in January, I lay awake in bed, mind abuzz, as Thea slept in the crib next to me. I was processing and synthesizing the flood of information I'd absorbed in recent months. I now had a basic idea of what a growing season in Illinois would look like and understood that my previous commune experience could apply to meaningful real-world work. Everything I was learning seemed to be weaving together with what I already knew and was leading me somewhere. But where? It struck me as strange that there were activists growing vegetables on abandoned city lots, literally on top of slabs of concrete, but there was not widespread food-growing activity in the suburbs, where residents had plenty of green space to work with. A large portion of these residents were also regularly buying organic produce at Whole Foods. And then it suddenly clicked: The North Shore needed not just organic food, but *homegrown* organic food. It struck me that maybe I could, in fact, start a business, as my friend Pammy Swartchild had suggested months earlier. I was ready now to think about how I might make that happen.

Early the next morning I set out on the kitchen table the pictures of the backyard garden my mother had snapped from the top of the stepladder. What made the garden a failure on a practical level—its sheer overabundance, the overcrowded plants that choked off paths and pushed against the fence—was also what made it so photogenic. Something about the angle of the photos taken from above—the garden's lushness set against the white house, the white picket fence, and the manicured lawn—made it look idyllic, almost implausibly so. The pictures showed twelve-foot-tall sunflowers, an explosion of greens, tomatoes, squash, pink cosmos, and marigolds. They gave me proof of what I'd done— proof that I could do something that other people in the suburbs might want for themselves.

Granted, I didn't know anything about running a business. I didn't know how I'd find clients, or how much I should charge them. I didn't know how I'd carry the cost of supplies until agreements were made and the gardens were planted and paid for. I

BACKYARD GARDEN AT MY PARENTS' HOUSE, 2004

didn't even know what to call myself. But the brainstorming started immediately. My dad pulled out a pad of paper and pen and urged me to hash out the practicalities one by one. In terms of finding clients, the garden photo itself made for a good advertisement and would work on a flyer. In terms of the cost structure, agreements with clients, and supplies, my father had a simple principle: *If you don't know what you're doing, find people who are already doing something similar and learn from them.* There were no specific models for my idea that I could find online in 2004—no gardening businesses in our area or anywhere nationally that were helping households grow vegetables, let alone *organic* vegetables. So I decided to call the landscapers who'd helped me construct the raised bed in the backyard, a local family-run company, to ask how they ran their season.

MY ONCE-QUIET SUBURBAN LIFE had suddenly become busy. I was juggling my office job at Abby's (I still had clerical responsibilities two

days a week) with the Edible Garden project at the zoo, and researching my business plan. But in the midst of it all, I decided to
take a trip I'd postponed for too long. My sister, Hallie, was living
in Santa Cruz, California, apprenticing with a home-birth midwife.
She and her son, Puma, had visited Winnetka once since I'd come
home, but it had been a brief, rushed visit soon after my return,
when I'd had little to offer emotionally. I wanted to spend more
time with her under better conditions, and to let Thea spend time
with her aunt and cousin.

In Santa Cruz, three-year-old Thea and four-year-old Puma connected instantly and with surprising intensity. As they talked and
played, Hallie and I felt a sense of relief: these two only children
with struggling moms could now inhabit their happy toddler world
without complexities. Hallie and I similarly took refuge in each
other and our memories, staying up late reminiscing about our
childhood and Hallie's visits to Zendik Farm. She had visited me
more often than anyone else, and did not judge or criticize the way
of life. She would roll up her sleeves and pitch in with whatever
work needed doing—farming, dishwashing, or carpentry. At one
point, Hallie had even thought about moving to the farm to serve
as resident midwife, but our mother, in a rare moment of putting
her foot down, forbade it.

After Arol's criticism of my close relationship with Hallie, I'd
started talking to my sister in cooler tones in public and on the
phone. But Hallie had never stopped trying to get through, and
though she had good reason to, she'd never blamed me for pushing
her away. I was happy to discover during my visit to Santa Cruz
that, after the years we had lost in our relationship, we could so
easily pick up where we'd left off. It felt like a confirmation of her
trust when she confided in me about her difficult relationship with
Puma's father and asked for advice. Sometimes, when you're trying
to pick up the pieces of your own life, there's no greater source of
strength than helping someone you love pick up the pieces of theirs.

I offered a quintessentially Pinsofian solution, pulling out a pen and a pad of paper and saying, "Let's make a list." We wrote down the things that were going right in her life, the things that were going wrong, and the changes she wanted to make within a year. Six months later, Hallie had followed through with the first change on her list: leaving her painful relationship and moving home to Chicago with her son.

After our list-making exercise, I asked Hallie for her take on my new plan: *Am I out of my mind to try to build a life and a business in the very community I'd turned my back on?* "There's no better place," she told me. "You went away in search of something and you found valuable knowledge. Now you're bringing it back to share among the people you can really reach." Then she reminded me of some of the harsh growing conditions I'd faced on the farm— the scorching Texas summers, the dry desert soil of Southern California, the infestations of fire ants, grasshoppers, Colorado potato beetles, and gophers—and the beautiful vegetable gardens that grew despite it all. If you made it through that, she told me, anything is possible.

SAYING GOOD-BYE TO HALLIE

SOON AFTER MY RETURN HOME—and for the first time in as long as I could remember, Chicago actually felt like home—I met with Bob Bertog, the owner of a local landscaping company. I arrived at his office armed with a page of typed questions about what it would take to succeed in the business of gardening for hire. He couldn't have been more generous with his advice. Within an hour, I'd gotten a soup-to-nuts tutorial in all aspects of my potential operation: how to prepare proposals for clients; how to predict the length of time a job would take (they always wind up taking longer than you think, he warned); how much to charge per hour; and how much supplies should be marked up to leave yourself with some profit.

Deciding on a name for the business did not come easily. I initially toyed with the words "farm" and "farmer" and even considered the cringe-worthy "Farm Girl," but quickly dismissed those as too far removed from the culture of the suburbs I was aiming at. The word "gardener" seemed more toned-down and suburban. My father kept reminding me not to overthink it and pick something simple, clear, and direct. "The Organic Gardener," I decided, was as clear as it gets.

With that settled, I moved on to the task of getting supplies. Any mechanical or heavy equipment I'd need, like a rototiller, I could rent on a per-job basis from Home Depot. The tools I'd need to start the business—hard rake, diamond-shaped hoe, round-nose shovel—were tools I'd already used on my parents' garden. I bought a top carrier for my station wagon from REI to cart the tools around in, and picked up some extra tools that I'd need for the zoo garden—trowels and dibblers that kids could use when they dropped by to plant and harvest.

I set up an account with Johnny's Selected Seeds, a gardening catalog I had used to order seeds at the farm, which had now expanded its reach through a website. (I had assumed that the farmers I'd met through Green City Market might have a local source, but most of them actually preferred Johnny's.) I started with a basic inventory of seeds, including romaine, oak-leaf, and butter lettuces, zucchini, spinach, Tuscan kale, rainbow chard, tricolor beans, butternut squash, and melons. Any plants that I planned to buy as seedlings—heirloom tomatoes, strawberries, herbs, and the like— I could get as needed through sources at the farmers market.

I worked up several designs for the flyer and decided on the heading VEGETABLES FROM YOUR OWN BACKYARD—THE ORGANIC GARDENER, with my mom's backyard garden photo in the center. Beneath that, the pitch:

- I WILL CREATE A CUSTOM ORGANIC GARDEN WITH VEGETABLES, HERBS, FRUITS, AND FLOWERS SUITED TO YOUR NEEDS: DESIGN, INSTALLATION, MAINTENANCE, AND TEACHING.
- A SANCTUARY FOR ALL OF YOUR FAMILY. KIDS/ADULTS CAN HELP.
- OVER 18 YEARS OF ORGANIC GARDENING/FARMING EXPERIENCE.
- COMPOSTING SYSTEM SET-UP AND INSTRUCTION; TURN YOUR KITCHEN WASTE INTO ORGANIC FERTILIZER.

At the bottom were tabs with my name and the number of the cell-phone I'd recently gotten.

I printed thirty-five flyers on an inkjet printer and then cut the phone number tabs at the bottom for easy detachment. Thea carried the box of tacks and Scotch tape as we ventured to grocery stores and coffee shops from Lake Forest to Evanston and affixed the flyers to windows and bulletin boards. After that, there was nothing I could do but wait.

Chapter 7

I T TOOK A YEAR OF PSYCHOLOGICAL BABY STEPS AFTER MY RETURN
home before I was able to think of myself as a woman, in a romantic sense. The change in my mindset was a result, in part, of physical progress—I had gained back some weight, I was getting pretty
regular sleep and exercise, and I was finally able to look at myself
in the mirror without flinching. And I could begin to think about
myself again now that Thea had begun to adjust to her new home.

By March 2005, a year after our return, Thea was doing well. In
fact, she was thriving. Bryan had moved to Evanston and wanted
to spend every minute he could with her. That gave me a chance,
for the first time since Thea's birth, to take long runs, linger in a hot
bath, and experience real, unencumbered solitude. It wasn't long
before I found myself standing in bookstores or coffee shops looking for a man I might find attractive. I hadn't been intimate with
anyone in a "real world" context since Mark. And having never
experienced the dating scene of bars, gyms, and coffee shops, I had
no idea how to go about finding a date. Surely there would be no
"sign-up sheet" at the Winnetka Starbucks.

My mother, as mothers do, had plenty of ideas, but most of the
men she suggested I date were divorcees with white-collar jobs who
belonged to Lake Shore Country Club. This made me feel irratio-
nally frustrated and hopeless—like I'd be signing up for exactly the

kind of life I'd rejected when I left home. Even though the commune had proved to be a false ideal, I still wanted and needed to find a different way to live. I didn't voice my frustration directly to my mother—my life, I realized, was my own responsibility, and if I wanted to date somebody different, it was up to me to find somebody different. First, I tried Match.com, an experiment that lasted all of two weeks. The first "match" I accepted—a reasonably attractive North Shore guy who'd graduated a year ahead of me at New Trier—was an immediate bust. We lurched through one awkward topic of conversation after another—movies I'd never seen, music I'd never heard of—and at the end he asked if I wanted to go golfing. I left the date so discouraged that I deleted my Match.com account the minute I got home.

In an effort to rebound—and this was admittedly a stretch—I sought out an unrealized crush from middle school: Mr. Wilson, my former eighth-grade English teacher, now in his early fifties. After looking up "Jay Kenneth Wilson" in the Evanston White Pages, I cold-called him and discovered that he was still single, remembered me well, and was happy to meet for dinner. We had a great conversation, discussing everything from the urban farming movement to the books we'd read in his class, and arranged to meet again. Jay was a Yale graduate, smart and articulate, still ruggedly handsome, and he dressed exactly as he had in the classroom: plaid shirt, denim jacket, Carhartt pants. But when he kissed me, I felt nothing. When we took it further—I was determined to find a spark—still, *nothing*.

The sexual apathy scared me. Arol and Wulf had often described the commune as a sanctuary for *real* sexual experience with open, honest communication, and had implied that living in the "death culture" saddled people with stresses and inhibitions that robbed them of true intimacy and deep sexual pleasure. Although I'd come to realize that almost all of the Zendik philosophy was a sham, my passionless encounter with Mr. Wilson left me worrying that this particular tenet might be true.

I felt achingly lonely after these dating fiascos. I doubted that it would ever be possible for me to connect intimately with someone who didn't fully understand my past. How could I explain what life on the commune—almost half of my life until then, and almost all of my adult life—had been like to someone who had not shared my experience there? How could I explain the utter conviction I'd had, for years, that the life I shared on a farm with three dozen people was the only life worth living? It would be equally difficult to convey how strange the wider world still felt to me at times, with its buzz and hectic pace, its omnipresent consumerism and cellphones.

Having Bryan nearby was more than a comfort; he was a lifeline. He was fiercely devoted to Thea, and always consistent and calm with her even as he endured the confusion and anguish of his own readjustment. Through long talks and commiseration, Bryan and I were able to encourage, focus, and steady each other. Still, I found myself craving the kind of intimacy that he and I had realized we would never really have between us.

On an early spring vacation to Pawleys Island in South Carolina with my parents, Thea, Hallie, and Puma, I couldn't shake my feelings of isolation and longing. We were having a good time—I'd never seen Thea happier than when she and Puma were jumping in and out of the waves and splashing each other on the beach. But on one of my first nights there, I found myself thinking about Verd. I returned over and over again to one particular memory I had of him from our time together. People at Zendik Farm were generally discouraged from spending the night together with any frequency, as it might lead to too close and exclusive of a bond. But we did spend the night together a few times in an airy one-room cabin with screened walls on the bank of the rushing river that bordered our property in Texas. One warm August evening, rain pounded on the cabin's tin roof as we lay on the blankets we'd spread on the mattress on the floor, and a cloudlike mist entered the room through the screens. Verd and I talked for hours into the night about our families and the common ground we'd shared as kids growing up in different parts of Chicago.

All of a sudden, he turned to me and said, "Let's go get drenched."

"Go on, Verdie," I replied. He jumped up and ran outside while I followed him out and stood watching him run naked through the downpour. When he returned, we fell upon each other with kisses, the wet earth beneath us.

Lying awake at night at Pawleys Island, I began to miss Verd so fiercely that my breathing grew tight and shallow. I walked across the hall to Hallie's room, woke her up, and told her my realization that I'd been missing Verd all along. Until then, I'd been in survival mode and hadn't allowed myself to open the door on my memories of him. Hallie had met Verd many times on the farm, and she told me without hesitation that it was clearly time to return his call.

The next day, I called Bryan so that Thea could talk to him as she did every day. Before I even mentioned my realization about Verd, he said, "It's the strangest thing: I just heard a comedian on the radio who sounded exactly like Verd." Bryan had been friends with Verd on the farm, acting as a kind of mentor to him. "I really think you two should reconnect," he added.

I was so surprised that I was silent for a moment. "But I don't know how to find him!" I finally said.

Bryan answered calmly, "I'll figure something out."

Chapter 8

HELD A BLANK YELLOW LEGAL PAD AGAINST MY CHEST LIKE A SHIELD as I started up the front walk of the large landscaped estate. It felt odd to be here on business—not only was this the first and only prospective client call I'd received to date for the Organic Gardener, but it was in Lake Forest, one of the most exclusive towns on the North Shore. Winnetka was wealthy, but Lake Forest, a stately suburb with houses and estates designed by noted architects such as Howard Van Doren Shaw and David Adler, had wealth plus a certain mystique—an aura of power, blue blood, and cultivated taste.

This particular house wasn't a mansion; it was a two-story wooden structure set back from the road. But the property itself was large, covering more than an acre, and it was meticulously landscaped, with an English country aesthetic that included an expansive bluestone terrace leading into a series of curved flower beds. The owner, the woman who'd called my cellphone a few days earlier asking for "the Organic Gardener," had told me she wanted "just a small garden," but I wasn't sure, in this context, what that meant. I had carefully chosen what to wear to the meeting—an indigo blue sweater, nice jeans, cowboy boots—and as I approached the door, my purse felt heavy on my shoulder from the weight of the tape measure, camera, and garden photos I'd packed the night before. The door opened before I could ring the bell, and suddenly an energetic, pretty woman in her fifties was smiling, leading me into the house. It was decorated in a way I liked, with a natural color palette and minimalist West Coast aesthetic. She pointed at my purse, exclaiming, "I have one just like it!"

"It's my mom's, actually," I said. "She wanted to help me look 'professional.'" The woman, Denise, laughed along with me. Though I'd been determined to present myself as businesslike and accomplished, the purse had broken the ice and I felt comfortable. We sat at the large marble island in the center of her kitchen, clearly the domain of someone who loved good food and cooking. "I'm a foodie," she said. "I go to Napa Valley and Sonoma at least once a year, and I've noticed how much *better* food tastes when it comes right out of the ground."

She asked how I'd gotten the idea for my business. I answered truthfully, omitting only the word "commune," saying, as I had to Abby Mandel, that I'd lived and worked on three different organic farms over seventeen years. Denise told me she was interested in growing mostly gourmet varieties of vegetables, such as green zebra tomatoes and Italian beans, arugula, golden beets, and butter-crunch lettuce. We had grown these plants at the farm from seed, but I hadn't known that they were considered delicacies until I came back to Illinois and saw them highlighted in displays at Whole Foods and Green City Market.

Denise led me out to an area behind her garage. She'd grown herbs and flowers before and knew where she wanted this garden to go—a sunny spot that had once been a horse paddock. She guided me through the dimensions of the plot as I knelt to take measurements. We agreed to do a raised bed like the one in the flyer photo—my parents' garden—rather than an in-ground garden, to help demarcate the space.

The meeting went smoothly, lasting about an hour, but at the very end—after I'd told Denise that I'd draw up a proposal for the work and send it for her approval—she asked how many other clients I had. I felt my face flush. "Actually . . . you're the first." She broke into a grin. "I'm so glad!" She'd been nothing but friendly, but given the high level of expertise that had clearly gone into her landscape design, that wasn't what I'd expected to hear. "I think your business is going to be a big hit," she said, "and I got you first."

DESPITE DENISE'S VOTE OF CONFIDENCE, I'd had no other bites yet for the Organic Gardener. I focused my energies instead on preparing the ground for the new Edible Garden at Lincoln Park Zoo. I began by relocating the few rugged sage and chive plants that had managed to survive the past years of neglect to a space just outside the fence. A landscaper friend of Abby's had volunteered his services to rototill the garden's depleted soil and bring in fresh compost, which eliminated two big concerns. But I knew I still had a lot of work ahead in building up the raised rows. At Zendik, preparing to plant had generally been a collaborative effort with at least a dozen people working together—first loosening the soil by rototilling, then using hand tools to heap the earth into the long rows we'd marked with string, raking and smoothing out the mounds we'd formed, and mixing in additional compost and fertilizer.

It was a strange feeling, doing in that city space the kind of in-ground farming that I'd done in rural areas, and the work took several days. The year before, when I'd planted my parents' garden, I'd been in survival mode and had only enough energy to focus on the tasks at hand. Now that I'd started looking forward—or at least not looking back as much as before—I was able to focus on my surroundings. There were high-rise buildings all around, and from the garden plot looking south, the iconic Hancock tower stood out against the backdrop of the city skyline. The visual contrast between the setting and the hands-in-the-dirt farming I was doing seemed to mirror the state of limbo I felt internally. I wasn't depressed—I enjoyed the physical labor, and was hopeful about my business—but the solitary work left room for reflection, and I was conscious that I had no idea where I'd be in a year's time.

I LABORED OVER THE PROPOSAL for Denise's garden. Sitting at the kitchen table, I worked out an estimate based on the garden's size, the supplies I'd need, and how long the preparation work would take. I approached Bertog about the cost of subcontracting his crew to construct the raised bed from untreated cedar timbers and to truck in a compost, sand, and soil mix. I also needed to purchase my own plant labels, organic seeds, seedlings, and fertilizer, and to factor in the cost of my own hours. I'd asked Denise for a 50 percent down payment to cover supplies. I'd assumed she would need some time to mull it over but was amazed when I received an envelope back from her with the first payment a few days later. I froze for a moment, feeling pride and disbelief as I held her check made out to "The Organic Gardener." That was *me, my* company. It was the strongest indication I'd had so far that this could, in fact, be a viable business, and—on a personal level—that I was getting back up on my feet.

Bertog's crew did an excellent job building the raised bed, finishing ahead of schedule, and I began raking and smoothing out the bed's rich mix of soil and compost. At the farm, I'd learned the importance of nutrient-dense compost to food growing. Making compost had been an intense, year-round operation involving ten-foot-high piles of food and farm waste that crews of a dozen or more people would periodically hand-turn with pitchforks and shovels. We'd layer rotten alfalfa hay, horse manure, food waste from the kitchen, garden waste, and straw atop a bottom layer of branches to elevate the pile off the ground, and we'd wet and turn the pile every few weeks to keep it aerated and moist. It was hard and messy work, but there was also a kind of beauty to the process that I started to appreciate the first time I used the rich, dark compost—we called it "black gold"—on a row we were preparing to plant. There was a certain texture, a smell, a visual, sensual *rightness* to it. And there was the gratification of knowing that the process of making and using compost is one that completes "the circle of life."

Compost is the single best way to build up a healthy soil that can generate lush, productive plant growth. The material we think of as dirt (a mixture of particles such as sand, silt, and clay, and minerals such as copper and iron) actually makes up less than half the content of healthy soil. Ideally, 25 percent of good soil is made up of water, 25 percent is air, and 5 percent is organic matter such as bacteria, fungi, and dead plant and animal residues. All these components of soil have to be in balance for garden plants to thrive. In natural environments, compost builds up gradually through the cycle of life as plants and animals die and decompose into the very nutrients that fuel the next generation of plant growth. But in cleared fields and suburban lawns, that natural cycle can get disrupted. Compost is a way of amending the soil to replenish what's been lost.

The method we'd used on the farm was a large-scale version of "hot" composting, in which the bacteria in a large, moist, well-aerated compost pile give off heat as they eat the organic material and help it decompose. This heat then invites in more bacteria and speeds the decomposition process, so that a fresh pile can be ready to use in a few months or less. The temperature of hot compost can reach as high as 160 degrees. On the farm, the compost piles would be steaming on cold days.

But composting can also be done on a much smaller scale, in a small heap of suburban yard waste, in a trash can with the bottom cut out, or in a plastic tumbler like the one I'd bought for my parents' house. The key is to give the helpful microorganisms in compost what they need to do the work of decomposition: most important, the right balance of materials that contain carbon and nitrogen. "Brown" materials such as dry leaves, cornstalks, straw, and shredded cardboard or paper have high amounts of carbon, and should make up about two-thirds of the compost mix; the other one-third should be "green" or wet materials, including kitchen scraps, garden waste, and fresh grass clippings, which have high amounts of nitrogen. The most common mistake in backyard composting is not adding enough "browns" to the mix. These materials have the added benefit of helping to manage moisture and odors. If you don't have access to a consistent supply of dried leaves, keep a bale of straw on hand to add to the pile as needed. (Make sure that the straw is seed free and not grass hay, which will sprout weeds.)

The compost I got from Bertog for Denise's garden didn't quite have the richness of scent and texture of the compost we'd produced on the farm, but it was more than adequate to do the job. By the first week of April, I'd finished my preparations for planting the Edible Garden, my parents' garden, and Denise's garden, and now just had to wait for the weather to turn warmer before putting in the first seeds.

THAT SAME WEEK, Bryan followed through on his promise to get Verd's phone number. My handwriting as I jotted it down on a loose scrap of paper in my parents' den looked jerky and unfamiliar. After I read the number back to Bryan twice to be sure I'd gotten it right, I hung up and dialed immediately, before I had time to think about it. I was nervous—beyond nervous, with my heart seeming to knock against my ribs. I closed my eyes when, after a few rings, I heard the familiar light tone of his voice. An answering machine. I fought the temptation to hang up. "Hi, Verd," I said, "Jeanne here." I was trying to keep it simple and cheery because I had no idea where he was living or who else, whether a girlfriend

or roommate, might be listening. "Well, it's a year later but I'm finally calling you back." My tone faltered. "I'd love to talk. Call me
when you can."

I kept my cellphone—the number I'd left him—with me at all
times for the rest of that day and for the next several days, obsessively checking the battery level on the small gray screen. For all my
nervousness about calling him, it hadn't occurred to me that Verd
wouldn't call me right back—until he didn't.

It was a welcome surprise when I suddenly got several calls for
the Organic Gardener. On a breezy spring day I drove due west
from Winnetka to the town of Northfield to meet with a woman
named Kate who'd asked me to come by to discuss a potential garden. Her road was heavily wooded, not like a typical suburban
neighborhood, and the houses on it were sheltered by curtains of
trees and spaced far apart. The directions she'd given me led me to
a sprawling white Colonial set back on a wide lot of at least three
acres, a stretch of jewel-green grass surrounded by oaks and maples.

I'd dressed comfortably, in nice jeans and a sweater, just as I
had with Denise, but I felt a stab of self-doubt as I approached the
house—and my insecurity deepened when I saw the woman who
answered the door. *Flawless* was the word that came to mind. She
was in her midthirties, thin, beautiful, with perfect posture, clear
blue eyes, and long, straight chestnut hair. A smile flickered across
her lips as she shook my hand. In her cool looks and demeanor, she
struck me in many ways as the embodiment of the North Shore
type I'd rejected when I'd left home for Zendik Farm.

As Kate led me inside, she directed the oldest of her three young
children, a towheaded boy, to watch the others while we talked.
We passed through a wide living room and kitchen area on the way
to a wood-paneled den. As we sat quietly across from each other on
the dark leather couch, several moments passed before I realized
that Kate wasn't going to interview me; it was, in fact, my job to
interview her. I threw out the first question that came to mind:

"What made you decide to plant a garden—what do you hope to get from it?"

I'm not sure what I expected for an answer, but I was floored when she said, "There's cancer in my family." When she hesitated before continuing, I realized that what I'd interpreted at first glance as coolness was, in fact, a combination of gravity and shyness. "My sister—she was diagnosed five years ago. Ovarian cancer. Our mother died of breast cancer. I started looking into cancer prevention because I wanted to know if there was something I could do. For myself—and even more for my children. To keep them healthy. The more I read, the more what I found out led me to question our lifestyle, what we're putting in our bodies, what we're breathing. . . . And all of that led to food."

I asked what books she felt she'd learned the most from and she mentioned Andrew Weil among other authors. Zendik Farm had kept an informal library of books and articles about food and nutrition, and I'd read about the chemicals in conventionally grown food and the health benefits of organic produce. I'd learned that since World War II, U.S. manufacturers had released an incredibly large number of synthetic compounds into the environment—more than eighty thousand of them—and that *only 2 percent* of these man-made chemicals have been tested for cancer-causing properties. The Centers for Disease Control and Prevention reports that the average American currently has detectable levels of 237 chemicals from the environment in her body, including the chemicals frequently used in pesticides.

Kate had good reason to be concerned about food and cancer risks. The EPA has approved the use of about 1,400 different kinds of pesticides, according to a recent U.S. Department of Health and Human Services report, and exposure to the chemicals in them "has been linked to brain/central nervous system (CNS), breast, colon, lung, ovarian . . . pancreatic, kidney, testicular, and stomach cancers, as well as Hodgkin's and non-Hodgkin's lymphoma, multiple myeloma, and soft tissue sarcoma." It's a stunning fact that roughly forty *known* carcinogens are currently used as ingredients in EPA-approved pesticides. Moreover, on average, eighteen new pesticides are submitted to the EPA for approval each year. The approval process hinges on a disturbing cost-benefit analysis: The agency green-lights new chemicals if it decides that the "benefits" of their crop and economic yield outweigh the potential "costs" to health and the environment. What's worse, chemical manufacturers often claim that they can't publicly reveal the ingredients in their products because it's proprietary information, which makes it "almost impossible," according to the Department of Health and Human Services report, "for scientists and environmentalists to challenge the release of new chemicals."

Cancer is far from the only serious health concern linked to the use of synthetic pesticides. These chemicals can have negative effects on the hormonal and neurological development of fetuses and young children in particular. A 1998 study by the Environmental Working Group found that nine out of ten children in the United States between six months and five years old were exposed to no fewer than thirteen different insecticides containing neurotoxic chemicals known as "organophosphates" in the foods they consumed on a daily basis. The EPA later tightened its standards for these harmful chemicals, but recent studies from Columbia University, the University of California at Berkeley, and Icahn School of Medicine at Mount Sinai have shown that organophosphates are still prevalent and continue to have serious health effects. All three studies found a direct link between prenatal exposure to organophosphates and diminished IQs in children. Another recent study in the medical journal *Pediatrics* showed that for every 10 percent increase in the concentration of these chemicals in the urine of children who participated in the study, there was a corresponding increase of *55 to 72 percent* in the likelihood that a child would have ADHD.

Some of the most popular fruits and veggies—celery, apples, bell peppers, spinach, strawberries, and potatoes—also have the highest measurable levels of pesticide residues when grown conven tionally. The good news is that switching to organic versions of these and other foods has been shown to reduce over time the amount of pesticide residues present in the body. A 2008 Emory University study found that when children shifted from conventionally grown to organically grown fruits and vegetables, the traces of organophosphate pesticides in their urine fell to zero.

Organic foods also offer a bonus health benefit: Several studies have shown that organic produce has a greater density of nutrients—including phytonutrients known to have cancer-preventing properties—compared to conventional produce. A recent study published jointly by the Organic Center and the University of Florida Department of Horticulture showed that organically grown food had an average concentration of eleven essential nutrients that was 25 percent higher than that of conventionally grown food. And a University of California at Davis study that focused on individual nutrients in specific crops found even more striking differences: The level of certain beneficial antioxidants (phenols) in corn that was sustainably grown, for instance, was found to be 58.5 percent higher than in conventionally grown corn.

I asked Kate about her sister. As she described her struggles, tears came to her eyes, and to mine, too. I was crying out of sadness for Kate's tragedies and fears, but also out of a sense of gratitude that though this woman was scared, perhaps I could help. We worked together to design the garden, beginning with the crucial first step of choosing its location. A garden needs at least six to eight hours of sun a day, a challenge in Kate's yard because the open stretch of grass was used by her children for sports and play, and the trees bordering the property created shade issues along the periphery. Kate wanted to grow vegetables that would be nutritious but also easy to maintain, and I gave her a rundown of the most "user-friendly" options. Lettuces are always easy to grow; snap peas (one of Thea's favorites) are fun for children to pull off the vine and eat right in the garden, and also typically easy; hot and

sweet peppers, cucumbers, butternut squash, and beans are relatively trouble-free (I suggested tricolor bush beans, because kids
love the mix of yellow, green, and purple shades). It's hard to imagine a lush summer garden without tomatoes, and if the underlying
health of the soil is good, they're also generally easy to maintain.

As we sketched out a plan for the space we estimated at ten feet
by fifteen feet, I explained some of the rationale involved in crop
placement: Certain plants will strangle or shade others if they get
too close—pole beans can get tangled up with tall, leafy greens
such as kale, for instance, and choke the plants off. Squash and
pumpkin plants spread out quickly and need lots of room to sprawl.
I included flowers in the design (kids especially love sunflowers)
and explained their importance in attracting beneficial insects.

It was an odd feeling to be standing on this elegant property in
the heart of Chicago's North Shore teaching the lessons I'd learned
in remote, rural locations to a dedicated suburban housewife and
mother. And it was an even stranger feeling to realize that I was
learning much more than I was teaching. I was beginning to see
that some real and lasting good could come out of a period of my
life I'd been interpreting as a failure. I was also beginning to see
how the business of gardening would enlarge my view of society—
erasing the either/or of the past judgments I'd cast on the North
Shore. Kate and I had taken different life paths, but I was able now
to appreciate the many things we had in common instead of seeing
only the things that set us apart. She was passionately committed to
creating a life for herself and her children that was healthier and
more in balance with and connected to the earth. Her drive to find
a more authentic life for her family was no less serious or urgent
than my own.

Kate's garden was not without its problems. The area of the
lawn that we decided was best for the garden had poor drainage.
This meant that though we'd initially discussed an in-ground design, the garden would have to be a raised bed. This wasn't in itself
a problem, but Bertog's business was heating up as the spring pro-

gressed and he had no spare personnel who could construct it. I
found a sometime-carpenter and general contractor to tear up the
sod and build the ten-by-fifteen-foot box of cedar timbers and a
rabbit-proof fence, but his crew didn't always show up on the days
I'd promised Kate and we fell behind schedule. I regretted that I
hadn't established a firm timeline and realized that, going forward,
I'd need to develop a more precise and demanding management
style.

I hit another snag when it was time to fill the garden with compost. I'd learned from Ken Dunn of the Resource Center that it was
possible to grow food entirely in compost. At the farm, I'd worked
with compost solely as an additive to soil, but I was excited to try
Ken's method. Given the amount of compost I'd need to fill the
space a foot deep, I knew there was no way I could manage it by
lugging in five-pound buckets, so I asked Ken if it would be possible for me to buy a large quantity from him and have it delivered.
My mistake was ordering seven cubic yards of compost—*way* too
much (I've since learned the handy rule that one cubic yard will
cover three inches of depth on one hundred square feet). Since the
lawn near the raised bed was somewhat soggy, there was no way it
could support the weight of Ken's large dump truck, so the compost had to be dumped out in a gigantic pile on several tarps I hur-
riedly spread at the end of Kate's driveway.

The pile of compost was much more than I could cart out to the
garden myself one wheelbarrow at a time, so I made panicked calls
both to Bryan and the general contractor to get their help.

For all those headaches, however, the planting itself went beautifully. The more time we spent together, the more I came to appreciate Kate's work ethic and lack of pretense. She wanted her
kids to be involved in every step so that they'd experience for themselves how food grew from the earth and the hard work involved in
gardening. Thea came with me to "help," and she happily showed
Kate's youngest how to pat-pat the soil back into place over the
seeds. I was glad that I'd brought along extra trowels so that all of

the jostling siblings could participate. The children listened raptly as I explained what kinds of vegetables would grow where in the garden, and they placed handwritten wooden markers to identify each vegetable with a touching sense of awe and ceremony.

The planting at Denise's garden had also gone well. I was starting to think that this business just might work.

A WEEK AFTER I LEFT my voice mail for Verd, just as I was giving up any hope of hearing back from him, he called. "I'm so sorry," he said when I picked up. "I just got your message. I would have called you back right away—I wasn't messing with you. I've been out of town." I felt a rush of excitement when I heard his voice and that unique combination of sincerity, gravity, and lightness that I'd nearly forgotten.

"I was starting to wonder," I said, smiling.

I'd been upstairs in my dad's office, organizing some of my bills and paperwork. I walked next door to pick up the phone in the more private guest room, closing the door and leaning against the couch by the window. "But I'm the one who's sorry," I continued. There was a pause as I tried to think of where to go from there.

Verd leaped in. "I want to see you," he said. "Even if it's just to have coffee. I want to see what there is between us. If there's anything still there."

"You do?" Coming suddenly and without the takeoff ramp of small talk, this was more than I'd expected.

"I've been with other women, but I keep thinking about you," he said. "I keep comparing them to you. Can I come see you?"

"Okay," I said. "Where are you, by the way?" I was trying to let my brain catch up to the sudden lurch and racing of my heart. The conversation then turned back to the place where in other circumstances it might have started, as we filled each other in on what we'd been doing for the past few years. Verd was living in Tampa, running a canvassing office for the environmental nonprofit organization Clean Water Action. I was happy and strangely relieved to hear that he was still trying to live out the ideals we'd shared on the commune. I told him about my work with the Edible Garden in the zoo and the business I'd just started, and my hopes and fears for these projects. "That's exactly what you should be doing," he said emphatically. "Of course it's going to work."

I felt a kind of transformation as we talked, an awakening of aspects of myself I hadn't fully realized had gone numb and that I'd only ever really experienced with Verd—equal parts the comfortable intimacy of friendship, playfulness, and sexual charge. At the end of our conversation, he promised that he'd come to see me in two weeks and that he'd call me back to let me know his flight details.

AS THE SPRING BEGAN to take hold, the Edible Garden started drawing visitors. The garden was located just inside the entrance to the farm exhibit in the zoo, which meant that as the weather warmed and people came in increasing numbers to see the farm animals,

THE EDIBLE GARDEN IN LINCOLN PARK ZOO, CHICAGO, 2005

they walked right past my garden. I'd hung up a handmade sign that read THE EDIBLE GARDEN: PLEASE JOIN IN!

From the first day of planting preparation, I had help from families with children ranging in age from two to twelve years old. I mixed up a batch of granulated organic fertilizer and put it in old yogurt containers so that the kids could shake out the fertilizer over the raised rows and then rake it into the top few inches of soil. I showed them a few sample seeds and explained how seeds "eat" the nutrients in the fertilizer and the soil as they "grow up" into vegetables and flowers.

I'd chosen vegetables that I thought the kids would find delicious and fun to grow: peas, potatoes, red and green lettuce, eggplant, edamame, peppers (green at first, ripening to red, yellow, and orange), watermelon, cucumbers, carrots, beets, and okra. Okra, with its gooey seedpods, had been a favorite of Thea's when she was a toddler, and the plant produces beautiful cream and burgundy flowers. To add more color and attract beneficial insects to the garden, I planned to grow a variety of flowers—purple hyacinth beans, zinnias, and sunflowers, as well as blue, white, and purple morning glories and red scarlet runner beans to create vines and blossoms along the border fence.

I taught the kids how to use their fingertips to poke holes in the soil between one-fourth and one and a half inches deep (depending on the type of seed), and explained why the holes for different plants were spaced apart at different intervals, from narrow spacing for the small lettuces to six-foot spacing between groupings of seeds for the large, sprawling watermelons. I showed them the difference in size between tiny carrot seeds—which are a third of the size of a grain of rice—and bulky squash seeds, letting them hold them side by side. I loved watching the varied looks of solemn concentration, amusement, and wonder on their faces as they handled and planted the seeds. It reminded me of the sense of discovery I'd felt myself when I'd learned these things for the first time. More than that, it made me feel, as I had with Kate and her children, that I had something of value to teach and contribute to others.

AS I PREPARED FOR Verd's visit, I found myself relieved that my parents were away on a long trip to Europe. I was nervous enough about seeing him for the first time in almost two years without having to worry about whether they would get along. I knew my parents would appreciate Verd's warmth and kindness—but I also knew, or at least thought I did, how important things like clothes and table manners were to them. Bryan had offered to take Thea for the weekend, and I was all alone in the house that Friday as I dressed to go pick up Verd from O'Hare. I struggled with what to wear. I was dressing in a more mainstream way than I had on the farm, and I wasn't sure what Verd would make of that. Beyond that, I was conscious of having aged since the last time I'd seen him, aware of the etching of lines at the corners of my mouth and eyes. I put on blush and lipstick, but then worried, scrutinizing myself in the mirror over the bathroom sink, that it was too much. I wiped it off. No amount of makeup would cover my doubt, on the most basic level, that he'd still find me physically attractive.

At the airport, as I drove up to the terminal, I spotted him immediately from the car, even though he, too, had edged notably closer to the conventional. Years of door-to-door canvassing had tamed his fashion eccentricities: He'd knocked on the doors of more than twenty-five thousand households in the previous two years and discovered, he later told me, that "nine times out of ten, you won't get a signature if you've got an eyebrow piercing or Salvador Dalí facial hair." Standing outside the main terminal next to a small brown leather suitcase, he was clean shaven and had short-cropped hair, almost prep-school style. Gone was the bling: no chunky rings, no piercings, no pendants or studded belt. He wore faded jeans, cowboy boots, and a red T-shirt with the logo

MONKEYWRENCH BOOKS, a hip bookstore in Austin—not North Shore attire exactly, but nothing too offbeat. I'd told him to look for the green and yellow magnets that said THE ORGANIC GARDENER attached to the car's front doors. He stepped toward me as I pulled up to the curb. I hopped out, and we hugged quickly, perfunctorily, before he tossed his bag in back and jumped into the car. But I lingered for a few moments before pulling out into traffic. I stared at him, taking in the physical reality of the face I'd spent so much time imagining. He smiled and I looked away, self-conscious.

Neither of us said anything as I put the car in gear, but at the first stop sign I turned toward him and blurted out, "How do I look to you—do I look okay?" I'd always been able to say whatever was on my mind to him without censoring myself, no matter how trivial.

"You look amazing," he said.

"Really?"

He grinned. I'd forgotten how his smile spread across his entire face and how good it felt to see it. "Hell, yes."

I slowed as we turned off the highway and approached my parents' house, remembering how daunting it had seemed to me when I'd first come home. I started to warn him, but he shrugged in response. "I've already seen it," he told me. When he'd tracked down my phone number last year, he'd also gotten my parents' address and at one point, when he realized I wouldn't be calling him back anytime soon, he'd considered simply showing up at the door with flowers. He'd located the house on Google Maps, but then abandoned that plan because he felt it would be wrong to pressure me.

I led him to the guest room where he'd be staying—the spare room with the couch and twin beds—and then took him on a tour, heading down to the living room, dining room, and kitchen, and finally to the basement where my parents kept toys for the grandkids.

"Wait," he said when I turned to lead him back upstairs.

He moved toward me, reaching his hands to my face. His touch, the light pressure of his hands, felt so familiar and so new all at once that I couldn't speak. He pulled me to him, kissing me lightly, barely grazing my lips, then deeply.

Soon he was leading me upstairs to the guest room. It wasn't until he pulled back to ask me what was wrong that I realized I was crying.

"I'm sorry," I said. I'd been feeling intensely happy but then suddenly overcome with sorrow—aware fully for the first time of the painful separation we'd endured, the tearing apart that he'd protested and that I had ultimately accepted.

He shook his head, smiling, brushing back my hair from my face. I asked if he could forgive me but he said he didn't have to. "I never held any of it against you." He kissed my forehead, then my lips, and told me he didn't want us to spend our time going back over the past; we had to look forward.

Chapter 9

B Y MID-MAY, TWO MONTHS AFTER I'D POSTED THE FIRST BATCH OF
flyers, it no longer felt strange to answer the phone and hear a request to speak with the Organic Gardener. I'd gotten more than
twenty calls from people who'd seen my flyers, and twelve had become clients. And some of those clients were becoming friends.
Soon after I met with Debbie Sobel about a garden, she insisted
that I bring Thea along to play with her four-year-old daughter,
Frankie, on planting day. It would become a ritual that continued
for many years to come, Debbie and I in the garden planting, weeding, or harvesting, with Thea and Frankie either helping out or
playing on the swing set, then the four of us, along with Frankie's
brother and father, splitting two large pizzas at the Sobels' picnic
table. I found myself watching Debbie and Frankie during our visits, just as I'd watched Kate with her kids, appreciating her style of
mothering. Debbie patiently let Frankie discover and explore the
garden on her own time, and she was equally patient with Thea,
wryly indulging her desire to drink from a particular blue cup every
visit.

Thea was making good headway, as she had been ever since
she'd started adjusting to life in my parents' house. The previous
spring she'd developed an uncannily explicit way of showing her
happiness in our new life, almost every day playing with my mom

and reenacting her birth. She would curl up in a ball under a blanket on the bed, then emerge very slowly, arms outstretched, as my mom shouted, "Oh, she's here! Thea is here!" My mother would pretend the phone was ringing, answer, and say, "Oh, Uncle Bill!" (or Aunt Suzan or Hallie). "Yes, we have a newborn. . . . Yes, you can come see her, and bring a present!" And my mother would describe the large circle of family Thea belonged to, listing names of grandparents, aunts, uncles, and cousins. Thea seemed to find it healing to relive her birth and imagine herself surrounded by a loving family, and they repeated this routine hundreds of times in our first year back.

While Thea was easing into her new life, I was also beginning to accept that the North Shore was somewhere we might actually stay. I had come home because I hadn't had anywhere else to go, without giving much thought to the longer term, but as we settled in and started building new lives, the thought of a real future in the area began to take hold. I still had questions about whether I could raise a child in Winnetka in the ways that I felt were important—*Would Thea grow up seeing wealth as a measure of happiness? Would she have a strong enough connection to nature? Would she be pressured to conform instead of be herself?* But I was also beginning to see that there were aspects of the community that were good for Thea's development, especially the support of extended family and close relationships with multigenerational family friends. I could see the value of giving Thea a life framed by family traditions and holiday gatherings. I was also beginning to appreciate the strengths of the school system, the safety and beauty of the neighborhoods, and the broader community I was coming to know that seemed willing, and even determined, to help us succeed.

It wasn't lost on me that I—a thirty-six-year-old living at home—needed this sense of safety, constancy, and support as much as Thea did as I began to build my business and reengage with the other parts of my life. Even though my schedule was getting ever busier as I juggled my work downtown at the Edible Garden with my twelve suburban clients, I was still unsure if the business would fly. And I was still in flux in my personal life, though hopeful about the possibility of building a relationship with Verd on our own terms. During his visit to Illinois, he'd filled me in more fully on what he'd been doing since leaving Zendik Farm, an epic journey across states, countries, and continents.

His departure from the farm, like mine, had been complicated, occurring in stages. When he first left in the fall of 2000, he went to live with his parents for a while in Chicago (they'd recently sold his childhood home in Oak Park). He had stopped communicating with his family for long stretches during his more than five years at Zendik, after Arol criticized him for being too emotionally connected to them; at one point, hoping to prove his loyalty, he'd even yelled at his sister in a phone call, in earshot of other farm members, for "tempting" him by inviting him away for a New Year's Eve trip to Thailand to celebrate her graduation from college. He felt like a failure for not having been able to make his life on the farm work, and apologized over and over to his family for having hurt them.

But Verd hadn't yet given up on the farm's guiding philosophy—or on me. In an effort to stay connected, he offered to become a kind of roving "evangelist." He borrowed more than a thousand dollars from his parents to buy boxes of Zendik Farm magazines, T-shirts, CDs, and bumper stickers, and a plane ticket to Germany, where he stayed with extended family in Hamburg and went on his own "selling trips" through nearby cities. He'd been one of the farm's highest earners (incorporating dance moves into his street corner riffs about Zendik philosophy), and despite the language and cultural barriers, he managed to do well abroad, at times making the equivalent of more than three hundred U.S. dollars a day. From Hamburg, he traveled to Copenhagen—in part to reconnect to his family's roots there, and in part because he'd seen a documentary that emphasized the remarkable openness and tolerance of Denmark's culture. His next leap was to Cape Town,

South Africa, where he lived for six months, both selling Zendik Farm gear in the city and working alongside a Zulu farmer and other interns on Bloublommetjieskloof Farm in nearby Wellington. It was an organic and biodynamic farm, and Verd's work focused on growing potatoes and beekeeping. He loved it—it was there, even more than at Zendik Farm, where he discovered a true love of organic gardening—and he thought about staying longer. But he'd sold the last of his Zendik gear, and when he called the farm to stock up, Arol (in one of her classic reversals) refused to sell him any more.

He wasn't ready yet to lose all connection to Zendik Farm, so he returned in the late fall of 2001. I was working in the field when he came back; I looked up, and he met my gaze. I quickly looked away, but what he saw in that "one look" was all he needed, he later said, to know that whatever it was between us was still alive.

At the time, Thea was still an infant, and I was struggling under the weight of Arol's criticism of my mothering. I simply couldn't handle any additional criticism for rekindling a relationship with Verd. And Verd himself had changed during his time away: As a teenager, he'd gone straight from his parents' house to Zendik Farm without ever having been on his own; now, seven years later, as a twenty-three-year-old, he'd been exposed to different cultures and had managed to make his way in strange cities thousands of miles from anyone who knew him. He wasn't willing to accept being characterized by Arol as passive, phony, or lazy. He still had his environmental ideals—but most other aspects of life on the farm, in particular Arol's critiques of farm members, now struck him as "bullshit." He started speaking up and answering back— a cardinal sin at the farm. After an argument with another seller during a trip with a Zendik Farm selling crew to Washington, D.C., he was given enough money for a bus ticket and found himself lit- erally pushed out of a van that was moving just under ten miles an hour.

He had no wallet or ID—nothing but the clothes on his back.

Verd knew his parents would have welcomed him, but he wanted to prove to himself that he could make it on his own. He bought a ticket to Northampton, Massachusetts, where a friend of his who'd left Zendik Farm the previous year was living. The ex-Zendik friend put him up for a night, but her apartment was cramped and she didn't have room for him to stay long-term. In a strange bit of luck, while Verd was walking down the street trying to figure out what to do next, an Amherst College student called out to him, "You're Verd from Zendik Farm! I bought a T-shirt from you in Harvard Square in Boston!" She offered to put him up for a few weeks.

He applied for food stamps and got some clothes from Goodwill, and one day looked up to see a poster that offered a solution: Clean Water Action was looking for canvassers. With his "sales" experience, his willingness to work hard, and his passion for the environment, it was the perfect fit. He started off in Northampton and did so well that he was quickly promoted to canvass director in Tampa, Florida.

He told his boss there, on his first day in June 2003, that there was a woman in his life he had unresolved issues with, and that if it became possible for him to reconnect with her, he might have to leave on short notice. When I finally called him back in the spring of 2005, he'd been getting ready to seek me out anyway. He needed to see if what he'd felt in that one look in the field at Zendik years earlier was still true. He knew that it was, he told me, the second he saw me step out of the car when I picked him up at O'Hare.

On the last day of his visit, before dropping him off at the airport, I'd taken him to have brunch with Grandma Rose to celebrate Mother's Day. The two of them were an unlikely pair—a twenty-something eco-activist who had a personal net worth of less than five hundred dollars, and an elderly Chicago grande dame who had never in six decades gone without a weekly manicure. But Verd was characteristically game. We stopped at Banana Republic first to buy him some clothes suitable for the dining room in Rose's high-rise retirement home and settled on a pair of black pants and a burgundy short-sleeved linen shirt with chest pockets and shoulder epaulets. He looked, we both agreed, shockingly presentable.

Grandma Rose greeted us with a cheerful "Hi, kids!" She was beautifully coiffed as always, wearing a fresh coat of pink lipstick and carefully coordinated jewelry. She needed to bring her oxygen tank, and Verd, whose mother and sister were nurses, was gentle and skilled as he helped her into her wheelchair and placed her feet, in their petite low-heeled pumps, onto the footrests. We hadn't been aware of the dining room requirement that men wear jackets, but the maître d' instantly appeared with a spare blue blazer for Verd. Almost as quickly, beneath the glitter of the chandeliers, he and Grandma Rose fell into a mutual reverie. They chatted at length about their travels throughout Europe, quipping and comparing notes. They complimented each other and the food. I listened and watched, sipping champagne on an empty stomach and giggling with pleasure at their rapport. It was another circle closing, as if by magic, in a way I couldn't have imagined.

I was still buzzing from brunch and from how the weekend as a whole had turned out when I dropped Verd off at the airport that afternoon. Standing in the atrium amid the chaos of O'Hare I could register nothing but the feel of his face in my hands and the sweetness of our kiss. I heard myself saying, in words that sounded inadequate even as I said them, "You made me feel like a woman again." He rested his chin on the top of my head and said, with a combination of gentle humor and utter seriousness, "The best is yet to come."

Watching him walk away through the crowd, I thought back to that skinny, plucky high school dropout streaking through the rain in Texas and felt again what I'd felt then: *I would not—could not—live without this person.* He had plans to visit again in two weeks, and each day leading up to his return seemed to crawl by.

KATE'S FAMILY WAS GOING out of town, and she'd asked me to maintain their garden while they were away. *Of course,* I'd said. I thought the work would be trouble-free until I arrived one morning to find two holes chewed through the supposedly rabbit-proof plastic mesh fencing I'd installed around the raised bed, and evidence that rabbits had eaten a big portion of the newly growing vegetables. Given the size of the holes, which had appeared overnight, it was clear that the barrier had been easily breached.

My initial reaction was out of proportion to the actual damage: some snap-pea plants nibbled bare; a few lettuce heads gnawed to their stumps; half a dozen carrots unearthed and pilfered. But somehow this gaffe made me doubt whether I was up to the task of running the business. I had, after all, been outwitted by a rabbit. And I felt that there was a lot at stake in this particular garden, including living up to Kate's trust and faith.

I'd dealt with pests before—it's impossible to work on any kind of farm, and certainly an organic farm, without facing them. In California in particular I'd encountered gophers who would eat entire rows of crops from underneath. In Texas, fire ants had been a menace. Aphids, locusts, caterpillars, Japanese beetles, tomato hornworms, cabbage loopers, squash vine borers—I'd seen and battled them all, almost always successfully. But I'd also always worked in a group on the farm, and there was a sense of shared responsibility and cooperation that made problem solving easier. Standing in Kate's yard that morning, it was just me. I alone was responsible for building a new fence and replanting (fixes that cost $265 in materials), as well as apologizing to the MacKenzies. Kate appreciated that I had caught the problem early and absorbed the expense. But the episode kept alive the nagging questions I'd had about the long-term prospects of my business.

When another new client, Susan Schlesinger, who had a beautifully landscaped property and a historic home, showed me the spot where she wanted to put her garden, I was uneasy but didn't voice my concerns. It was between two small trees, and although there was enough sunlight, I could see that it would be hard to prepare the soil because the roots from the trees would compete with the plants. I knew that the only way to make it work was a raised bed, but that didn't fit with Susan's aesthetic vision. I wanted her business and didn't say no—and then kicked myself when, just as I'd thought, the leaf crops did fine but all of the root crops (carrots, beets, radishes, and potatoes) failed. It was a lesson in how I would have to make tougher, more practical decisions in the future, but it was also a kind of confirmation that I actually did know what I was doing, and just needed to trust my knowledge and experience.

For the most part, the other gardens I planted that year succeeded. Chris Kennedy, then the president of Chicago's Merchandise Mart, approached our gardening sessions with amazing rigor. He insisted on doing all the work himself—aerating the soil, making the rows, weeding, and planting—often bringing his young children out to dig and yank and sweat alongside him for hours at a time. When, at one point, Chris's wife called to him from the kitchen window to take an important phone call, he called back to her: "Tell them I've got to get the peas in before I can talk!"

I still had a number of technical challenges to sort out, including, crucially, finding subcontractors to build the raised beds and bring in the compost, but the enthusiasm of my clients that first year more than compensated for the setbacks. I came to suspect, by midseason, that the business of planting gardens might have more growth potential than I'd imagined.

ONE WEDNESDAY MORNING, as I was racing down Lake Shore Drive to the Edible Garden, I saw my cellphone light up on the passenger seat and display the words "I lov u madly. cant w8 2 c u 2morw, V." I was baffled. I'd never sent or received a text message before—I didn't even know what one was—which made the words, once I'd deciphered them, all the more exciting.

Verd and I had spoken by phone almost every night since his visit. Our conversations were usually brief, because by evening we were both exhausted, but they were long enough to share our experiences and to build on the power and excitement of his first visit. This second trip would be an important step forward for us, because Verd was going to get the chance to spend time with Thea.

After picking him up at the airport, I drove him straight to the Edible Garden, which was growing well, both in terms of the early spring crops and the number of visitors. Verd took it all in and immediately got to work, fixing a glitch in the sprinkler system, turning the compost, and helping out with weeding, while Thea played with other kids who were there with their parents. For me, it was a concrete example of how far she'd come since our return.

Back at the house, Verd kicked a soccer ball around with Thea, spotted her as she bounced on a small trampoline, and splashed her in the kiddie pool. Listening to them laugh together made me happy in the way that every parent knows can only come from hearing your child experience deep pleasure. The visit could not have been going better until 2 A.M. on Sunday, when the phone rang with the terrible news that Grandma Rose had taken a sudden turn for the worse; she had been sick during the past week, but now her caregiver was calling to say that she might not survive the night.

I called my parents in Europe, who immediately booked the next flight home, woke Verd and told him what was happening, and then called Bryan and gave him the update. Verd wrapped Thea in a heavy blanket and carried her to the car. We dropped her off at Bryan's, then drove on to Rose's apartment, where it was clear that she was dying. Her breathing, which had long been a problem, was increasingly labored, and the hospice nurse had her on a morphine drip. She was in and out of consciousness and unable to talk. Verd had been waiting in the hall, and I went to him and told him I wasn't sure how to handle the situation—I didn't know what to *do*. "Let's go in," he said quietly, "and you just sit on the bed and hold her hand and talk to her." Verd pulled up a chair beside me and held my left hand as I held onto my grandmother with my right. Though I couldn't be certain if she recognized me, I knew that she wasn't in pain.

I told her about my childhood memories of her and our family: the smell of brisket with carrots and onions and potatoes that filled her home during my weekend visits; the fresh orange juice she squeezed for us in the morning; her signature dessert, red Jell-O with sliced bananas on top; my visits to her Florida home and my fishing trips with my dad. I laughed about her visit to the farm in Texas, when she'd rolled up her pants legs, grabbed her stainless steel walking stick, and toured the property on foot. I remembered taking a trip myself by train to see her in my senior year of high school, just before I'd left home. We'd sat in her kitchen during a storm and admired the way the palm tree leaves were twisting and rippling in the wind, the astonishing beauty of something that simple.

GRANDMA ROSE, MOM, AND ME, WALKING ZENDIK FARM
IN BASTROP, TEXAS, 1993

Rose Greengrass Rachlin was ninety-two and died gracefully. I felt release and gratitude that I had been able to be with her, my grandma who had loved me so much and done so much for me, in her last moments.

The nurse told me that she'd handle arrangements while we awaited my parents' arrival later that morning. To pass the time, Verd and I walked to Lincoln Park, down by the lake. He was due to fly out that evening, and we sat on the grass leaning against the thick trunk of a tree and felt the weight of the moment. I told him that Rose had lost many of the people she loved most prematurely— her sister to rheumatic fever as a child, her son to leukemia at twenty-nine, her husband to a stroke—and that what I admired most about her was that she knew how to move on and move forward and be happy, how to have a good laugh. As I let go of Grandma Rose, I felt at the same time that she was urging me to move forward. It also wasn't lost on me that Verd and I were sitting in Lincoln Park, not far from the zoo where my new career had begun to take root.

At that moment, Verd also had his eye on the future. He told me that he'd made some decisions. He said he planned to visit me every two weeks, that he'd move to Chicago within six months, and, most important, that eventually we'd get married. It was only the second time we'd been together in three years, but I knew that I wanted that, too. With equal clarity I also knew what I *didn't* want. I didn't ever want to go back to the depressed, disorganized state I'd been in a year earlier. I told Verd that in order to build a life that would work on the North Shore, in which our basic needs and Thea's needs would be covered, we'd have to get serious about our income. "I don't need a big house or fancy cars, just to have a decent life, but we've got to realize what that will take," I said. Real estate would be expensive on the North Shore. As she grew older, Thea would need everything that came with being in school and playing sports and having friends; and though we hadn't yet discussed it, I knew that once we were married and our family was stable, we might want to have another child.

Verd had never put much thought into money and was perfectly happy making a minimal salary at his canvassing job in Florida and living a simple life. Though he seemed open to my concerns, later I worried that I might have scared him with my sudden financial pragmatism—a U-turn from the money-be-damned philosophy of the Jeanne he'd known at the farm. But when we spoke the next day, he immediately said, "I've thought about becoming an acupuncturist." The notion was funny on a certain level—he'd never shown an interest in acupuncture before, and there wasn't exactly a huge demand for alternative medicine on the North Shore, but I loved his response. He hadn't been scared off at all. He'd been thinking through his possibilities.

Chapter 10

———————————

EVERY WEDNESDAY AND SATURDAY WHEN I ARRIVED AT LINCOLN
Park Zoo, I would park next to the buildings that served as a sort
of stage set for the zoo's farm exhibit, which was next to the Edible
Garden. There was a barn that housed a large demonstration John
Deere tractor, along with educational displays about farm life,
growing methods, and plant biology. The barn's silo was actually a
storage room, and the animals that lived in nearby stalls included
chickens, eight dairy cows, a dozen goats, two Flemish giant rabbits, a half-dozen sheep, two ponies, and a sow and her piglets.
This was the backdrop for my nearby miniature vegetable "farm,"
where dozens of kids stopped by each day to help me with ongoing
tasks like fertilizing, weeding, pruning, mulching with straw, thinning the carrots, and mounding hills of dirt around the corn and
potatoes (the more dirt you pile up around a potato plant, the more
tubers will form and the more potatoes you'll grow).

One Saturday, a young boy and his father noticed me working
in the garden and stopped by on their way to see the farm animals.
Some of the early crops were ready to be harvested, and Tommy, a
city kid, thrust his hands into the dirt and worked happily. After a
short while, when his father announced that they wouldn't have
time to see the animals if they didn't leave, Tommy wouldn't budge.
He fell into a hypnotic rhythm snapping beans off their vines, pull-

ing up one weed and then the next. An hour passed before his father finally convinced him to leave, with Tommy having decisively
chosen the plants over the animals.

They returned the following two Saturdays, and Tommy continued to be focused and absorbed. He listened to me and followed
my instructions—*You can pull up three beets, one of each color,
red, golden, and pink-and-white striped. . . . Just a little bit of fertilizer, and sprinkle evenly*—and enjoyed the harvesting most of all.
He would chomp excitedly into raw vegetables still gritty with dirt,
and he loved in particular the long, striped, funny-shaped Arme-
nian cucumbers. Every task drew questions—*How did this plant
make a cucumber? How did a seed become a watermelon?* I did my
best to answer him.

On their fourth visit, Tommy showed up wearing fist-size head-
phones that looked too big for his five-year-old head. His father
explained that they'd just come out of occupational therapy for
Tommy's early stage attention deficit/hyperactivity disorder. I was
stunned—Tommy had been by far the most attentive and engaged
visitor to the garden and seemed to me anything but distracted.
"It's a surprise to me, too," his father said. "He's a handful at
home and at school, but there's something about gardening that
seems to help him."

A growing body of research shows that there *is*, in fact, something about gardening—and, more generally, being in nature—that
helps people with attention deficit/hyperactivity disorder. ADHD is
shockingly prevalent in the United States, affecting roughly one in
every fourteen children. One recent study by the University of Illinois at Urbana-Champaign explored how gardening and other activities in green outdoor settings influenced the behavior of more
than four hundred kids nationally, aged five to eighteen, diagnosed
with ADHD. It found that these activities reduced "impulsivity"
and "inattention," among other symptoms of ADHD, by a "significant or marginally significant" measure.

The results echo the work of Stephen and Rachel Kaplan, professors of psychology at the University of Michigan who have spent decades researching the attention restoration theory, which holds that humans concentrate better after spending time in nature. The Kaplans distinguish between voluntary attention, when a person must actively focus to solve problems, and involuntary attention, when a person's focus is effortlessly engaged by the surroundings. Nature, with its varieties of sound, smell, and texture, has the unique power to highly engage a person's *involuntary* attention, which, in turn, rests and restores the person's ability to exert *voluntary* attention. This explained so well to me much of what I'd felt as a nine-year-old in the first garden I'd wandered into, and the joys of my summers at camp in the woods.

Frances E. Kuo, a coauthor of the University of Illinois study, concluded that nature appears to offer "a way to help manage ADHD symptoms that is readily available, doesn't have any stigma associated with it, doesn't cost anything, and doesn't have any side effects." It amazed me to learn about these quantifiable human impacts of gardening, but it also confirmed what I'd known on a gut level from years of experience—that growing food could be useful to all of us, adults and children, in ways that went beyond the obvious.

WHEN VERD RETURNED FOR his third visit in late June, a lot seemed to be at stake, not just because our relationship had been evolving at warp speed, but because this man I loved—twenty-seven and still without a high school diploma—was going to meet my parents. In my mind, he was perfect for me, but he was very different from the kind of son-in-law my parents had envisioned, and like any daughter, I wanted their approval. I had put them through hell, and the last thing I wanted was to cause more pain or create more distance between us; I needed them to see Verd as exactly the person I should build my future with.

I briefed both parties before the visit. "They really care how people dress," I cautioned Verd, trying not to insult the offbeat spirit in him I loved so much. "They really care about table manners." My parents also got a warning: "He doesn't care about clothes the way you do; he doesn't pay attention to table manners; he's endlessly gracious, but probably not in the ways you'd expect." With my parents, I closed by saying the only thing that I ultimately felt mattered: "Please keep in mind that I've never felt so loved and understood by a man."

The visit had its ups and downs. My parents both made a point of mentioning how late Verd, who'd worked long hours that week, slept in; my mother scolded him directly when he took a shower and left a damp towel draped on the couch in his room. I saw that her comments stung him, but he didn't give up. He kept trying to engage her, wearing her down with the kind of friendly banter he had so easily shared with Grandma Rose, and by the end of the visit, she was saying, "It's like talking to a good girlfriend!"

Finding common ground with my dad was more difficult. The night before he left, Verd took a cocktail out to the patio where my father stood, and accepted a proffered cigar. Verd not only delicately inhaled, but kept on going down to the nub. I watched the scene from the kitchen window, aware that he had never before smoked a cigar in his life, and found his efforts to fit in immensely endearing. The next morning, he woke up with an allergic reaction to the smoke, with sores all over the inside of his mouth. Instead of complaining, he teased, "I'd swallow fire for you."

BY THE TIME VERD moved to Chicago a few months later, I had saved up some money and was ready to move out of my parents' guest room and into a place of my own. I had made some important headway in my time at my parents' house, getting back on my feet psychically and emotionally, establishing Thea in a new town with lots of friends and relatives, breaking into the wider food and urban farming world of Chicago through my work with Abby Mandel and the Edible Garden, and starting my own business. There were times when it was dizzying to remember how things had looked a year and a half earlier, when my parents had taken me in during my time of extreme vulnerability and helped me get back on track. Now I was ready to create a life of my own with Thea and Verd. But moving Thea out of my parents' house—out of the rhythms and rituals she had become so accustomed to—would be a big step. An even bigger step both for Thea and me was going to be moving in with Verd, who, despite the inroads he'd made with my parents, was not someone they knew well. I was nervous about discussing my plan with them, unsure of how they'd react, especially given the change it represented for Thea.

But as it turned out, they'd been thinking along similar lines and agreed that it was time. I searched for apartments online while Verd looked for work. He'd realized that his plan of studying acupuncture would take years to pay off, and he needed to start making money right away. The answer was almost too obvious to notice: Verd had helped me at the Edible Garden on several of his visits, and I tentatively asked if he'd be willing to do some work for the Organic Gardener the next season. I wasn't sure how much I could pay him; I wasn't even sure yet how much money I'd netted in my first year and had no way of knowing how many clients I'd have the following year. But I did know that if I had any hope of growing my business, I'd never find a more competent and trustworthy collaborator. I'd already taught Verd most of what I knew about growing food at the farm, and he also had the skills to install irrigation systems and work on the soil-tilling-and-preparation side of things—tasks I would otherwise have to contract out. Equally important, in his years as a canvasser, he had knocked on thousands of doors and learned how to enter people's homes and instantly strike up a rapport; he had launched flyer and public outreach campaigns to build precisely the kind of grassroots network I would need in order to expand. When we hit upon the idea, we were both amazed that it had taken us so long to consider it. He agreed to give things a try, and promised to find whatever other part-time jobs he could to make money on the side.

He also suggested that Kord, his best friend from the farm, who had left a few years earlier and was now looking for work, join us as a housemate and collaborator. Kord was a kind, funny, hard-working guy in his early thirties who had a warm smile and a bear-ish build. He was trusted and respected by everyone at the farm, including me. This would save money on rent, and would also help solve the problems that had been the most frustrating and costly in my first year of business: building the fences and raised beds and transporting soil and compost. Kord was a skilled carpenter and had an F-150 pickup truck. The Organic Gardener now had a crew, and we were going to see if we could make it work.

On the first of October, Verd, Thea, Kord, and I moved into a three-bedroom apartment in Evanston on the ground floor of a nineteenth-century peaked-roof house with a sunny front yard. It was a short distance from a school that I'd liked for Thea. Evanston was also convenient because it was close to our client base and close to my parents. There wasn't much to move—a kitchen table and chairs from my parents' basement, a desk, a used television, a bed for me and Verd, and a bunk bed for Thea. The apartment was a thousand square feet, with cramped rooms and a tiny kitchen, but it got ample light and they were *my* cramped rooms and *my* tiny kitchen. That first night I stayed up for hours, wide awake in the dark, sipping a mug of peppermint tea and realizing with a strange sense of surprise that this was the first time I'd had a home I could call my own since I'd lived in the small Wilmette apartment with Mark at the age of seventeen.

This was also the first time since my years with Mark that I'd had a chance to pursue a romantic relationship on my own, outside my parents' home and beyond the scrutiny of the commune. In the days and weeks after we moved in I often lay awake at night watching Verd sleep, savoring the privacy of our room, knowing that the next morning we wouldn't have to report anything to anyone.

Most nights I fell asleep with my hand resting on top of his, think-ing *You're here. Nobody can take you away from me.* The instant I woke up, even before opening my eyes I'd rummage through the sheets to find him again. *You're still here.*

Verd and Kord managed to land part-time jobs quickly. Verd worked as an Arthur Murray ballroom dance instructor in the eve-nings, and in the daytime as a dog walker and a UPS holiday shift worker. Kord worked as a clerk at the local Foodstuffs gourmet grocery and joined Verd at UPS. Both of them committed twenty hours a week to the Organic Gardener. Even with our demanding schedules, we quickly settled into a comfortable routine as room-mates, sharing household tasks. Verd would get the groceries while I'd cook (with Thea "sous-cheffing") and Kord would wash the dishes; I'd tally household expenses while Kord fixed a leaky faucet and Verd mowed the lawn. Soon after we moved, Bryan found an apartment across the street and became part of our group meals and routines. We'd created, inadvertently, a microcosm of our for-mer communal life, where we were able, within the safety of our group, to begin processing memories of our shared experience on the farm.

A few months after we moved, our old friend Helen Zuman came to visit. Helen had joined Zendik Farm in the fall of 1999, just after graduating from Harvard. She'd won a fellowship to spend a year visiting intentional communities, and though she'd intended only to pass through Zendik, she ended up staying for five years. Some other Zendik members had been to elite universities like Dartmouth and MIT, but most of us had dropped out of high school or college. Helen was admired for her Harvard education but also snubbed for it: *That's not real intelligence,* the criticism went. After years of struggling internally with the farm's philoso-phy and mores, Helen began noticing contradictions in Arol's be-havior; as her trust in the leadership eroded, she sold fewer and fewer Zendik CDs and magazines. In 2004, Arol had her expelled. Helen hitchhiked to the West Coast, supporting herself with odd jobs until she got a position working at an organic farm in Northern California. She saved up wages to take a forty-day trip through Hawaii, New Zealand, Australia, and South Africa, before moving to Brooklyn, where she had grown up. Six months later, she came to Chicago to visit us.

The first night of her visit, Helen showed me a book she'd just read entitled *Combatting Cult Mind Control* by Steven Hassan, a former cult member turned counselor. Some of the patterns of cult leadership identified in the book closely resembled behaviors of the leaders at Zendik, she said, adding that while Arol and Wulf hadn't used overtly cultish tactics such as planning a collective suicide, portending an apocalypse, or requiring a formal "marriage" to the group, they had used a subtler form of psychological manipulation that the book identified as typical of cults. They'd controlled us by convincing us that the outside world was toxic—deathly so—and that we, personally, were deeply tainted and in need of purification that only they and the farm could provide.

I internally resisted Helen's argument at first, recalling that the San Diego police had sent a cult investigator to our California location who'd concluded that we were a functional commune, not a cult. But over the course of Helen's visit, in discussions that lasted hours at a time, Verd, Kord, Bryan, and I began hashing out questions that none of us had had the courage or clarity to address until then: Why had Arol and Wulf forced people in loving relationships apart? Why had they demanded to know the details of our sexual lives? Why were parent-child bonds constantly criticized and threatened? Why had they insisted that we uproot and move the commune so frequently just when we were finally settling into homesteads we'd labored over for years? Why did almost everyone who left the farm have degrading and painful departures? Helen, for instance, who'd given thirteen thousand dollars of her fellowship money to the commune, received a ten-dollar bill from Arol on the day she was told to leave, and was then dropped off to hitch a ride on the side of Highway 64.

Why had every one of us struggled with a chronic and profound sense that we were fundamentally *bad,* even disgraceful people, doubting aspects of ourselves that were, in fact, our strengths? Verd, for instance, who was one of the hardest working members of the commune, was continually criticized for being lazy and un-committed. Kord, who'd grown up in rural Illinois and had a truly friendly Midwestern disposition, was often publicly humiliated for "smiling too much" on the grounds that this was "phony" and belied his true feelings. Helen, who'd graduated from Harvard with a degree in visual art, gave up on making art at Zendik because her talents were dismissed as useless.

As our group sorted through these questions, we began to real-ize that even though we were now much happier than we'd been at the farm, we were all suffering from a kind of post-traumatic stress disorder. I told the group that more often than not, after I had sex with Verd, I'd hallucinate hearing Arol's voice demanding to know every detail; I'd even whip my head around to look behind me and see if she was there to misinterpret, criticize, and threaten us. Verd confessed that every time he made a careless mistake—if he nicked himself shaving, broke a glass, or missed a step on the dance floor—he'd reflexively cringe, waiting to be accused of having deliberately screwed up, as he had routinely been at the farm: *There are no ac-cidents,* his mind would echo.

Kord, for his part, was still mourning a crippling loss of love. He had arrived at the commune in April 1994, on his twenty-first birthday. He'd been miserable in his previous job at a factory hon-ing steel tubing in Somonauk, Illinois. Within a day of discovering a Zendik magazine at Blues Fest in Chicago, he'd packed up his belongings, cashed his two-hundred-dollar paycheck, and begun driving to Texas to join the "revolution."

Kord was handsome, affable, and a skilled musician, and he had been immediately drawn into the commune's inner circle. He'd be-come a leader of the Zendik band and improv comedy troupe. He'd fallen in love with Fawn, Arol and Wulf's daughter, and during most of their intensive four-year relationship he was adored by Zendik's leaders. But when Fawn began pulling away from him to seriously date another guy, and then became pregnant with her new partner, Kord collapsed emotionally and was ostracized for his depression. In 2001, he was dropped off on the side of the highway with his dog on a rope, one change of clothes in his backpack, and seven dollars in his pocket. He enlisted in the army, but less than a year into his service, he found himself questioning the morality of the Iraq invasion and managed to get discharged. He worked as a carpenter and moved in with some other ex-Zendiks in Massachusetts, where he learned that, adding insult to injury, Arol had removed his name from the many albums of music he'd helped to produce over seven years.

Every one of us rehashed painful memories during Helen's visit. As we did so, we alternated between states of quiet grief, fidgety discomfort, and explosive fits of laughter at the absurdity of our experience. Ultimately, our collective realization that the farm was, for all intents and purposes, a cult, came to be freeing. It signaled a shift in our thinking: Rather than hanging on to the belief that we were deeply and fundamentally flawed as people, we'd come to understand that the psychological gamesmanship at Zendik Farm had been deeply and fundamentally flawed. We'd made a grave mistake when we'd bought into a corrupt system, but we had begun to overcome our mistake by opting out of that system.

In the weeks after Helen's visit, laughter became our most effective form of group therapy. When Kord smiled his gentle Midwestern smile, Verd or I would deadpan, "You phony," and we'd all crack up. And when Verd would come home from twelve straight hours of dance lessons and dog walking, Kord would look at him and say, "You're such a lazy ass," and we would, without fail, howl with laughter.

VERD, KORD, AND I worked together throughout the fall to wrap up my initial twelve gardens. After the first hard frost, we cleared out the dead plants, removed plant supports, tidied the garden spaces, and prepped the soil for replanting the following spring. While the season certainly had its ups and downs, it ended on a high note, with ten of my twelve clients voicing interest in contracts for the following year. Verd began plotting a flyer campaign that would span a twenty-mile radius around Winnetka.

Chapter 11

ONE SETBACK IN THE NEW APARTMENT CAME IN THE LATE FALL AS I started planning for a huge full-sun vegetable garden to go in our front yard. There was plenty of room for it—the yard measured twenty feet by thirty feet—and since our street bordered the commercial heart of Evanston and had lots of pedestrian traffic, this garden had the potential to be an important showpiece. Our landlord had agreed to let us put up a sign with contact information for the Organic Gardener. But as I was out walking the yard taking measurements, a neighbor dropped by to caution me about lead in the soil, explaining that her own yard had tested high. She suggested that I dig up a sample and send it to a lab in Chicago for testing.

Lead can be found anywhere—in urban and rural soil, in neighborhoods of all socioeconomic stripes—but there's a particular danger near painted structures built before 1978, when lead-based paint was banned, or on any building site where a structure this old has been torn down. Lead can also be found near fruit orchards, since lead arsenate pesticides were often used on fruit trees, and in the soil around busy roadways.

Lead is a serious human health concern, a neurotoxin that can cause brain damage and disorders even in adults; babies and small children are especially sensitive to lead exposure because their nervous systems are developing rapidly. When fruits and vegetables are grown in contaminated earth, they absorb lead into their flesh, and when people eat these tainted foods, the toxin is, in turn, absorbed into their systems. It stunned me to learn that millions of metric tons of lead lurk in U.S. soil from the use and disposal of products such as leaded gasoline and lead-acid batteries.

Ken Dunn of the Resource Center told me that lead-laced soil can be even more of a problem in cities such as Chicago that have a history of waste incineration. That type of garbage disposal, which is now banned, produced fly ash with high concentrations of heavy metals, including lead. The ash would drift from the incinerator on wind currents and then settle into the soil, where it still lingers today.

Lead is measured in ppm (parts per million), and the general rule of thumb is that with soil measurements of less than 250 ppm, you're okay to garden if you add at least six inches of compost. The compost neutralizes the soil's pH, and this reduces the amount of lead that's taken up by the plants. If your soil has more than 250 ppm, the best solution is to build a raised bed and to line it with a heavy-duty landscape fabric that will keep the lead sealed off from the soil and plants above it.

The lab results for the lead content in our front yard soil were sky-high—990 ppm, nearly four times the safe levels. This instantly ruled out our front-yard garden plan, since we didn't have the extra money to spend on timbers for a large raised bed. But there was a far bigger concern in that I suddenly realized I hadn't yet tested the soil in the Edible Garden for lead, even though children had been planting vegetables there and eating the harvest for months. I immediately had it tested, and it was a huge relief when no lead was detected. But I'd come to realize that there were hidden risks and complexities to successful urban farming, and I still had a lot to learn.

ONE EVENING IN FEBRUARY, Verd and I were on our way to the city for an early Valentine's Day dinner. Though the evening had been his idea, I was also looking forward to a rare night out before the new gardening season kicked into high gear. Verd was acting strangely. To begin with, he'd never opened car doors for me, but that night he did; then, with an air of chivalry he called me "my true love," something I'd never heard before. Things had been going well that winter. Our business collaboration was off to a good start, and Thea, after an expected tough adjustment to all the change, had settled happily into her new routines.

I'd made our dinner reservations through Green City Market. Verd had said two weeks earlier that he wanted to take me someplace nice and I'd mentioned that a friend who sold fresh pasta at the market had a new Italian bistro where he was offering a free night's dinner to work out any kinks in the service before opening for business. Verd was working long hours in his various part-time jobs, but we were still barely making ends meet. I knew that if I hadn't found an opportunity for a free meal, he would have taken on extra work to pay for a fancy dinner. As we drove, he looked over at me, smiling, and said, "I think Les might like this place." It was an odd non sequitur—what did my father have to do with this?—but after a minute I thought I understood. *Verd must be planning to pop the question.* This would explain the extra care he'd taken in shaving and the three shirts he'd tried on before settling on unusually serious attire: dress shoes, black pants, and a black velvet jacket I'd bought for him at Kohl's that he wore when teaching his ballroom dancing classes.

I wasn't ready. There was no way, practically speaking, that *we* were ready, with so much still up in the air in our work lives and finances. We'd been back together for less than ten months. We'd talked about marriage, but always in vague, general, won't-that-be-great-in-the-future terms, and I'd thought of it as something "out there" when we'd be settled and secure with two undented cars, a house we owned, and consistent paychecks. But at the same time, Verd was *Verd*—the man I'd known for ten years, who was infinitely more than the sum total of moments we'd spent together and of any spreadsheet breakdown of our circumstances. I knew what my answer would be.

We debated about where to sit when the waitress led us to our table. There was more than enough room to put the chairs side by side, and I said, "Let's move so we can sit together." Verd shook his head no. We went back and forth, with him becoming more adamant in his noes until I realized that he must have rehearsed the marriage proposal scene in his mind and had pictured a more formal tableau with us sitting eye to eye rather than hand in hand.

Everyone at the bistro was eating for free on this trial-run night, and after our slightly rocky start the festive air among the other patrons and staff helped us relax. Verd insisted on buying champagne, remembering how I'd giggled my way through our champagne brunch with Grandma Rose, and before long both of us were laughing, reminiscing about that day and talking about everything from our first night together in our new apartment to our plans for expanding the business in the coming season.

Our conversation rolled along for more than an hour, and when the waiter brought us the dessert menu and a lengthy scorecard to rate the service, it occurred to me that I'd been wrong about the proposal and had given in to my own fantasies. *No matter,* I thought, *we'll take our time.* But then, suddenly, there was Verd, out of his chair on one knee beside me, saying, "Jeanne, will you marry me?" He held out not one but two rings, one with a red garnet and the other a gold band with a tiny diamond. His nervousness had returned; he was smiling with emotion in his eyes. "This is my grandma Charlotte's," he said, pointing at the garnet, "and this is my mom's. I didn't know which one you'd like better."

I PULLED HIM TOWARD me to kiss him; I was laughing and crying all at once, so overwhelmed with a feeling of relief and the *rightness* of it that I didn't realize I hadn't given him an answer until I saw his questioning expression when I finally sat back. I picked up the ring with the diamond, smiling, and he slid it onto my finger.

IN LATE FEBRUARY, Verd took to the streets to post flyers for the up-coming gardening season. He spent hours roaming the North Shore with tacks, Scotch tape, and a thick sheaf of Organic Gardener fly-ers, gathering local knowledge from librarians, store owners, and chambers of commerce about the shops and bulletin boards with the highest foot traffic of retirees who might be interested in or-ganic food and of families with young children. He found out which bakeries in Wilmette, Glenview, Lake Forest, Deerfield, and Highland Park were the most popular places to buy kids' birthday cakes, which restaurants were the most and least child friendly, which coffee shops were where young moms liked to grab a break with friends after dropping their kids off at school.

As February turned to March and the calls started coming in, his hard work, combined with word of mouth from the previous year, paid off: The number of clients jumped to thirty—more than double the number of the previous year. I scrambled to meet with prospective clients and draft proposals for their gardens, often staying up until 2 A.M. at the old fold-out desk we'd set up in a corner of our bedroom before waking at 6:30 A.M. to get Thea ready for kindergarten.

I faced a new challenge in writing those proposals: With Verd and Kord now doing most of the physical work of building the raised beds, constructing fences, and trucking in compost they picked up from Ken Dunn's Resource Center in Kord's F-150 (which kept bottoming out under the weight), estimating the cost of individual gardens was more difficult than it had been when I'd worked with subcontractors who'd charged a set fee. The three of us spent hours sitting at the kitchen table poring over the garden designs I'd sketched out and trying to calculate the cost of supplies and the amount of time the bed and fence construction would take. Still, somehow, we always wound up underestimating, and the business lost money in the first few weeks—sometimes hundreds of dollars per garden.

Verd and Kord did beautiful work, though, and I never had to worry about whether they'd be where they said they'd be or how they'd interact with clients. Over time, I learned to track and compare similar gardens and our estimates got much better. My designs were improving, too, as I became more comfortable working in new towns and neighborhoods, interacted more easily with clients, and got more skilled at balancing the beauty and the functionality of the gardens. My relative inexperience, though, led to some near disasters.

One of my first calls for the season brought me to a castlelike stone house less than half a block from Lake Michigan in the town of Kenilworth. The Mullens were an intensely charismatic couple in their early fifties. Outgoing in manner but also brisk, they were used to getting their way (I came to realize) through a combination of assertiveness and charm. The husband led me out to the backyard, which was small in comparison to the house, consisting of a sunny, grassy central area bordered by low-hanging trees and shrubs. "This is perfect," I said, pacing out a spot just off the center.

"No, no," he said. "It has to be here." He was pointing at a corner of the yard overhung by tree branches, in near total shade. I told him that I doubted the area would get enough sun, but he insisted this wasn't the case. I squinted up at the branches, trying to gauge from which if any angle the sun's rays could possibly peek through. "I'm the one who waters the lawn," he continued, "and that corner always dries out first. It definitely gets enough sun."

The planting session with the Mullens's two bright, talkative daughters went well. I'd planned a smaller garden than I otherwise might have because of my concerns about the light, but there was still enough room for a variety of seeds—lettuces, cucumbers, and peas—and seedlings. The garden itself, however, turned out to be a total failure—the first garden I'd ever planted where absolutely nothing grew. When I came back in two weeks' time to check on and tend to the plants while the Mullens were away, no seeds had sprouted, and the seedlings had withered and died. The soil was moist, so it was clear the plants were getting enough water from the sprinkler I'd set up on a timer. But there simply wasn't enough sun.

I stayed up late composing an email to the family, apologizing for my mistake in agreeing to a spot where there wasn't adequate light, and letting them know that I wouldn't charge them. I felt worst of all for the daughters, who when they returned from their trip would see a bare patch where they'd expected plants to grow. It was another lesson for me in learning to trust my judgment and stand my ground.

AT THE HEIGHT OF the planting season a few weeks later, when I was running behind schedule and got careless rushing from one garden to the next, I slammed my thumb in the car door while trying to juggle an armload of supplies. It hurt, but I didn't want to keep Chris Kennedy—who'd signed on again from the previous year— waiting. I yanked on a garden glove over the already-swelling right thumb and managed to make my way through that session, with Chris's ever-present intensity keeping me focused.

But by the time I got home that evening, I had a throbbing head- ache. Verd took one look at me and said, "What's wrong?" I held out my hand, and he gave a low whistle at the sight of my purplish sausage-size thumb. He told me he was taking me to the hospital.

"It just needs some ice, to bring the swelling down," I said. Verd tried to convince me to go to the doctor, but I was adamant that I'd be better by the next day, when I had a full slate of plantings lined up. In the morning my thumb was worse, and the now constant pain made me lightheaded. I still refused to go to the doctor, feeling something close to panic at the thought of canceling with my clients. Aside from the bad form of breaking appointments, I wasn't sure if I'd be able to catch up before the window had passed for planting strawberries and snap peas and other cold-weather crops—some of the favorites for kids. In this second season, every new client's positive word of mouth would be crucial to the survival and growth of the business.

Verd offered to do the planting sessions himself. He'd seen enough plantings at the Edible Garden to know how I talked to children about plants. When I started to say no, he insisted: "Look, I can't force you not to go, but whether you do go or don't, *I'm* going." He made me laugh when he added, "How good would it be for the business if you passed out face-first in the dirt?"

He was right, but I hated to burden him with my work given his already jam-packed schedule. Aside from his part-time jobs, he'd started studying for his GED. He was interested in medicine and was planning to take science classes at nearby Oakton Community College in the fall. I'd cheered on his studies; it seemed to me that he needlessly doubted his abilities at times because he'd never finished school. As he sat next to me on the bed, I launched into a lengthy apology for all of it—for the household chaos, for my short temper, for not having enough time to give to him in general, and now for making him take on even more work because of a careless injury.

He stopped me. "Being busy is a *good* thing. We're trying to build something. And the worst part of it only lasts for what, a hundred days?" (Bryan, who had picked up on my frayed nerves, eventually started referring to the height of the gardening season, from April through July, as the "hundred days of hell.") "After that we'll have time to regroup. And get married." He fingered the ring I'd had reinforced so I could wear it during planting season. We were planning the wedding for the following March. "It's going to be fine."

I conceded, eventually, that taking care of myself was part and parcel of taking care of the business—and something I owed on a personal level to Verd and Thea. Verd jumped in the station wagon to go tackle my client meetings while I headed in his car to the hospital. As I watched him drive off, I finally felt, after so many years of isolation, what it meant to have a partner who could anticipate my needs and back me up—as he had done from the moment he'd first returned my call just over a year earlier.

Chapter 12

As THE PACE AND RESPONSIBILITIES OF BUILDING THE ORGANIC GAR-
dener brought on a more and more hectic schedule, I came to covet
the predictable Wednesday and Saturday routine of my work in the
farm at Lincoln Park Zoo. On Mondays, Tuesdays, Thursdays, and
Fridays I would pinball between five different yards in various
towns after getting Thea to school and putting in my hours with
Abby. The quiet regularity of my routine at the Edible Garden reminded me of the rhythms of my work at Zendik Farm—check the
moisture level of the garden's soil at dawn, harvest at meal-times,
milk the goats twice a day, turn the compost pile every three weeks.
In the same way, on Wednesdays and Saturdays at the zoo I would
always start by checking the soil moisture and inspecting the plants
to see what they might need (more water, fertilizer, or pruning),
then work with the visiting children to plant, weed, and harvest.

A growing group of kids had begun to visit the Edible Garden
on a regular basis. Tommy came every Saturday, and his family
was so moved by his response to the garden that they eventually
started growing food at home and helped to build a large garden at
Tommy's school. He was joined by other weekend regulars, including two-year-old India, who loved to munch on raw okra, four-
year-old Emma, who would fill her mouth with cherry tomatoes
until her cheeks bulged out, and eight-year-old Audrey, who made

it her responsibility to deadhead the calendula and cosmos (pulling off the spent heads of flowers to encourage more growth).

I hadn't expected to love teaching children to garden so much. Putting a fresh bean in a child's hand and seeing him eat and enjoy it felt like a far more gratifying and tangible act of *doing good* than anything I'd done at the farm. When I watched a kid dig up a potato or pull a carrot from the ground for the first time, I could see written on her face the sheer miracle of growth from seed to food. And I loved the questions—sometimes hilarious, sometimes heartfelt—from Tommy and the other children. One little girl who particularly liked vegetables of unexpected colors unearthed a blue potato and asked, "Is this what happens when a potato loves a blueberry?" I began to realize that my goals as a gardener would be in large part to connect with and educate kids.

I found a perfect collaborator when I met Melissa Graham, a chef dedicated to helping kids eat more healthy fresh foods. Together on the porch of a cottage next to the zoo garden, we offered simple cooking workshops. The kids would pick their favorite vegetables—purple beans, pink Easter egg radishes, multicolored carrots, peppers, tomatoes, and herbs. We'd whip up salsas and sauces and spreads with whatever was harvested. Melissa brought cookie cutters for the kids to cut stars, hearts, and diamonds from bell peppers, which they ate with fresh hummus. These demos drew larger and larger crowds.

One morning in May, a teacher from a public school three blocks from the zoo stopped by to ask me if her first-grade students could visit the garden for a field trip. I agreed—then wondered what we'd do with twenty-five kids at once in that small space. We divided the kids into groups of five with two parent chaperones, and rotated them through the garden for a hands-on experience in twenty-minute shifts. It went so well that I reached out to other area schools; by the next fall, we had as many as eighty kids visiting on field trips per week. I would describe to these groups in simple terms how seeds grow and the basic steps of garden care.

More often than not I'd hear a student say: "I hate tomatoes!" "But have you ever seen a *gold* tomato?" I'd ask. "You get to choose whichever one you want if you'll pop it in your mouth." The kid would chew hesitantly, eyes widening, and shout, "Wow! Tastes kinda like a grape!" prompting the others to try it, too.

I HADN'T TOLD ABBY much about the Organic Gardener's suburban work because I didn't want her to doubt my dedication to the market. Which is why I was surprised to get an email from her one day during our second season saying that an old oak had died in her yard, and where they'd removed the tree she now had an open, sunny space: *It's screaming for a garden,* she wrote.

The garden plot was circular and small, ten feet in diameter. We decided to surround it with a fence made of bendable willow latticework that would match a trellis in the backyard. Kord installed the fence while Abby and I worked on a crop list with the specialty vegetables she wanted—French breakfast radishes, yellow Hungarian wax peppers, Black Beauty eggplants, haricots verts. But when I emailed Abby to ask how the new fence looked, her reply was brief: "Have *you* seen it?"

I drove over and saw that while the fence itself looked exactly as we'd planned, Kord had built a gate out of thick cedar boards that was perfectly functional but out of keeping with the aesthetic of the rest of the garden: It looked like nothing so much as a patch of burlap on a piece of lace. It was a fairly easy fix—after a good laugh, we constructed a more delicate gate and moved on. But it triggered a moment of realization for me: I saw clearly that I wanted to offer people not just a source of organic food, but also something beautiful to look at and experience. In order for the grow-your-own trend to succeed in the well-ordered suburbs, the gardens I grew had to complement the architecture of the homes and blend into the existing green space. They needed to look like a seamless part of that landscape, like they'd always been there. Even on the farm, beauty had been an important concern, with flowers planted among the vegetables, and the placement of crops determined not just by the best conditions for productivity but also by how their colors and textures would play off one another.

A single heirloom pepper or tomato or eggplant—even, and perhaps especially, the ones of irregular shape and mottled color—was for me the very definition of perfect design. Fruits and vegetables, after all, have spent hundreds of thousands of years evolving to become more edible and visually appealing. Their varieties of shapes and colors have been studied in portrait after still-life portrait. It felt essential to try to showcase them in gardens designed to celebrate their beauty.

THE SECOND SEASON of the Organic Gardener was a mild summer with good rains, and nearly every garden I planted that year did well. I didn't yet have the sense that I'd mastered the conditions for gardening in northern Illinois—the seasons, the pests, the soil composition—but I'd begun to get a feel for them. And when Jaime Zaplatosch from Openlands asked me to give a presentation on gardening at the Garfield Park Conservatory, a large greenhouse on Chicago's West Side, I realized that I actually had something to say. Through my experience on the farm and my gardening mistakes and adjustments in the year and a half since coming home, I'd formed a base of knowledge and certain general guidelines for success—five principles that will help you grow food anywhere, whether on a rural farm, in the city, or in the suburbs: sunlight, soil, fencing, paths, and irrigation.

Sunlight. The failure of the Mullens's garden confirmed for me that growing plants need a minimum of six hours of sun a day, eight or more if possible. When growing in the lower range of sun exposure, it's safe to plant beans, peas, herbs, all of the leafy greens, and some small fruiting plants such as cherry tomatoes and cucumbers. In these limited-sun gardens, seedlings and big seeds (for peas and beans) do best; tiny seeds often don't come up. I've found that carrots, potatoes, and other root vegetables need at least eight hours of sunshine, and plants such as tomatoes, peppers, melons, and squash will not produce large fruits that ripen to color without full sun. Plants draw energy from sunlight, and producing a large, colorful fruit requires much more energy than producing a small fruit or leafy vegetable.

The sun also affects a fruit's flavors, textures, and aromas. In a tomato, for instance, the sun activates the key ripening enzymes amylase, pectinase, kinase, and hydrolase. As these enzymes release into the fruit, the starches in the flesh become sugars, and essential oils develop that create the tomato's complex flavors, scents, and nutrients. The enzymes also break down cell walls, softening the flesh and creating juiciness. These subtleties of flavor and texture can't be achieved without sun.

Amazingly, of the more than one billion pounds of tomatoes grown annually on commercial farms in Florida alone, almost none are ripened by the sun; these field-grown tomatoes, like most other fruits sold in grocery stores, are picked while still unripe and hard for ease of transport, and then chemically ripened in warehouses with ethylene gas. But the ethylene completes only part of the ripening process—mostly aspects such as skin color that make the fruit look, but not taste, ripe—which is why so many fruits and vegetables sold in U.S. markets can taste mealy, watery, flavorless, or bitter. In essence, they are sun starved.

I'd never faced a shortage of sunlight at Zendik Farm, where I'd grown food in open fields, but sufficient sun is one of the most challenging issues in urban and suburban settings, where the density of buildings and trees can create shade. Furthermore, I've found over and over again that clients are prone to wishful thinking, imagining that the spot where they want the garden to go receives more sunlight than it actually does. It was a huge relief when Verd eventually found a small, inexpensive "sun calculator" device I could place in a particular area of a yard to measure the amount of sunlight it received over the course of a day, and then offer my clients clear data before we made a decision. Another option is to draw up a simple map of your backyard, pick a day when you'll be home, and go out every hour throughout the morning and afternoon, noting where it's sunny. It doesn't matter if the sunlight occurs in one concentrated block or at scattered times; all that matters is the total number of hours of sun an area gets from dawn to dusk.

Soil. Well-prepared soil acts as the immune system of the plants. Ideally, you want to have twelve to eighteen inches of nutrient dense, deeply aerated soil to give plants what they need to thrive. If a plant is well nourished by healthy soil, it's less susceptible to disease and less appealing to insects because pests attack sick or weak plants first. Compost supercharges the soil with beneficial bacteria, carbon, and nutrients. I prefer to use sifted compost to ensure that there are not too many twigs or branches in it, and I typically add extra nutrients with organic granulated fertilizer. People often ask me about the difference between compost and granulated fertilizer: The compost is the bulk additive (for a new in-ground garden, we bring in a three- to six-inch layer; more for a raised bed), and granulated fertilizer is a topping, sprinkled on the soil lightly like a seasoning on food and then worked into the top few inches.

Clients often assume that if their soil has been well prepared the first year there's no need to work the soil in the following years, but a garden's nutrients get depleted throughout the season by plant growth, and the earth can get compressed with the passage of time by rains and by the weight of snow. It's important every year to aerate the soil with a rototiller, shovel, pitchfork, or broadfork, and then replenish it by adding compost and fertilizer.

Fencing. My experience with rabbits at the MacKenzies' made it clear to me early on that gardening in the suburbs without well-engineered fencing would be an expensive and losing proposition. (Critters can vary widely by locale, but rabbits are virtually everywhere, and deer are more and more pervasive.) Rabbit-proof fencing typically extends two and a half to three and a half feet high, and between four and twelve inches below ground. There's no consensus on deer-proof fencing—some people insist it should go as high as seven or eight feet, and this is, in fact, necessary in places where the deer can get a running jump, but in enclosed spaces a lower fence is often effective. I've frequently used five-foot fencing with success in smaller suburban gardens with low deer pressure.

Keep in mind that the fence is a part of the garden that you'll see year-round, even after the plants are gone, so you should like the way it looks. Fences made of iron and painted wood can be expensive, but there are many more affordable options out there, including a basic raw-wood frame and a simple wire mesh with openings no larger than one inch by two inches. In other words, you aren't limited to rusty metal posts and chicken wire: A little extra creativity and effort can make a critter-proof fence both functional and attractive.

Paths. Paths provide room to work comfortably in the garden, and, more important, they allow the garden to breathe—without them, the rows can get trampled and the tiny air pockets that are essential to soil health can get choked off. In the garden in my parents' yard the first year, I'd lost my paths because I overplanted, which made working in the garden harder than it had to be.

I've always liked to use straw to mark the paths (and to keep weeds from invading them); that's what I was accustomed to on the farm, and what I chose to use at the Edible Garden. But many of my suburban clients think straw looks too "farmy," so I've also used wood chips, bluestone pavers, brick, and stepping stones with success. I've had good results using gravel in raised-bed gardens but find it messy and hard to manage in in-ground gardens.

Irrigation. During my first year at the farm in California, we hand-watered two acres of vegetables—a two-hour daily ordeal—but we later installed drip-line irrigation. Often in charge of repairs, I would walk out in the fields carrying spare pieces of tubing to replace what animals had chewed through.

In my first year at the Edible Garden, when I went in only two or three days a week, I was unable to water the plants as much as I'd have liked to and found that the best method for irrigation is a system that's on a timer. My favorite is drip-line irrigation because it waters the plants at the roots and conserves water, but some of my clients have successfully chosen to modify the height of their existing automatic lawn sprinkling systems so that the spray reaches their gardens. Ordinary sprinklers hooked onto a garden hose can work as well. I generally recommend installing water-sensitive automatic timers that measure soil moisture and then prompt the system to irrigate as needed, allowing you to "set and forget"; this kind of automated irrigation saves resources by preventing overwatering. But a basic battery-operated timer purchased from any hardware store is also a good option. I've always told my clients that if they have a free hour to tend to the garden, I'd rather they engage with the plants than spend the time hand-watering.

AFTER I BRIEFED JAIME ZAPLATOSCH on my "five keys to gardening success" outline, she suggested that I put together a PowerPoint presentation—another fixture of life in the digital age that had passed me by. I confessed that I didn't have any idea how to do it, and she generously met me at her office and worked through my outline and some photos I'd taken of the Edible Garden and client gardens. I also brought some crude charts I'd made about what crops to plant when for the best results. In a couple of hours, Jaime and I cobbled together the foundations of a one-hour gardening presentation that I shared with an audience of community activists and urban farmers-in-training at the Garfield Park Conservatory. Since then, the presentation has continued to evolve and I've shared it with hundreds of audiences.

AT THE END OF our second season, as I was trying my hand at public speaking, I got two pieces of good news about the Edible Garden.

First, Abby told me that she'd found funding for my position as the Green City Market's organic gardener, which meant I no longer had to work in an office. The funding would come through Steve Balsamo, a retired financial industry executive who happened to live directly across the street from Abby's Glencoe home and whose enormous garden I'd often gazed at.

I also learned that the Edible Garden might quadruple its size in the 2007 season. Lincoln Park Zoo had just hired a new programming director who saw the value of our project and wanted to find a way to expand it into the nearby four-thousand-square-foot plot that had been used as a John Deere showcase for soybean and corn crops. Abby and I put together a proposal for a huge in-ground garden with straw paths and three-foot rows that would showcase more than one hundred varieties of fruits and vegetables. We included a plan for handicapped-accessible raised beds where wheelchair-bound participants could do virtually all the tasks of gardening—digging, planting, watering, weeding, and harvesting. There would be fragrant herbs so that the disabled and vision-impaired could smell the plants, touch them, and taste them, engaging in a rich sensory experience. The project was approved, and the Edible Garden was scheduled, to my great excitement, to become the Edible *Gardens* the following spring.

III.

TENDING

Chapter 13

LATE IN THE SUMMER OF 2006, VERD AND I SAT IN A THEATER WATCH-
ing the climate-change documentary *An Inconvenient Truth*. I'd
known for years about climate change, which was first brought to
public attention following NASA scientist James Hansen's 1988
testimony before Congress, and had been widely discussed at Zendik Farm. We saw planetary warming as yet another example of the
destructive impact of the "death culture" on the natural world. But
before watching the film I hadn't known just how severe the effects
of global warming had already become, and how fast the crisis was
accelerating.

As I listened to Al Gore list fact after scientific fact detailing the
effects of greenhouse gas emissions on the environment, and saw
image after image of crumbling glaciers, violent storms, flooding,
and drought, I experienced a kind of system overload—a physically
sickening feeling of helplessness and dread. It was a stronger version of what I'd felt two decades earlier, during the booming
Reagan-era economy, when I'd left Winnetka with the deep conviction that the natural world was in peril. Back then, I was focused
on specific issues such as deforestation and species extinction and
had only a vague sense that there was a broader threat to the planet
as a whole. In my initial phone call to Zendik Farm, Bryan's phrase

"The earth is dying" had made me feel for the first time that my concerns were shared, and were connected to something larger.

Gore had made the case that the resource demands of mainstream consumers were driving the planet toward systemic collapse—a core belief at the commune. The movie seemed to validate my motives for clinging so stubbornly for so long to a way of life that was efficient and self-sustaining. But the movie also begged for real, meaningful solutions that could motivate change on a national and global scale, and in this regard the Zendik experiment had completely failed. In no way had our model of living inspired the broader "revolution" we'd imagined.

Now, without the false hope that the farm had offered, I felt afraid. I no longer had the consolation of living outside the mainstream with a bare-minimum impact on the earth. I lived in suburbia and spent hours each day burning gas in a station wagon. I'd read that suburbanites, on average, emit 70 percent more carbon dioxide from transit than city dwellers, and knew full well that I could have chosen a more efficient lifestyle after the farm. Instead, I'd gone from one extreme to another. Sitting in the theater, I had to wonder if I'd left my ideals behind. It had felt good and rewarding to help my clients improve their health and deepen their connection to nature. But how, I wondered, could this have any effect on the big picture? The movie's image of the pixel-size Earth taken from the *Voyager* 1 spacecraft made me feel small and insignificant in the face of such a huge crisis, and made my enterprise growing backyard vegetables seem futile.

My angst lingered as I wrapped up the 2006 gardening season and prepared for the start of 2007. One October afternoon, I voiced my concerns about global warming to a new friend I'd made, Meredith Lownes, a relaxed, bohemian educator who ran a progressive children's education center out of her house that Thea was attending. "But you're offering one of the most effective solutions out there," she rejoined. "A gateway to sustainable living in communities that need it most." She recounted an article she'd read arguing that one of the single best things families could do to shrink their carbon footprints was to grow their own food. Her comment inspired me to start researching how and why homegrown food could have such a positive effect.

The three critical factors that determine a person's carbon footprint, I learned, are transportation (primarily car and air travel), home energy, and food. Food alone accounts for about 20 percent of the total carbon footprint of the average American household— a higher percentage, for some of us, than that of the cars we drive. One recent study by two Carnegie Mellon professors found that a typical family will release around four and a half metric tons of greenhouse gases from driving roughly twelve thousand miles per year. By comparison, the process of growing all the conventional food in their diet will generate almost twice that amount of carbon emissions, about eight metric tons.

Growing your own organic food can shrink your carbon footprint in a number of ways. For one thing, it shaves down your "food miles." While it's true that certain local foods grown in heated greenhouses can actually have a higher carbon footprint than imported foods, it's generally a reliable equation that the shorter the distance your food has to travel from farm to market, the smaller its carbon impact. On average, produce sold in the Chicago region travels 1,500 miles before it gets to store shelves, and each gallon of fuel burned by the trucks, ships, and airplanes that transport this food releases twenty or more pounds of carbon dioxide into the atmosphere.

But transportation is only a small part of the total carbon footprint of our food system. Most of the carbon impact of our food— about 85 percent—comes from the process of growing and producing it. That's in part because American farmers douse their fruit, vegetable, and grain crops with roughly 6.2 billion pounds of nitrogen-based fertilizers each year, and huge amounts of fossil fuels are needed to manufacture these chemical substances. In addition, when nitrogen-based fertilizers are applied to soil, they release into the atmosphere nitrous oxide, a greenhouse gas that has three hundred times the global warming impact of carbon dioxide. When PepsiCo launched a study of the carbon footprint of its Tropicana orange juice, it found that synthetic fertilizer accounted for more than a third of the total carbon footprint of the juice—much more than the impact of its manufacturing, packaging, distribution, or use.

There's another good reason why homegrown food can reduce your carbon footprint: When you grow your own supply of delicious produce, you tend to eat more fruits and vegetables and less meat. By far the highest greenhouse gas–emitting food is meat. Beef generates 14.8 pounds of carbon dioxide per pound consumed—significantly more than chicken, and more than fifty times as much as soybeans and potatoes. Eating just one red meat– and dairy-free meal each week would have the annual carbon-reducing impact of driving 1,160 fewer miles—roughly the distance from Chicago to Tampa. If the vegetables in that meal were grown organically rather than by conventional methods, the impact would be even greater—and not just because organic methods cut down on fossil fuel inputs, but also because organic farms can actually *remove* carbon dioxide from the atmosphere. Organic soils capture and store carbon dioxide in a process known as sequestration. The high amount of active organic matter that's present in healthy, chemical-free soil tends to bind carbon. Glomalin, for instance, which is a gluelike substance that's produced by soil fungi, is responsible for storing roughly a third of the carbon present in soil.

In a thirty-year study of farming practices, the Rodale Institute found that the carbon content of soil that was farmed organically increased up to 28 percent more than the carbon content of conventionally treated soil. This fact, as the institute's chairman stated, "puts agriculture into a lead role in regenerating the environment." If the 160 million acres of U.S. farmland devoted to growing soybeans and corn alone were farmed organically, a total of 580 billion pounds of carbon dioxide could be effectively scrubbed from the atmosphere each year. And anyone—as a simple first step—can turn part of her backyard into a beneficial carbon sink by planting an organic garden.

The more I researched the environmental impact of food production, the more clearly I understood that after all the miles I'd trekked trying to live out my principles on the commune, I was, in fact, fulfilling my ideals more fully through my business. I admired the activists and politicians who were fighting at the national level for legislative change and now understood that there was also critical work to be done at the grassroots level—putting gardens in the ground, helping people make more informed choices about the food they eat and how it is grown, and teaching skills that would help them live lives more connected to and in balance with the earth—person by person, family by family, and yard by yard.

IN THE BRIEF PERIOD of quiet following the 2006 season, my family and Verd's finally had the chance to meet. In 2000, after Verd's parents had retired, they had moved away from the Chicago area to their family farm in Waupaca, Wisconsin, where Verd's great-grandfather had run a tree nursery. It was important to us that our parents meet before the wedding, and Thanksgiving at my parents' house seemed to be just the right occasion—but we were both on edge about the gathering. There was little chance that our families would find common ground in terms of their politics, interests, and values.

The day got off to a fine start—our parents greeted one another cheerfully, not seeming to notice their sartorial differences (my father was in his usual khakis and tweed, my mother in her black heels and crisp white blouse, while Annette had on a brightly colored holiday sweater and Phil was wearing a flannel shirt with suspenders and sneakers). Things began to get awkward when Phil and Annette's close friend Dorothy, an eccentric activist in her eighties whom they'd brought along with them, pulled out a stack of feminist political pamphlets and proceeded to distribute them among the dinner guests. And when Verd and Phil went out to join "the boys"—my father and a few of his friends and their sons who were out back smoking cigars and deep-frying a turkey while discussing stock portfolios—they laughed about how little they fit in.

But over the course of the meal our parents began to find that they had much more in common than we'd thought. Our mothers spoke at length about the work they'd both done in psychiatric hospitals. Our fathers had a heart-to-heart on the terrace about the fears they'd had about the commune, and Phil wept when talking about how relieved he was that Verd had found stability and love after struggling so much as a teenager. Annette and Phil also went out of their way to engage Thea, and succeeded so well that she accepted big bear hugs as they left. At the end of the Thanksgiving feast, my father sealed the new friendship between the Pinsofs and Nolans when he raised his glass and said, "Cheers to Jeanne and Verd—and to us all. Their marriage is not just a joining of two great people, but a joining of two families who love them very much."

Chapter 14

O N THE MORNING OF MARCH 10, 2007, I WOKE WITH A START TO A clamor of thoughts. A pale predawn light filled the bedroom of our Evanston apartment as I lay beside Verd, eyeing my wedding dress, a long white gown hanging on the door of the closet, ready to be worn that afternoon. From my high school years into my thirties, I'd outwardly dismissed the convention of marriage as constricting and unnecessary. But privately over the course of my time at the commune, I'd begun to crave the commitment I couldn't have. *Without him, I'm half of myself,* I wrote in my journal after Verd left the farm for the first time. *All I think and feel he intuited and understood. How can I hope to change the world for the better if I'm so diminished a person without him? . . . Verd is home. I need him for me to be me.*

My misgivings about marriage stemmed back to my early childhood when I'd routinely heard my parents arguing; by the time I was seventeen, I'd concluded that my parents were imprisoned by their marriage, and that my mother, in the traditional role of the wife, was living solely to please my father. But after returning home from the farm, I came to appreciate how well matched my parents really were, and how hard they'd fought to protect and deepen their bond over nearly forty years of marriage. "Mom and I were each other's lifeline during your absence," my father had told me.

It wasn't the prospect of marriage that had me on edge the morning of our wedding—Verd and I had known each other for more than twelve years, and the idea of publicly committing to each other felt good and empowering. But I worried that we'd gotten in over our heads when we'd decided to have a traditional white-gown ceremony—one that would play out, by most standards, on a very grand scale. When Verd and I first met with my parents to begin planning our wedding, my father had offered to give us a portion of the money he would have spent on a wedding in lieu of a ceremony. We could have used the money to pay off debt, send Verd to school, or grow the business. But still we wanted—in fact, felt we *needed*—to celebrate our commitment with friends and family.

Neither Verd nor I had ever been to a traditional wedding (we'd both been living on the farm during the years when our childhood friends had gotten married), so researching what went into a typical ceremony felt like a kind of anthropological study. We considered a range of locations including a state park, a rented barn, and my parents' backyard, but finally decided, in part as a gesture of respect and appreciation for my parents, to hold the ceremony at Lake Shore Country Club. We knew full well that this was a major plot twist. The notion that we—having spent half of our lives renouncing material wealth—would get married at an upscale golf club would have been heretical to our old way of thinking. But somehow the idea of getting married there no longer held a threat—in fact, it felt liberating. "We can do this," Verd said, "and still be ourselves." We resolved to plan the event to balance traditional aspects we knew were important to my parents with elements that reflected our own values.

The setting of our ceremony was by the book: Thirty rows of chairs divided by a center aisle had been set up for us in a large living room that looked out onto a terrace and sloping lawn, with Lake Michigan in the distance. Chandeliers hung from the vaulted ceilings, and flower arrangements, white and pale green, had been set topiary style atop bases made of birch bark. Verd wore a tuxedo (a definite nod to my dad). Thea, the flower girl, wore a satin-sashed dress and white floral headband. Even Bryan sported a tweed jacket and tie.

It felt at once strangely exciting and humbling to share the same rituals that people had been practicing for hundreds of years. But Verd and I also tried to interpret the ceremony in our own way. We composed our own vows and sourced the food at the reception from local organic farmers. The ten-piece band that played everything from rock to blues and jazz was 100 percent Verd. The guest list was an eclectic mix of past and present that included family friends, colleagues from Green City Market and Verd's ballroom dance studio, and a group of Zendik expats.

As the time for the ceremony drew closer, I wanted to rehearse the poem I'd chosen as part of my vows, but I couldn't find the printout I'd made and realized that Verd had it. Though we'd forgone the tradition of not seeing each other at all before the ceremony that day, we'd agreed that he wouldn't see me in my dress. When Hallie, whom I'd chosen to be my maid of honor, finally arrived with the sheet of paper, I saw that Verd had scrawled *I love you* across the top.

As the ceremony started, I stood just outside the room beside my dad, watching Thea set off down the aisle next to her cousin, Puma, the ring bearer. Thea was grinning and waving at the people she knew in the assembled group. My father squeezed my hand for a moment before I slid my arm through his. My hands were shaking as I held the bouquet, but I relaxed when I got close enough to see Verd, who was clear-eyed and smiling, meeting my eyes with his.

We'd asked my uncle Bill, my father's brother, to perform the ceremony. He was a prominent family-and-couples therapist who'd visited me on the farm and had been a friend and mentor to us both. "Today we are celebrating the miracle of a long journey," he said as he began a moving commentary about what he'd learned it took to sustain a marriage in his more than thirty-year career.

"Jeanne and Verd, you're combining your love of the earth and community with your capacity to dance—your roots and your wings—which will sustain the spirit within you and between you." The poem I'd chosen to read as part of my vows was Ogden Nash's "Tin Wedding Whistle":

> *Though you know it anyhow,*
> *Listen to me, darling, now,*
> *Proving what I need not prove . . .*

Verd was nodding and my voice became louder and clearer as I read two lines:

> *Yet how worth the waiting for,*
> *To see you coming through the door.*

FINALLY MARRIED! MARCH 10, 2007,
LAKE SHORE COUNTRY CLUB

It had truly been a long road to reach this point, and looking out at our friends and family, I thought about how simply and uncomplicatedly *good* it felt—after so many years of uncertainty and doubt—to have arrived on this safe and solid ground. I realized then that this celebration was only in part about a union between Verd and me; we were also pledging our commitment to the communities we had left behind and then rediscovered, letting go of mistakes we'd made and freeing ourselves up to move forward. At the end of the ceremony, after Verd and I shared a victorious kiss, he shouted "Finally!" We held up our clasped hands in celebration, and the room erupted in loud cheers.

Half a dozen ex-Zendik friends had come from around the country to attend the wedding: Helen Zuman, who was working as a writer in New York; Bugz, an independent photographer in Hawaii; Clay, a property manager in San Diego; Anya, a craniosacral massage therapist; Teca, Anya's daughter, who'd grown up on the farm and left at age sixteen and was now a model and actress in Los Angeles; and Mazz, a talented violinist in New York who performed an original piece as part of our ceremony. Along with Verd, Bryan, and Kord, this was the largest group of Zendik members I'd been around since leaving the farm. The night before the wedding, we'd had a party at our apartment where we all had a chance to catch up and reflect. Everyone's experiences, like mine, had been mixed—but the instant, effortless rapport we shared that weekend reminded us of what we'd loved most about communal life.

VERD AND I HAD decided to put off a honeymoon in favor of getting a head start on the gardening season, but when the alarm clock went off on Monday morning, I pressed the pillow against my ears. Still, I didn't regret our decision to delay the honeymoon. We'd just made a big investment in the Organic Gardener, taking out a loan to buy a used Ford F-550 dump truck that would be able to haul compost without bottoming out. It was more truck than we needed at the moment (a smaller model would have gotten us through the season), but I'd decided to buy for the business I hoped we would become. The weather was warming, and the number of clients had grown again since the previous season, from thirty to forty-five.

There was also much work to be done at the Edible Gardens. Cleared of the wheat, alfalfa, soybeans, and field corn that had once grown there, the new garden plot at Lincoln Park Zoo appeared bigger than its fifty-by-eighty-foot dimensions. The older garden looked small in comparison, tucked beside the yellow cottage and wrapped in its white picket fence. The new space had no adjacent buildings and was bordered by a weathered cedar split-rail fence. Above it loomed the city skyline—a vivid reminder that this metaphorical blank canvas stood in the heart of Chicago's downtown. The added four thousand square feet of growing space gave us much more room for educational programming and represented more opportunity for me to share the things I'd learned about food and the environment with the wider community.

I sketched the layout on paper, knowing that I wanted to plant the space just as we had at the farm, with three-foot-wide raised rows and straw paths. I planned to do a large patch of sweet corn and a perimeter bed of fruit (blackberries, raspberries, and different types of grapes), and to roughly divide the rest of the garden into four quadrants highlighting the vegetables that grow best in each season—one for the cold-tolerant early spring crops, two for heat-loving summer crops, and one for a succession planting of late fall crops. At the far end of the garden were two giant compost bins and bales of alfalfa hay for mulching.

The plot had not been treated with chemical fertilizers or herbicides, which was a definite plus, but it also hadn't been regularly tended, and as a result the soil was compacted and weeds were rampant. The wheat and field corn crops that had grown there previously were nutrient greedy and had stripped the soil of nitrogen, so I planned to nourish it with compost and organic fertilizer. I asked Kord to pass over the plot twice and then a third time with our rented rototiller to deeply aerate the soil and grind up the weeds and traces of the old crops.

We'd planned to haul in three tons of compost—about two or three big truckloads—but we hit a snag with the first load. The new F-550 truck was much heavier than the old pickup, and when Verd backed it into the space, the wheels sank axle deep. Kord had to bring in his F-150 to try to pull the new truck out, and eventually succeeded, but stripped his gears and bent the frame of his truck in the process.

It was an inauspicious start, but enough was going right that I didn't worry. We had a new team member: Helen Zuman had decided to join our crew for the season. At one point, after marking out the rows I'd sketched with string and orange flags, I glanced at Verd, Kord, and Helen raking the compost into the soil beside me. At the farm, I'd always worked with a crew of at least three or four; here I was with a team of the same size but without any of the commune's shadows, and I savored the simple pleasure of working closely with a group of like-minded people.

It was still too cold and too early in the season for visitors to come in large numbers, but we'd advertised the planting day through Green City Market, and Tommy and several other regulars

KORD (IN HAT), VERD, AND OUR BELOVED DUMP TRUCK, 2007

showed up to help as we put in dozens of varieties of vegetables, including chard, beets, lettuce, potatoes, carrots, and peas. Everything seemed to bode well for a good season ahead. But ten days later, after steady spring rains, I came back and found an insurrection. Weeds had sprouted thickly over the entire four-thousand-square-foot bed. The whole plot looked like it was covered in grass. It was not just a visual disturbance but a threat to the crops we'd planted. Weeds compete hungrily for nutrients, water, sunlight, and space and can beat out seeds and seedlings for those resources.

With a sense of panic, I sank to my knees in the muddy soil and began yanking up the weeds. They were young but already coarse and sturdy. A passerby told me that I was looking at nut grass, a particularly noxious weed. It took me just a few moments to realize that the rototilling, rather than eliminating the weeds as I'd hoped, must have pulled thousands of dormant seeds up to the surface, causing the weeds to spread and multiply. My mistake had put all of the work that had gone into this garden at risk. If this year's crops failed, there was little chance that the funding for the project would be renewed; and even if it was, the weeds, if they weren't handled correctly, would continue to plague the garden space for years to come. After hand-weeding for several hours on my own and barely making a dent, I called Verd. "It's hopeless," I told him. "There is no conceivable way to get on top of this."

"You're seeing it all wrong," he said. "This is perfect. Now we have something for every visitor to do when they come to the garden." The saving grace of nut grass is that it is relatively easy to pull up. All we needed to do, he said, was give visitors a few tips on weeding, help them understand it as a key part of the growing process, and steer them toward a patch of nut grass.

I put together a quick tutorial for kids on the threats and marvels of weeds. Weeds are smart and highly successful from an evolutionary standpoint. They thrive because they're so adept at stealing away what other plants need to grow—water, nutrients, sunlight, and root space. They also reproduce quickly. Vegetables and fruits produce seeds at the very end of their life cycles, but weeds often produce a huge number of seeds when they're young, so they multiply even if they don't live very long. A single dandelion can produce 175 seeds, each with its own tiny parachute that can carry it through the air several hundred yards.

One good method to prevent weed growth is to put a barrier on top of the soil—a sheet of landscape cloth or a four- to eight-inch-thick layer of straw mulch—that essentially starves the weeds of sunlight, though if weeds have already started growing before the straw or sheeting is applied, or if that protective layer gets torn, this method can fall short. By far the most effective way to kill weeds without herbicides is to pull them up as soon as you notice them, roots and all, one by one. It sounds more time consuming than it is: If you prepare your soil properly by adding a generous amount of compost every year and stay on top of the weeds, never letting them get established, you will win the weed battle.

In the first few weeks, as the new garden started to grow, hundreds of people pitched in to help us tackle the nut grass. Everyone from three-year-olds to senior citizens knelt down in the dirt beside me. Witnessing that effort among friends and total strangers alike, I was amazed by the number of people—many more than I'd realized—who felt a part of the Edible Gardens. It was a community in the truest sense.

MOST OF MY NEW CLIENTS in 2007 were, as they'd been in past years, suburban parents roughly my age with young children. But two new clients came on board who helped me understand the therapeutic benefits of gardening in a new light. Georgette Shabaz was in her sixties and Joan Silvern in her eighties; both were struggling with grief and loneliness after having lost their husbands.

In my darkest times at the farm and after my return home, I'd always had the conviction that I could feel the soil—literally, almost instantly—absorbing some of my emotional pain when I placed my hands in the damp, cool earth. It's one of those things you can't exactly quantify but that you just *know* is true. Over the course of the season, both Georgette and Joan described a similar experience—finding that the rhythms of gardening helped them refocus their energy. So it felt like a momentous confirmation—surprising and obvious in equal measure—when I stumbled on an article in *Discover Magazine* entitled "Is Dirt the New Prozac?" It described a study released by the University of Bristol in England in 2007 showing that when injected in mice, a specific soil bacterium, *Mycobacterium vaccae,* targets immune cells that stimulate the serotonin-releasing neurons in the brain—the very same neurons activated by Prozac. The study concluded that this soil bacterium could play a role in the "regulation of emotional behavior."

Therapeutic gardening has been practiced for hundreds of years. In the early nineteenth century, Dr. Benjamin Rush, a pioneer of American psychiatry and physiology, reported that gardening was one of the most effective therapies for people suffering from mental illness. In the 1940s and '50s, therapists used gardens to help rehabilitate tens of thousands of World War II veterans. Today, the field of "horticultural therapy" is widely researched and taught at universities. The American Horticultural Therapy Association and other groups promote the practice of therapeutic gardening in hospitals and prisons. One of the leading practitioners of horticultural therapy is the Legacy Health System in Portland, Oregon, a five-hospital system that manages seven gardens. In recent years, retirement homes and community centers across the country have started "senior gardening" programs that are often located indoors for year-round tending. The elderly, in particular, can benefit not just from the chemical effects of gardening on mood, but also from the gentle exercise and steady rhythms of garden maintenance.

AS MY BUSINESS GREW, I had come to see that my success or failure would be tied almost as much to my instinct for people and relationships as it would to my knowledge of gardening. I was learning to fairly accurately predict how new clients would relate to the process of gardening. Some people, like Chris Kennedy, couldn't wait to get down in the dirt and work. Often these hands-on clients would want every inch of their garden jam-packed with growth. One, for instance, envisioned a pumpkin patch with dozens of pumpkins and wanted to plant just as many seeds. I warned him that each seed would spring a vine that could carry half a dozen pumpkins or more, but he still wanted to plant a whole packet as a kind of insurance policy. When the vines started to grow, I had to guide him in thinning a majority of them out, since the crowded plants would have had to compete for limited sun, water, root space, and nutrients.

I've also encountered gardeners who like to experiment with innovative techniques. One woman I worked with filled a hypodermic needle with *Bacillus thuringiensis,* a liquid organic insecticide, and injected it into the stalks of young zucchini and squash plants to protect them from vine root borers. The method worked well, but it required huge amounts of time and patience. That same gardener got the idea that the best way to plant the tiny seeds of carrots would be to put them with sand in a salt shaker to disperse them. (Carrot seeds are normally spaced roughly an inch apart, and even then require much thinning as they grow.) The resulting growth was so abundant, dense, and tangled that we had to drag a hard rake through the plot to thin the plants.

The plus side of the do-it-yourself experience is that the lessons learned that way tend to stick. I generally encourage learning by doing, in part because I've found my own mistakes so instructive. But I've also worked with clients who take a more cautious approach and prefer that I do most or all of the work myself, either because they lack experience or just don't like to get their hands dirty. I've always been willing to do the whole process, but I still try to find ways to persuade people that vegetable gardening is universally *doable*—that virtually everyone, everywhere, can grow their own food.

Some clients are comfortable with the growing part but get nervous about the harvesting. If you miss the harvesting window, fruits and vegetables can dry out, toughen, become bitter or mealy, or even sprout roots and flowers. The difference between an unripe or overly ripe tomato and a ripe tomato is the difference between nothing and everything—and that can be intimidating. I like to encourage new growers not to sweat it and to learn from trial and error. I remind them that their gardens will go through multiple cycles of birth and death: Strawberries and lettuce and other early crops will fade just as peppers and cucumbers will be starting to thrive; tomatoes will phase out just as butternut squash and Brussels sprouts are coming in. These cycles will then turn into the larger cycles of the season and year, as dried stalks and faded leaves become part of the compost creating nutrients to fuel the next year's growth.

AS THE ORGANIC GARDENER GREW, the increasing workload and scale of our projects stepped up the pressure on our personal lives. In March, just at the start of the season, Kord moved out of our apartment to live with his girlfriend, which gave Verd, Thea, and me a bit more living space. It wasn't until I moved my desk into Kord's old room, a sunny space with windows on three sides, that I realized how unbelievably cramped I'd been pounding out proposals on my PC with client folders stacked next to the overflowing laundry hamper. But the new room quickly started filling up with paperwork, office equipment, and supplies. Our thousand-square-foot apartment was starting to feel much too small for a family and growing business. I also wanted more green space and badly missed having my own garden. Without a place to grow food, our apartment was feeling less and less like home.

IN LATE JULY 2007, after our busy planting phase, Abby Mandel asked me as a favor to consult for a neighbor directly across the street from her. This was Steve Balsamo, who'd provided the funding for me to work at the Edible Gardens, and whose garden I'd gazed at from the window of Abby's home office. I drove over on a weekend morning, taking Thea with me, and was even more enamored with the space up close. The sprawling five-thousand-square-foot rectangular plot felt like a farm in the middle of suburban Glencoe, with its maze of in-ground beds bordered by wood timbers. Fringing the old stone perimeter fence were giant clusters of peonies and forsythia. But the vegetables inside the beds were failing. While I walked the garden with Steve, his mother-in-law, who was harvesting gooseberries for a pie from a thick stand of bushes on the far side, invited Thea to come help her. It was the first time I'd ever seen gooseberries, which look like small grapes and have a taste both tart and sweet. Thea was quickly absorbed by the task of gathering them.

I immediately saw what was wrong with the garden. For one thing, there was no high perimeter fence, and deer had clearly been damaging the plants—the tomatoes in particular. In addition, the pale color and stunted growth of the vegetables told me that there was a problem with the soil's nutrients. I recommended an organic fertilizer mix and told Steve how to work it into the earth around the plant roots. Another problem was that he'd been relying solely on landscape cloth with wood chips over it to control the weeds; for the next season, he needed to pull up the eroded cloth, add a generous amount of compost, turn the open, flat expanse of the garden into a series of mounded rows, and then apply a layer of straw between the rows to mark walking paths and for weed control.

Steve then offered to give me a tour of his house, a large David Adler estate built in 1921, set back down a long, tree-lined road from the garden. The house's décor was stunning. Despite its size and grandeur, Steve and his wife, Susan, had given it a warm, homey feel that was in keeping with their down-to-earth style, and it felt like something you might see in the Normandy countryside.

Steve walked Thea and me back to where we'd parked by the garden, and I noticed a charming ivy-covered building directly facing the garden that had once been a carriage house. As we said our good-byes I asked him who lived there. He told me that an artist had recently moved out and the place was now vacant. He added, just as I was leaving, that he'd fantasized about having a master gardener live there who could update and maintain the growing space we'd just been discussing.

Having fantasized, myself, about *being* the master gardener in precisely that space, I was dumbstruck. That afternoon, I called Steve to tell him we were interested.

A few days later I returned to tour the house. It was full of quirks, and I loved it instantly: Downstairs, the small kitchen opened onto a central living-dining room with a fireplace, terracotta-tiled floors, and floor-to-ceiling arched windows. The two upstairs bedrooms were small and cozy, with dormer windows and a common area that could hold desks for the business. The backyard, full of old-growth oak and elm trees, was a leafy haven for Thea to play in and explore.

Aching to find a way to make it work, Verd and I hashed out the numbers. The rent was lower than we'd thought it would be, but it was still a reach for us. We decided it was worth it, as Steve would turn the garden over to us and we could use it to showcase our work for prospective clients and as a minilab to try new varieties of vegetables. I met Steve at a coffee shop in Winnetka at the end of August to sign the lease. I could barely breathe as he handed me my copy, telling me, with a decisive nod, that it was ours starting on October 1.

Chapter 15

I N SEPTEMBER, I LEARNED THAT CHEF AND ACTIVIST ALICE WATERS, A close friend of Abby Mandel's, would be giving a talk at Green City Market the following month, and that she wanted to tour the Edible Gardens while she was there. The national discussion on sustainable foods had been heating up with the release of Michael Pollan's book *The Omnivore's Dilemma* and Barbara Kingsolver's *Animal, Vegetable, Miracle*. Waters's visit had the potential to give our local attraction national visibility. I was also looking forward to meeting and learning from someone who had helped build the sustainable food movement from the ground up.

Alice Waters had been a food activist for almost four decades. *60 Minutes* had dubbed her the "mother of slow food," and *The New York Times* had said she'd "single-handedly changed the American palate." I'd first read about her work with the Berkeley, California, Edible Schoolyard when I was researching the zoo garden project in 2004, and since then, I'd read more about her guiding philosophy. Food is "the one central thing about human experience," she'd written, "that can open up both our senses and our conscience to our place in the world."

Born in 1944, Waters grew up tending the World War II victory garden her parents had planted in her childhood backyard in Chatham, New Jersey. As an undergraduate majoring in French cultural studies at the University of California at Berkeley, she traveled to France and was inspired by the way Europeans savored their meals and valued fresh local ingredients. After she graduated in 1967, Waters spent time studying early childhood education in London and traveling again through Europe to experience its culture and cuisine. She returned to Berkeley and, in 1971, raised ten thousand dollars to start her own restaurant, Chez Panisse, on the bottom floor of an old house. She grew her own lettuce in the backyard and purchased her other ingredients from local farmers—a radical practice in that age of swelling U.S. food miles. She published the first of several cookbooks in 1984, and soon began winning prestigious awards.

She used her national platform to write and speak out about the benefits of organic foods and local farmers markets, pushing the rapid growth of those trends across the country. In 1994, she helped launch another national trend after she visited a local Berkeley middle school and was shocked by the prevalence of junk food and the lack of fresh, healthy options for lunch. She planted a garden on the grounds of the school and drew on her experience in childhood education to start teaching the students about fresh food, nutrition, the environment, and health. She went on to establish the Edible Schoolyard Project to encourage similar programs in schools across the country.

Without Waters's work championing local and organic food sources throughout the United States, it was very possible that I would never have been able to start the Edible Gardens or launch my business. She and other leaders of the sustainable food movement such as Michael Pollan, celebrity chef Jamie Oliver, *New York Times* food columnist Mark Bittman, and the nutritional sciences professor Marion Nestle—all of whom were building on the efforts of Wendell Berry, Wes Jackson, and other early leaders—helped bring about a sea change in the way Americans perceive themselves and their relationship to food and the environment.

———

THE EDIBLE GARDENS WERE still blooming in early October, one week before Waters was scheduled to arrive, and I was holding out hope that we wouldn't get a cold snap in the meantime that would kill the growth, since a hard frost freezes the water in the cells of plants and essentially dehydrates them. I wanted to do everything I could—weeding, staking, thinning, mulching, pruning—to prepare for her visit, but I knew that in gardening, perfection is rarely, if ever, possible.

The warm fall that had been a boon to the gardens had also extended the growing season for the Organic Gardener. Though we'd moved into the coach house on October 1, we hadn't had time to begin settling in, and unpacked boxes still covered the floors. In those early October weeks I juggled repeated trips to the zoo with visits to clients who needed help with garden maintenance. Verd, who was taking time-intensive fall classes at the local community college, pitched in as much as he could, promising me that we'd do everything necessary to get ready. "It's doable," he said matter-of-factly.

The morning of Alice's visit, the weather was not just unseasonably warm but hot. I'd been told she might arrive any time before 1 P.M., after touring Green City Market. I worked with kids harvesting squash and beans until just before 11 A.M., when a petite woman with windswept gray-brown hair carrying an armload of goods from the market came toward me with a hand outstretched. I was immediately struck by her dynamism. I'd seen pictures of Alice Waters before, but in them she'd always radiated quietness and calm; in person she was wide-eyed and animated. She wore a flowing skirt, black cotton shoes, and a rose-colored tunic. As she shook my hand and apologized for the delay, she conveyed a kind of electric idealism and an intensely purposeful air. Before I could offer to show her around she was already in motion, wandering the straw paths, complimenting the raised rows, the farmlike feel, and the variety of vegetables we'd managed to grow in five thousand square feet. Everything was thriving—the red, green, and orange peppers; the scarlet and yellow heirloom tomatoes; the sprawling melons, squashes, and pumpkins; the eggplants, beets, carrots, spinach, collard greens, kale, and chard; the red and green lettuces (oak-leaf, butterhead, romaine); and the more exotic greens that Chez Panisse had helped popularize: mâche, mizuna, and arugula.

Alice particularly liked the green, yellow, and purple string beans that I'd planted in the corn patch after the summer harvest; the spent corn stalks now served as support poles for the vining beans. But it was the flowers that struck her most of all—the mammoth sunflowers, the crimson zinnias, and the blue, white, and purple morning glories that had established themselves in slender vines extending all along the perimeter fence. One variety of morning glory in particular stood out, cream-colored with periwinkle streaks emanating from the center. Alice took pictures of the blooms and then asked if I could send her its seeds. She turned to look back out over the gardens as we headed to the nearby farmhouse to get out of the heat, and I turned mental cartwheels when she said, "I wish my garden looked that good!"

We spent the next hour at the wooden dining table in the main room of the farmhouse sharing ideas about food-growing curricula for children. As we headed back outside, she said she wanted to put me in touch with "other leaders" so that we could join forces and share ideas, including Josh Viertel, then codirector of the Yale Sustainable Food Project, who would later serve a term as the president of Slow Food USA, and Eliot Coleman, a hero of mine ever since I'd read his book *The New Organic Grower* in the library at the farm. "There aren't that many of us," she said. "We need to bring more people into this, and big change can only happen if we reach out to our communities like you're doing here."

After she left, I sat for a while on the porch of the farmhouse with my mind reeling. After years of living outside the mainstream, deeply skeptical of conventional life, I'd rejoined traditional society just in time to discover America's surging interest in sustainable foods—and to find that I had a part to play in that movement.

OVER THE NEXT FEW days, as the excitement of the visit faded, I began wrestling with some serious questions I hadn't fully considered before. Alice had mentioned, just before leaving, the possibility of speaking with the mayor about getting support for gardening programs in underprivileged city schools that could work with the Edible Gardens, using it as a model and a learning resource. I loved the idea, but it also made me aware of the relatively narrow demographic I'd been working with to that point. Most of my suburban clients were well-off, and a majority of the families with young children who made regular visits to the Edible Gardens were also generally middle and upper income. Many of the field trips we'd hosted were from schools with means. The few experiences I'd had with children from underfunded city schools had made me aware of how rarely their circumstances allowed them to engage with the natural world.

One field trip in particular stood out to me: Several eighth-grade girls had been so upset by the sight of a few bugs on the leaves of plants, and by the bare soil of the garden rows, that they'd had to watch my demonstration from the gravel path outside the garden and were unable to take part in the hands-on work. They were an extreme example, but many of the other children I'd worked with from inner-city areas, who'd had little or no exposure to green space, had also been reluctant to walk through the garden and put their hands in the dirt.

Child advocate Richard Louv called this kind of alienation from the natural world "nature deficit disorder," a term he first used in his 2005 book *Last Child in the Woods*. Children from inner-city areas who lack access to green outdoor space are among the most vulnerable. But Louv noted that American children across the board are spending much less time in nature than previous generations and argued that this trend is causing or intensifying a range of problems, including rising rates of obesity, attention deficit disorder, anxiety disorders, and depression.

Since the 1950s, as American populations have shifted from rural to more urban landscapes, the rates of depression among adults and children have increased dramatically. According to the Centers for Disease Control, 16 percent of American adults today— almost one in six—have met the criteria for depression. "Human beings," writes Dr. Andrew Weil, "evolved to thrive in natural environments. . . . Few of us today can enjoy such a life and the emotional equilibrium it engenders, but our genetic predisposition for it has not changed." A study of more than 1,200 participants published in the journal *Environmental Science and Technology* showed that as little as five minutes of exercise (including gardening) in green outdoor spaces notably improved mood and self-esteem.

I began to wonder how plausible it was that residents of downtown Chicago could apply the lessons of the Edible Gardens to their lives. Did the work I was doing really mean anything if having a garden was restricted, by definition, to those with access to green space—at a time when a sizable majority of Americans lived in densely developed cities? Was the healthier, more connected life my suburban clients were discovering possible for people who lived in apartment buildings and townhouses surrounded by concrete? And if not, was that sense of connectedness itself an illusion?

Alice Waters had written, "We can't think narrowly. We have to think in the biggest possible way." But could city residents, I wondered, really participate en masse in growing their own food? Could any meaningful amount of fresh produce be grown in dense urban areas?

THERE WAS PERHAPS NO better place for me to investigate these questions than in Chicago, a city on the front lines of the nation's urban farming movement. Richard M. Daley, Chicago's mayor at the time, had pledged to make his city "the greenest in America," and

Ken Dunn, the founder of the Resource Center and City Farm, had identified twenty thousand vacant acres in Chicago that he estimated could create between one hundred thousand and five hundred thousand agriculture-related jobs while growing more than half of the city's fruits and vegetables.

I began researching similar efforts that had been launched in major cities across the country. In New York City, John Ameroso started urban farming in 1976 and the numerous organizations and initiatives he helped create grow more than eighteen tons of produce per year within city limits. In Los Angeles, the Urban Homestead was producing six thousand pounds of organic food per year on just one-fifth of an acre, and offered a working model for similar programs. In Detroit, Malik Yakini had founded the Black Community Food Security Network, which ran a productive three-acre farm, and Edith Floyd had started the Growing Joy Community Garden, which would eventually span twenty-eight city lots in her inner-city neighborhood. A Michigan State University study had identified nearly five thousand acres of land in Detroit that could eventually supply residents with more than two-thirds of their vegetables and nearly half of their fruit.

What moved me most about what I was learning was the debt that many urban farming innovators felt they owed the past. Will Allen of Milwaukee's Growing Power was inspired by the urban growing techniques that were used in nineteenth-century Paris, when gardeners grew enough produce to supply the city's entire population and export excess vegetables to England while using only 6 percent of municipal land. They relied on multiple applications of rich compost (much of it "recycled" manure from the city's horses) to thickly planted beds that were covered in the winter with movable glass panes to extend the growing season. It was incredibly encouraging to learn that city farming had occurred successfully on such a large scale—that the concept wasn't a radical possibility, but a tried-and-true reality.

America has its own rich history of urban farming. During the economic depression of the 1890s, gardening programs were launched as part of poverty relief efforts in cities from Buffalo to Denver. During the Great Depression a successful round of urban farming efforts drew local and federal funding, and in New York City alone, more than five thousand new food gardens were started in vacant lots, producing about one million pounds of vegetables a year. During World War I and II, Americans grew victory gardens to help the war effort by reducing food-related rail traffic and freeing up commercially produced and canned vegetables to feed the troops. The number of garden plots in backyards and vacant lots nationwide rose to more than five million in 1918, yielding more than half a billion pounds of produce that year. During World War II, more than *twenty million* gardens were planted, producing more than 40 percent of all the vegetables consumed in the United States.

All of these efforts were born of necessity, and all of them did much more than anyone could have thought to meet the need at hand. Looking to the future, it's possible that urban farming will no longer be optional, but necessary. In recent years, a growing number of new clients have told me that they wanted gardens because they feared a future of environmental and economic volatility, and that growing food was a practical survival skill they wanted their children to have. By 2050, the global population is expected to increase to more than nine billion, with roughly 70 percent of the world's people living in urban centers. The UN Food and Agriculture Organization has predicted that global food production will have to jump by 70 percent in order to feed this expanded population. Meeting this demand using today's farming methods would require far more arable farmland than currently exists.

One part of the solution may be to cultivate food in the suburban "green belt" areas surrounding cities; another approach may be to create new arable space within cities on the buildings themselves. The concept of rooftop gardens dates back at least as far as the sixth century BCE, to the Hanging Gardens of Babylon, a series of terraced platforms where flowers, ferns, cypress, and broad-leafed trees were grown. The Renaissance saw another surge in the popularity of rooftop gardens, with the Medicis of Florence and other prominent families growing rare plants in ornate rooftop arrangements. In the centuries that followed, rooftop gardens came in and out of fashion until, in recent years, there's been a surge of interest among environmentally conscious city dwellers. Today, vegetables can be seen growing in cities across the country on rooftops, terraces, windowsills, and even fire escapes.

Rooftop gardens can be grown in containers or in a layer of soil poured directly on top of the roof's surface (lined with a waterproof barrier, and often equipped with irrigation and drainage systems). These food-growing "green roof" installations can be warehouse-size endeavors: The green roof of Chicago's Gary Comer Youth Center measures 8,160 square feet and grows a range of vegetables, fruits, flowers, and herbs. The Brooklyn Grange farm in New York City is cultivating fruits and vegetables on a warehouse rooftop that spans an entire acre, complete with beehives and egg-laying hens. New York City alone has an estimated *fourteen thousand acres* of rooftop space where food could be grown. Here and in an increasing number of U.S. cities, activists and city officials are working to improve incentives for green roof projects, which require large investments on the front end but save money and resources over time: They cut down the heating and cooling needs of buildings by providing insulation and transpiration (the loss of water vapor from plants, which has a cooling effect). Rooftop gardens can also absorb rainwater and significantly reduce storm water runoff. And as plants absorb carbon dioxide and release oxygen, they can improve urban air quality.

The further I researched urban farming, the more convinced I became that gardens grown in urban lots, on rooftops, and in large enclosed spaces will have to be a part of any long-term solution to the world's most pressing environmental problems. I was encouraged by these possibilities—and wanted a hands-on understanding of them. Whether on the farm (with its many ups and downs) or in my work life (with its many mistakes and adjustments), I'd always learned by doing. And part of why I felt I'd been able to connect in helpful ways with my suburban clients and with visitors to the Edible Gardens was because I believed that gardening at its core was basic and simple. If I could perform a task and fully understand it, anybody could. If urban gardening was going to be widely embraced by city dwellers—enough to have significant positive effects on health and the environment—it would, I realized, have to be easy to grasp.

While the Edible Gardens were technically an urban effort, grown within city limits, they were ensconced in Lincoln Park and therefore set apart from the urban landscape. I'd had one brief experience with rooftop growing a year earlier—advising a family friend who lived in a downtown apartment on planting vegetables in self-watering containers (small pots with a bottom reservoir of water that's in constant contact with the soil and keeps it moist, essentially watering the plants on demand) on her four-story roof. The project didn't count as a substantial garden, but it convinced me that the five basic keys to success I'd learned—sunlight, soil, fencing, paths, and irrigation—could, in theory, still apply to urban lots and rooftop gardens. I was eager to test that theory, and, as it turned out, I didn't have long to wait for the opportunity.

Late in the fall of 2007, I received two calls that presented new challenges for me. One—surprisingly, from my father—was a request, through his volunteer work with Outward Bound, that I help the new Polaris Charter Academy on the West Side of Chicago design and plant a school garden the following spring. It would be entirely new territory for me because the garden space itself would be set on top of a concrete lot adjacent to the school. The second call came from one of the best-loved and most prestigious "green" restaurants in Chicago, Uncommon Ground. The owners, Helen and Michael Cameron, asked me to come meet with them to discuss their plans for growing some of their vegetables and herbs on the roof of their restaurant. This would prove to be perhaps the biggest of the many big steps I'd taken since returning to Illinois.

Chapter 16

From the outside, Uncommon Ground looked like just another urban storefront on Devon Avenue. It was on a busy street with a few Bradford pear trees planted at intervals along the concrete sidewalk in the heart of Edgewater, a diverse neighborhood seven miles north of downtown Chicago, near Loyola University. I could see, pulling into the parking lot behind the restaurant, that a rooftop farm there would get plenty of sun, but the dense city landscape still felt like a crowded and chaotic place to grow food.

Once I stepped inside, however, the project started to make sense. The restaurant's interior was an oasis. It felt warm and tranquil, with its wood-paneled walls, canvas booths, and ample natural light. Helen and Michael Cameron gave me a brief tour as they talked about their vision for the space. They were just a few years older than I was, established professionals with a hipster edge that was reflected both in their manner, which was confident and infused with idealism, and in their style—Helen wore a printed wrap dress, with her long auburn hair hanging loose; Michael wore jeans and a button-down with rolled-up sleeves. They were committed to sustainability in even the smallest details of their business, and had designed every aspect of the retrofitted building to follow the standards required for certification with the Green Restaurant Association. The restaurant's tables were made from white oak and silver maple trees that had fallen in Chicago's Jackson Park. All of the wood used in the building, in fact—from its wall panels to its doors and fireplace mantel—was locally harvested, and the varnishes and paints were nontoxic. The art deco bar was a century old. The kitchen appliances were energy efficient; the walls and windows were superinsulated; the lights were compact fluorescents and LEDs on motion detectors set to automatically switch off when people left the room. They had even carefully chosen the compostable takeout boxes, biodegradable cleaning supplies, and the brown cloth napkins that don't require bleaching.

Helen and Michael had opened Uncommon Ground's first location on Clark Street near Wrigley Field in 1991 after working for decades in the restaurant industry—he as a manager, she as an executive chef. Helen, who grew up on Chicago's West Side eating from her family's large backyard garden, had begun sourcing local, organic ingredients for their Clark Street location from day one. Having just opened their second location on Devon, Helen wanted to ratchet up their commitment to local foods, sourcing produce that would be grown not just fifty miles away but fifty steps away. Her goal was to build not just any rooftop garden but the nation's first certified organic rooftop farm.

I followed Helen and Michael up the exterior steps to see the unfinished roof. One of the challenges for a rooftop garden of any size is to make sure that the structure can support the substantial weight of the soil, since each cubic yard of soil weighs around two thousand pounds, and you have to consider the potential winter snow load as well. Michael had anticipated this, and had the roof's steel undergirding reinforced. Though the deck they planned to build on top of the undergirding hadn't been laid yet, I was still able to scope out the space, a 2,500-square-foot rectangular expanse that, despite my initial concerns, appeared to have great growing potential.

When Michael showed me the architect's plans for the roof, he pointed out five large solar-thermal panels that would heat the building's water, a huge benefit for a restaurant, with its constantly running dishwashers. He also pointed out the spot where they intended to keep rooftop beehives and a large composter for the rooftop farm's plant waste. He showed me a sample of the decking material they'd use—a composite made of recycled plastic and wood—to help me visualize the space.

I admired the Camerons' commitment and the breadth of their vision and wanted to be a part of it. Though it wasn't the kind of growing space I was used to, I tried to think of it as I would any other farm or garden space. I asked my standard first question: *Why do you want to grow food here?* Did they want something purely functional, to maximize food production, or did they want more of a flexible space where they could host educational and social events? Helen said they definitely wanted to raise awareness about the power of local production, to partner with schools, and, especially, to work with kids.

My first piece of advice was that the farm would need paths, the most crucial component for any educational space, once the basics of sunlight, soil, and water have been met. At the Edible Gardens, I'd seen firsthand that kids need clearly defined space to move around in without trampling the soil or otherwise interfering with plant growth. Visitors to Uncommon Ground wouldn't step on the plants or soil—Helen wanted the garden beds to be a series of wooden planter boxes raised up from the deck—but there still needed to be room to easily maneuver between the beds and to have the best access to the plants. Fencing clearly wouldn't be an issue, either, since rabbits and deer weren't a factor, but the city's building code required that any rooftop space used by the public have a perimeter wall of at least four feet high. Spacing the beds properly would make the rooftop not just more functional, but also more beautiful. Helen wanted the rooftop farm to attract and engage the community, and we all agreed that its visual appeal would enhance its educational value.

Right away, Verd, Kord, and I began working closely with

Helen, Michael, and a metalworker they'd hired to construct the planter boxes. Our team of six met several times over meals at the restaurant to plan and design the space. Sunlight would be ample; in fact, the constant sun was likely to put extra demands on the irrigation system. The soil of a rooftop growing space can become hot and dry much more quickly than the soil of an in-ground garden. Growing food on a full-sun rooftop can be almost like growing in a Floridian climate, with the plants growing quickly and requiring frequent and plentiful watering.

The Camerons planned to bring plumbing and a water spigot to the roof to irrigate the garden, but I was concerned about the tubing leading to the planter boxes—I didn't want a tangle of hoses that would look messy and pose potential safety hazards when young visitors moved between the beds. Kord came up with a plan to extend and organize the tubes the way you'd organize computer wires under a desk—bundling them together and running them discreetly under the deck and up the sides of the beds. Fertilizing the soil would also be a tricky issue. Nutrients can drain out much more quickly from a garden box that is not in direct contact with the earth. We settled on a soil depth of twelve inches, which would give the roots sufficient room to grow and absorb nutrients, provided that the soil was regularly replenished with compost.

Our biggest concern from both a practical and aesthetic standpoint was the planter boxes. The six of us brainstormed a design that would be practical and elegant, with a combination of steel frames and cedar beds with a fabric lining on the bottom to help retain moisture. The beds would be four feet wide by ten feet long and about two feet tall so that both children and adults could work comfortably.

Helen was particularly interested in the possibility of extending the growing season. Just as rooftop gardens heat up more quickly than in-ground gardens in the summer, they're also more sensitive to cold in the late fall and early spring. I had done a good deal of season extension at the farm, where we'd built low enclosures around the plants that protected them from harsh weather. We'd taken bendable PVC pipes and stuck them into the ground like giant croquet wickets arching above our crops and then covered those arches (about four feet high and four feet wide) with sheets of plastic, creating tunnels over the entire row that we could crawl through to reach the plants. The plastic let in the warm sun during the day and retained much of the warmth overnight, protecting the plants from frost and the soil from freezing.

I worked with the metalworker on a plan that would make it easy to install similar mini-greenhouses above the planter boxes at Uncommon Ground. He designed sockets on the steel frames that could be used to anchor metal hoops; plastic sheeting could then be draped over the hoops in the late fall and early spring months. (The sockets could also be used in the summer as a base for a trellis to support tall plants.) As winter set in, I wasn't quite sure how our plans would translate into the actual hands-on work, but I was looking forward to the challenge.

IN DECEMBER, AFTER THE busy 2007 season came to an end, Verd, Thea, and I were settling into our lives in the coach house. Two months earlier, I'd found out I was pregnant with a second child. We were excited about the prospect of growing our family and felt grateful to be in a home with room enough for four. We splurged on a couch and a rustic dining room table, and finally had enough cupboard space for the pots, pans, and umpteen serving bowls we'd received as wedding gifts. I loved spending time in the kitchen, making blueberry pancakes for Thea, or cooking beef-and-vegetable stews. Thea, now six, was excited to have a living room big enough to hold a Christmas tree. Verd, for his part, loved the upstairs alcove where he could burrow into his studies.

I met with Steve Balsamo to discuss plans for the rabbit- and deer-proof fence that would border the garden. We purchased 150 yards of Benner's deer fencing (a durable polypropylene mesh), which we planned to attach to a cedar split-rail fence (painted white, to match the existing fencing on the property) that we ordered from the Walpole catalog. I spent long happy evenings that winter with a yellow legal pad sketching out different garden layouts, fantasizing about a large stand of sweet corn, big melon and pumpkin patches, raspberries to go next to the gooseberries, and expanding a bed of strawberries next to the asparagus that had been planted years ago and was still thriving.

The drawback of our move from Evanston to Glencoe was that we were now living twenty minutes away from Bryan. Thea loved her regular movie nights and sleepovers at his apartment, but Bryan and I worried that shuttling her between two homes would disrupt her new routine and friendships. We decided instead that Bryan would have dinner with us as a family every other night and spend time with Thea at our house. When I mentioned the arrangement to friends, they thought it was, at best, unusual—*a two-father household?* But Verd supported the arrangement without any hesitation. Bryan and Verd had developed a great relationship and a wry, jocular way of interacting. Each of them had taken on distinct, noncompetitive roles in Thea's life—Verd more the responsible buddy and adviser, and Bryan more the decision maker and teacher. Thea has always been, unmistakably, Bryan's daughter. She inherited his love of sports—he taught her at an early age how to dribble a basketball, and to this day they play hoops together in the local park almost every week and revel in their shared devotion to the Chicago Bulls. Bryan also reads books almost obsessively, on topics from quantum physics to human genetics, and by the time Thea was in kindergarten he had taught her to read and had built her a library.

My parents admire Bryan's devotion to Thea and include him in family events whenever they can. One evening when Verd, Thea, Bryan, and I joined my parents for dinner at Lake Shore, I heard my father introducing both Verd and Bryan to his friends as his "sons-in-law." It perfectly summed up our family dynamic and made me feel deeply glad.

IN FEBRUARY 2008, just before the start of a new season and almost exactly a year after we got married, Verd and I boarded a flight to Cancún. It wasn't the ideal time for a tropical honeymoon—I was five months pregnant, and having already gained fifteen pounds, I wasn't feeling very bikini ready. But I was well past the period of morning sickness and was otherwise able to savor the prospect of taking my first real vacation in more than twenty years.

On the commune, the concept of "vacation" had been viewed as an inexcusable waste of time and resources. The act of burning huge amounts of fuel to drive or fly somewhere to rest for a week seemed to us indulgent, irresponsible, and even absurd. *The planet is in crisis and Americans are going to Disney World,* our thinking went. *Revolutionaries don't have time for vacations—there's too much work to be done.* Verd and I found that some of those assumptions lingered as we debated whether it was ethical to fly all the way to Mexico rather than go somewhere closer to home. We felt better

THE COACH HOUSE AND GARDEN AT HARVESTTIME

about the plan when we found a rustic place online called the Hemingway Eco Resort in Tulum, something between a resort and a campground with thatched-roof huts right on the ocean. We booked a six-night trip, the longest I'd been away from Thea, and I felt nervous about leaving her. But when I called Bryan after we had arrived and settled in, expecting anguished sounds in the background, instead I heard Thea laughing. She told me when we spoke that she was so busy she didn't have time to stay on the phone for long.

In the year since our wedding day, Verd and I had occasionally managed to go out to dinner, but things had been so chaotic with work that we'd had almost no waking time alone together. In Cancún we snorkeled in the early mornings, and during the day we hopped into the jalopy we rented and searched out cenotes—the gorgeous, clear freshwater pools in deep natural sinkholes that the region is known for. We walked mile after mile of Mayan ruins. We spent lazy hours every evening chatting in bed under our king-size mosquito net, and came to understand for the first time in our adult lives the virtues of rest.

We talked about the year ahead. Verd had been getting excellent grades in college, but we weren't sure yet where his path would take him. He ended up enrolling in the University of Illinois at Chicago's Honors College to pursue a bachelor's of neuroscience the following fall. Financially, we had no choice other than for Verd to continue working full-time for the business alongside his studies, especially with a baby girl on the way. The last evening of our trip, as we lounged in bed, Verd curled his hands to make a pretend loudspeaker and, directing his voice into my swelling belly, promised our daughter that he'd teach her every dance step he knew, from the moonwalk to the merengue. He reassured me that it would all work out, reminding me that we'd hired extra hands to pitch in for the upcoming season in preparation for my due date in early June. I marveled yet again at his steady optimism, which always kept me looking forward.

WE RETURNED FROM OUR HONEYMOON TO THE FEVER PITCH OF a new season, with our client numbers rising from forty-five to sixty-five, over half of them through word of mouth. There were more proposals to write, more garden beds to prepare, more buzz around our business than ever before—but also more pressure on our home life. The downside of discovering the virtues of rest was confronting the pain of giving it up. Verd and I returned from seven days of bliss to commence our hundred days of hell, and the transition wasn't easy. Suddenly I faced eighty-hour weeks as I fielded new clients, negotiated contracts, sourced supplies, and organized crews for soil preparation. Now in the third trimester of pregnancy, I felt utterly overwhelmed. "I can't do this, Verd," I said in those early weeks of spring. "This is physically and emotionally impossible." He responded with a pep talk: "Imagine you're a bear in a river, Jeanne. There's a salmon run, and you have to keep opening your jaws and catching the salmon. It's a seasonal feast."

The business was not only devouring our time, but also physically taking over our household—and taking its toll on Thea. When shipments came in—sacks of seeds, huge boxes of tomato cages, five-gallon buckets of liquid fertilizer, big bundles of bamboo stakes—they glutted the front hall and then spilled over into our living room. When crate after crate of seedlings came in, we had to build a makeshift plant shelter in the backyard. The second floor of our house was also cramped. Just outside Thea's bedroom, our desks and filing cabinets overflowed with client files and papers. There was never any time to tackle all the dirty dishes in the kitchen sink, or to clean the dirt and debris from our car, which was always filled with the heavy scent of compost.

Thea, understandably, began to retaliate. "This house is disgusting!" she screamed one morning. "We can't live like this! Why are you doing this to me?" My attempts to console her drove her into a deeper spiral. "I hate you," she screamed. "I hate Verdie." This triggered a reaction in Verd to protect me—to try and talk some sense into Thea—and I, in turn, felt the need to protect my daughter. I shot back at Verd: "Let her speak her mind! It's not your place to discipline her!"

It hurt Verd that I shut him down like that and limited his role in Thea's life, but I wanted, above all, for Thea to be honest with me—to be able to share her feelings freely in a way that I hadn't with my parents. We all retreated to our corners, injured and exhausted. It was Bryan who drew us back together and brokered peace. The four of us sat down in our living room and talked through the conflict. Thea was able to explain how hard and confusing it was to face so many sudden demands on her mom and her household, especially when in only three months, her new sister would arrive; Verd was able to discuss the need for clarity in his role as a father figure; I was able to voice my feelings of guilt for having hurt both Thea and Verd. Bryan mediated the discussion with care and patience, and by the end of it, we were more aware of ourselves and of one another, and understood that our family would be our most important source of strength as we faced the changes and challenges ahead.

Once we had our contracts signed and the soil prepared at our sixty-five gardens, the season began to roll smoothly. I continued to meet with clients and do basic gardening tasks through early May. As my belly grew bigger and bigger, my pace slowed and it became harder to carry heavy loads of tools and compost. Still, it felt good to kneel down in the soil and plant. The spring was mild with good rains, and our gardens were off to a strong start. The logistical challenges we faced were all fairly easily resolved, and some of them were more amusing than frustrating. While weeding the garden of an established client with Verd, I came across a spike-leafed plant in a far corner—marijuana, not exactly a native weed of Illinois. The plant looked as though it had recently been tended, with the soil around it carefully smoothed out. I called Verd over and asked if he thought we should just pull it up. He laughed and said it would probably be a good idea to ask first.

The owner explained to me that her teenage son was "experimenting," and that she and her husband wanted to be supportive of him. Verd mentioned that she might want to look into the legal implications of growing pot in Illinois. By the next time we showed up, the plant had disappeared. Apparently, a quick Internet search had been enough to convince her that the potential costs outweighed the credit to be gained for being cool parents.

My favorite encounters with quirkiness always had to do with children. I planted a garden for the Gandhi family, a Lake Forest couple with two small children. At 1,500 square feet, it was the largest residential garden I'd installed at that point. The parents, Kavitha and Sanjay, were second-generation Indian Americans and liked to cook Indian cuisine that included rarer fruits and vegetables such as bitter melon, which we helped them grow, along with multiple varieties of eggplant (Rosa Bianca, Nadia, Raveena, Barbarella, and Kermit), many varieties of beans (tricolor bush beans, Asian long beans, and red noodle beans), Thai basil, and Thai hot peppers. Since the start of the Organic Gardener, I'd found that one of the tasks children enjoy most is writing out the wooden labels for the plant rows. Usually, one or both parents hover nearby to answer spelling questions and prompt corrections, but these children attended a Montessori school and the parents were ultrafirm believers in letting them find their own way in sounding out words.

The labels they drew up for these complicated, multipart vegetable names were the most wonderfully creative I'd ever seen, jumbles of consonants sprinkled with random vowels: "dcanrahds" for daikon radish; "reedkabige" for red cabbage. Even when I later ran into a fencing problem and other glitches there (a new type of wire mesh advertised as rustproof had rusted through and I had to replace it), I never left that distinctly labeled garden without a huge smile.

HEADING INTO THE 2008 SEASON, I faced a new challenge at the Polaris Charter Academy, where, for the first time, I'd be planting directly on top of concrete. The recently opened charter school was located on the site of an old public school that the city had judged to be "failing" and shut down. The three teachers who founded Polaris had won a prize for teaching excellence at other Chicago schools, and they wanted to incorporate cutting-edge methods of experiential learning into their new school's curriculum. They saw a garden as a way for the children to get firsthand experience with earth science and biology, and a good dose of the green outdoors.

The hands-on gardening education trend has been booming in recent years. In the state of California alone there are now more than six thousand school gardens, and there are tens of thousands more nationwide. Though it's "new" in the modern era, this trend has a history that goes back to the nineteenth century. The German term *kindergarten,* which translates to "child-garden," was coined by education pioneer Friedrich Froebel as the name for the children's teaching institute he created in 1837. Froebel thought of children as figurative flowers to be tended and nurtured; he also educated children in actual gardens, and stressed that a connection to nature would help them develop their powers of observation. Froebel's philosophy was based on his notion that if a person "is to attain fully his destiny . . . he must feel and know himself to be one . . . with nature."

The late-nineteenth-century educators Maria Montessori and John Dewey shared Froebel's belief in school gardening. By the early twentieth century, when the U.S. economy was still mostly agrarian, and food-growing skills were viewed as essential for young Americans, there were more than seventy-five thousand school gardens in the United States. During World War I, the federal Bureau of Education introduced the "United States School Garden Army," a program it advertised with an image of two smiling children planting seeds and the motto "We eat because we work." Schools were also enlisted to join the victory garden movement during World War II. But in the postwar era, as farms became bigger and more mechanized, school gardens plunged in number.

The reemergence of school gardens since the late 1990s has been driven mostly by grassroots efforts by parents, local activists, and teachers. But in certain cities and states, lawmakers have joined in to move the trend forward. California, Oregon, and Alaska, for instance, have passed state legislation to encourage and fund school gardens. Chicago, Boston, and Denver are among dozens of cities that are pushing the school garden movement at the municipal level. In 1998, former mayor Richard M. Daley began to fund campus parks at Chicago public schools that provide open green spaces for students and the wider community. The city then used funding from this program to support the Chicago Botanic Garden's School Gardens Initiative. Daley also helped build new school gardens through his Greencorps job training program. By 2008, 312 public schools had campus parks or food gardens thanks to these and other programs. Daley's successor, Mayor Rahm Emanuel, has been working with nonprofits to secure the funding to continue this installation effort.

The educational benefits of school gardens can be vast and varied. In a garden-based science class, for instance, students can learn about plant life cycles and the soil ecosystem, and test different conditions of moisture and sun to figure out why some kinds of plants thrive and others don't. English teachers can bring students into the garden space to observe details and write descriptive passages and poems; art teachers can use the plants as subject matter for drawing and painting; math teachers can work with students in the garden to apply counting and measuring skills, to examine the geometric shapes hidden within flowers and fruits, and to chart plant growth and variability.

One recent study published by the American Society for Horticultural Science found that students who participated in hands-on science lessons in a school garden scored higher on science tests than students who learned in a typical classroom. A garden can also provide an incentive for a school to insert new classes about nutrition and food preparation into its curriculum. The *Journal of the American Dietetic Association* published a study that found that students involved in a garden-based nutrition education program increased their fruit and vegetable consumption by 2.5 servings per day, more than doubling their overall consumption of fresh produce.

AT POLARIS, BECAUSE OF concerns about lead in the soil, there was no choice but to grow on top of the concrete lot next to the school. We planned to build six four-by-eight-foot raised cedar beds. We would line the base of the beds with heavy-duty landscape cloth as a barrier, then add gravel for better water drainage before filling them with compost. The work would be done with the help of a group of volunteers from the school and from Outward Bound, including my parents.

At the time of the Polaris planting, I was well into my seventh month of pregnancy, already feeling hippo-size, my belly straining against a large pair of overalls. Kord and Verd had trucked in the gravel, four-by-four-inch cedar timbers, and compost, and set to work assembling the raised beds with the help of construction-oriented teachers and other volunteers. I was amused to see my father, the consummate take-charge businessman, directing Kord and Verd on carpentry details. They had constructed hundreds of beds by that time, but they gamely let my father take the lead.

My parents had, for the most part, stayed out of the hands-on aspects of my business. They'd given me encouragement and advice in the beginning and whenever I'd asked for it in later years, but they wanted to let me find my own way, and the only installation they'd visited at that point was the Edible Gardens. At Polaris, they both dove right into the hard physical work of moving wheelbarrows of compost alongside the other volunteers. It took two dozen of us all morning and well into the afternoon to finish the work of installing and preparing the beds for planting.

Toward the end of the day, I looked up from the stoop where I sat taking a break and saw my mom shoveling compost from a pile into a wheelbarrow to finish filling one of the beds. Petite and elegant as always, she wore dark corduroys, a fleece jacket, and hiking boots. I remembered watching her at work harvesting beets on one of her first visits to the farm in Texas. Even at the height of my estrangement from my parents, I'd been struck by her determination. But it wasn't until now, standing on the concrete lot at Polaris, that I was able to understand just how determined a person she was, how much strength and resolve it had taken this proud, meticulous woman to stand by me as I barely completed high school, shrugged off college, shunned society for seventeen years, bore a child out of wedlock, and married a much younger man with a tenth-grade education and three part-time jobs. Over and over I'd rejected the ideals and hopes she had for me. I felt a stab of nauseating shame as I remembered the time I'd refused to let my mom hold four-week-old Thea when she'd first visited the farm to meet her new granddaughter. I'd watched her swallow back tears, injured by the understanding of one of the lessons I'd internalized from Arol's many speeches on the subject that she might damage or somehow taint her own grandchild. My mom looked up from her shoveling to see me watching her; I smiled and got up to hug her for a moment, and then set back to work beside her.

Chapter 18

ON JUNE 9, 2008, RIGHT ON SCHEDULE, I WENT INTO LABOR WITH MY
second daughter. I had tried to be prepared: We'd set up a nursery
in a tiny sunny room on the second floor of the house with a
wooden crib we'd found on Craigslist and a hand-me-down rock-
ing chair from Verd's mom. At the Organic Gardener, we'd brought
in two extra employees for the summer to help cover for me, and
we'd made plans for child care so that I could get back to work by
midsummer. And though I'd been busy scheduling plantings and
troubleshooting the gardens that were already in process up until
the afternoon my labor began, I'd also taken time to rest and reflect
on who I had become and how I'd gotten there.

All things considered, my life had never been more stable. I was
excited and felt ready for a second child, but memories of my first
birth chafed at my confidence. Almost all the women at the commune had given birth in their own beds with a midwife attending.
Arol had told me and others that our own births, during which our
mothers had been "drugged" with pain medication, were the first
traumas of our lives. She saw epidurals as the embodiment of everything that was wrong with Western medicine—a procedure that
would numb the body, mind, and spirit, and interfere with a woman's most important rite of passage. Natural childbirth, I'd been led

to believe, would be a test of my inner strength and a test of my loyalty to the commune.

Ten days after Thea's due date, with no signs of labor, my midwife had told me that I would soon have to get induced, according to North Carolina state law. The morning I was scheduled for induction, I went into labor naturally on the way to the hospital. Fifteen hours into my labor, after taking long soaks in a warm tub and working through breathing techniques with the two women I was closest to on the farm, Kare and Lore, while Arol stood by, I spiraled into a panic. My legs trembled uncontrollably and I began to sob. Lore held my shoulders and tried to help me get control of my breathing, until Arol cut in. "Forget it," she said. "Shey's not with us, Lore—she's not going to let us help her. Just give up." They left the room when the anesthesiologist administered the epidural.

I now think of Thea's birth as the beginning of the end of my identification as a Zendik—not because I had failed the labor test of loyalty, but because I suddenly had a new understanding of what loyalty, in fact, was. The sense of belonging I felt toward Thea within moments of her birth was different from anything I'd ever known. When I first looked at her she was wide-eyed and returned my gaze squarely and intently. I experienced a rush of recognition, like we'd known each other for a lifetime. Her face seemed to me to be preternaturally serene (*Her beauty is animal and delicate,* I wrote in my journal; *she seems wholly at peace and unaffected by my own shame and frustration*).

Two days after I returned from the hospital, Arol arrived in my bedroom with six other people to discuss "what happened" at the birth. She sat on the edge of my bed and opened up a notebook to a fresh page. On it she drew two large adjacent circles overlapping slightly in the middle. "This circle is Zendik—our culture, our values, our way of life," she said, retracing the circumference of one with her pen. "This other circle is the death culture—it's Les Pinsof and his material goals, it's mainstream medicine and the doctors with their epidurals who believe birth is unnatural and women can't do it. When push came to shove, you chose your father's world. You put your daughter at risk and handed yourself over to them." Instead of reacting angrily and defensively, as I would have before Thea's birth, I felt nothing and said nothing in response.

I'd largely worked through and let go of the shame and defeat I'd felt during my labor with Thea, but seven years later, traces of doubt persisted as I went into labor for the second time. Throughout my pregnancy, Verd and I had discussed attempting a home birth. After my return to Illinois I'd been amazed to learn that home births had become increasingly popular. But I'd also come to realize that it wasn't for me—I'd be more relaxed in a hospital and wanted the option to have an epidural if I needed one.

I found a midwife-doctor team that I liked at Evanston Hospital, and I asked my sister, Hallie, who had a decade's worth of experience attending births, to be with me during the birth.

Thea, who'd soon be turning seven, had told me emphatically that she wanted to be there, too. Bryan, Verd, and I talked about this at length with her, cautioning that it could be difficult. We told her that she might get grossed out by the physical realities of the birth, or she might become distressed to see her mom struggling with a great deal of pain. But the midwife assured me that it wasn't unusual for older siblings to be involved, and I arranged for a teacher to come to the house and give a demonstration of labor and delivery—complete with props representing a baby and the birth canal. Thea was undaunted and felt certain she wanted to be included.

After a few hours of carefully timing contractions, I arrived at the hospital with Debbie, the midwife, Verd, Hallie, Bryan, and Thea. Verd stood next to me, keeping his hands on my back and body at all times, pressing on my hips during contractions to ease the discomfort. Hallie also gave enormous support. Like a trainer in a boxer's corner, she fed me Emergen-C through a straw to keep me hydrated and to keep my energy up, coached me on slow, steady breathing, and kept me focused on her eyes and off the pain as she repeated, *You can do this.* I was able to get through the labor without an epidural. Thea watched everything as it unfolded, with Bryan standing beside her to take her out of the room if she got uncomfortable. She didn't—and when her baby sister arrived red-faced, blue-eyed, fair-haired—Verd's spitting image—Thea was the first family member to make eye contact with her. She greeted her sister, whom we'd decided to name Kisten after Verd's sister, with the very same open, fearless gaze she had fixed on me when we'd first met.

WHILE I WAS ON MATERNITY LEAVE, Verd was busier than ever. His paternity leave lasted all of eighteen hours. After rallying through the labor and birth, he was up the next morning at 5:30 A.M.—as he would be on many mornings over the next few months—taking on my role as the lead negotiator, designer, planter, harvester, coordinator, and client liaison for the sixty-five gardens we were planting that season. He also worked with Kord to oversee the team we'd assembled to do the heavy lifting of raised-bed construction, fence building, and soil preparation.

The most challenging project slated for the month of June was the Uncommon Ground restaurant rooftop farm installation. A delay in the construction of the raised beds had pushed the project back by several weeks, and we were anxious to plant as soon as possible. I called Helen Cameron with last-minute adjustments to the crop list, and we eliminated spinach, butterhead lettuce, and other cold-weather spring crops that might not do well if they were planted late (particularly given that rooftop gardens are in a warmer "climate zone"), and added more heat-loving summer crops such as peppers, cucumbers, and eggplants.

The biggest technical challenge once the raised beds were in place was how to fill them with dirt. I'd decided to work with organic potting soil instead of compost. Potting soil has compost in it, but it also contains peat moss or coir (from coconut husks) and vermiculite (a lightweight natural mineral), which hold moisture and act as "lighteners" to prevent the compost from getting too dense (a key concern, as overly compacted soil prohibits roots from traveling freely to get the nutrients they need). The question remained of how to get the potting soil up to the roof. We'd need to transport no less than six tons of soil—twelve thousand pounds—to fill the beds. Michael Cameron had initially suggested that we use a crane that would be on-site for the final stages of the roof's construction, but because of the various delays the equipment was no longer available when we were ready, and a crane rental was beyond the scope of our budget. After brainstorming, Verd, Kord, and I saw only one solution: carry the soil, bag by bag, up the two flights of stairs. The task of hauling three hundred bags of potting soil up to the roof would have been backbreaking work for our small team, but Michael and Helen asked members of their community—school parents, college students, church members—for help. Five people volunteered, and in half a day the total crew of eight, under Verd and Kord's leadership, carried all of the soil to the roof and deposited it into the freshly lined beds. Throughout that morning, as I nursed Kisten and drifted in and out of a sleepy haze, Verd texted me updates with pictures showing their steady progress.

ONE MORNING IN EARLY JULY, I was pushing Kisten in her stroller down a quiet summer street when I got a call from a cheerful woman who introduced herself as "a representative of Hidden Valley." She said that the makers of the popular salad dressing had heard about the Edible Gardens and wanted me to be their national organic gardening expert. Her marketing team had recently launched a national "Love Your Veggies" campaign aimed at getting American kids more interested in eating vegetables (and the dressings they can be dipped in). The company would also be committing more than one million dollars to schools and organizations to help them grow vegetable gardens, and awarding grants to ten mothers around the United States to start community gardens.

I was amazed, on the one hand, that a major company even knew that I existed. I was also intrigued by the possibilities of a vegetable-advocacy campaign on a national level, with a grassroots, one-garden-at-a-time approach. On the other hand, I'd spent the better part of two decades learning to question the impacts of big business on the American food system. I knew full well that even if I wasn't directly promoting Hidden Valley products, I'd be doing so indirectly.

But I'd also evolved in my thinking and understood that big companies were not by definition "bad." Walmart, for instance, has become one of the world's biggest purchasers of locally grown foods—not so much out of loyalty to local farmers but because, among other reasons, the company realized it could save millions of dollars on fuel for its trucking fleet if it sourced food grown closer to its stores. In 2010, the company committed to sourcing one billion dollars' worth of food from farms under fifty acres, and this has helped keep many small farmers in business. Walmart had become the biggest organic foods distributor in the world by 2007, and had helped make organic products affordable for millions of Americans who otherwise would have found them out of reach. That didn't make Walmart wholly a "good guy." But it did convince me that large corporations have immense power to improve our food system—and to make healthier food more affordable.

The Clorox Company, which owns Hidden Valley, had recently purchased Burt's Bees, Green Works, and Brita in an effort to move its product line in a greener, less chemical direction, and Hidden Valley had introduced a line of organic dressings. While my clients on the North Shore tended to be people who shopped at health food stores and knew a lot about good nutrition, and whose kids already, for the most part, had healthy diets, Hidden Valley's products and its campaign were aimed at a different audience: people who didn't have the money to hire help for their gardens but who were committed to improving their children's health and well-being. I wanted to help them do that. I decided to accept the offer.

SEVERAL WEEKS AFTER the planting at Uncommon Ground, I returned to work. One of the first things I did was visit the farm there, and for the first time I took in the whole picture of the rooftop space that I'd only been able to imagine through sketches and plans—the five big solar panels, the beehives, the composter, the growing farm, the surrounding urban landscape. Helen and Michael Cameron were creating a small but workable, replicable model for sustainable agriculture, right in the city, twenty-five feet above the street and sidewalk.

In spite of the relatively late start, the warm rooftop conditions had helped fuel a growth that was quicker and lusher than we'd expected. The eggplant was flowering with bright splashes of lav-

UNCOMMON GROUND RESTAURANT ROOFTOP FARM, 2008

ender; the basil, lettuces, beans, and snap peas were growing in countless shades of green. The tomatoes and peppers in particular, which tend to love heat, were almost excessively plump on the vine. Only one part of the garden had not done well: In the two-foot-wide beds set against the perimeter wall on the front side of the roof, the plants had come up stunted and had stopped growing. It didn't make sense—the nutrients in the soil and the amount of water and sunlight were the same as in every other part of the garden.

Over the course of the summer, Kord, Verd, and I made several more visits to the Uncommon Ground rooftop farm and finally found an answer: the wind. In the Windy City, we realized, one hazard of rooftop gardens was that strong air currents could develop even more speed along the urban landscape's slick surfaces—becoming particularly fierce, for instance, at the corner of a second-story garden with no windbreak. It was an easy fix—eventually the Camerons installed bamboo windscreens along the roof's perimeter, and all the plants thrived.

Chapter 19

———————————

DURING THE UNCOMMON GROUND PROJECT, AS OUR WORK HOURS started adding up, I'd suggested to Helen that a portion of the restaurant's payment to us could be given in trade, as credit toward future meals. By September, when I tallied the finances, I realized we'd racked up enough credit to eat out every night for a month. I would be turning forty in October, and Verd suggested that we use the credit to throw a birthday party at the restaurant. I shot down the idea at first, thinking of forty as something to hide, not celebrate. But over the next few days I started realizing that the party would be an opportunity to gather and thank everyone who had welcomed me back home when I'd first returned, and the people who'd given me crucial support in the years since.

I invited thirty-five guests—family members mixed with old friends from childhood and new friends from work—who spanned three generations. The night of the party turned out to be chilly but clear, and when people arrived I took them upstairs to the rooftop, where the beds of greens and fall vegetables were still flourishing. The space had just gotten its official certification from the Midwest Organic Services Association as the nation's first organic rooftop farm.

Our group filled up the room that had been set aside for the party, with Thea and the other kids chasing one another between tables and trading crayons to write on the white paper tablecloths. Helen and I had worked up a menu that included their signature artichoke dip and pepper-encrusted beef tenderloin, three-cheese macaroni, mixed green salads, and fall vegetable dishes with roast potatoes, carrots, broccoli, beets, and onions, some of them grown upstairs. We served the food family style, in large platters that we passed around the tables. Halfway through dinner, before I'd had a chance to thank my guests, Uncle Bill's wife, Aunt Suzan, stood up to make a toast. "I heard a story once about a Zen Buddhist monk who renounced everything—his home and possessions, his family, his community—and went away to live on a mountain in isolation," she began, and the room got very quiet. "His family was hurt, but decades later he returned home and was able to share lessons he'd learned while away. His family and community came to see that his absence had been worthwhile—that they needed what he'd learned, just as we need what you went to find, Jeanne—the skills and knowledge you brought home."

I was deeply affected by Suzan's story and the effort she was making to absolve me for the pain and confusion I'd caused. As the night wore on, several other friends and family members made toasts that similarly moved me to tears, and I couldn't collect myself in time to make a toast myself. My father spoke last. "Jeanne, you're a person who had a strong conviction long ago for what you wanted that none of us could understand," he said. "You didn't know exactly what it was or how to get it done, but you set about trying to make it happen anyway. Now, so many years later, it's beginning to happen, and we feel an overflowing pride."

I managed to thank my dad and went to hug him, and it hit me then as I looked around the room that the people surrounding me were almost exactly the same in number as the people I'd shared meals with at the farm. And that these people—who'd been patient and steadfast and accepted me back without judgment no matter how judgmental I'd been—were the community I'd been seeking all along. Things had come full circle.

―――――

THERE WERE TWO PEOPLE who'd been crucial to my journey whose absence I felt strongly that night at Uncommon Ground—Mark Peterson, my high school love who'd helped me wander off the beaten path, and Abby Mandel, the woman who'd pulled me back toward it.

After my return home, I'd thought about Mark almost daily—every time I drove past the Cook County Forest Preserve where we'd spent so much of our time in high school. At the age of twenty-two, after his long struggle with depression, Mark had packed a gun in his guitar case, walked into the forest preserve, and ended his life. I never knew all the details of what had happened but I felt I knew where he'd gone. Shortly after I'd left for the farm, Mark had built a hut of tree branches and prairie grasses deep in the forest. It was based on a shelter design we'd learned at Tom Brown Jr.'s Tracker School in the Pine Barrens of New Jersey, where we'd gone for a week to learn wilderness skills after coming home from Arizona. He'd framed the hut with long straight branches leaning together at the top, and filled the space between the poles with bundles of prairie grasses he'd collected and bound together. He showed it to me on my first visit home from the farm—noticeably proud of the secret space he'd built. "Here, the world feels right," he'd said. The hut was surprisingly spacious, with a lantern, books, foam sleeping pad, and blankets inside. We spent hours there during my visit talking and rediscovering our friendship. I told him about life on the commune and pressed him to move there with me, but he said the rules and the lack of privacy would suffocate him.

I wished mightily that I'd had the chance to show Mark that the community we'd rejected was, in fact, capable of change, and to introduce him to change makers like Abby. She was as singularly passionate as Mark—a nonconformist thinker unafraid to do things her way. After a yearlong struggle with lymphoma, Abby had passed away in August 2008 at the age of seventy-five. Under

Abby's direction, Green City Market had grown from its initial nine farmers in 1998 to almost fifty, and the range of products sold there had broadened each year. The number of visitors to the market had jumped from 40,000 in the 2007 season to more than 80,000 in 2008, and it would continue to grow over the next few years, with up to 200,000 visitors recorded in 2010. The growth of Green City Market's popularity mirrored national trends: In 1998, there were about 2,600 farmers markets in America; in 2010, there would be more than 6,000.

Abby had lived to see her project succeed, and had instilled in me her optimism. After sifting through my memories of Mark on my fortieth birthday, I felt as though I owed it to him, as much as to anyone—my children, my husband, my parents, my friends—to do all I could to keep cultivating a sense of hope and possibility.

AS THE 2009 GARDENING season got under way, the number of our clients jumped again, from sixty-five to one hundred, and we had no choice but to hire more people. At the peak of the season, our staff increased to eight, and the new hands helped in particular on raised bed construction and soil preparation. The baby was, fortunately, sleeping through most of the night, getting more sleep than Verd and me combined. Despite the difficulties of a busy season, I was happy. I felt more settled than I had in past years, more secure in myself and more confident that the business, however hectic, would continue growing and moving forward.

Late that April, I drove to the Gary Comer Youth Center in Chicago to give a hands-on gardening demonstration to the ten mothers who'd won Hidden Valley's "Search for Veggie Champions" contest. Each woman had been awarded five thousand dollars to apply toward starting or supporting an existing nonprofit garden in her community. Jean Marie Gunner, a mother of two from New York, used her grant to launch a community garden at her local elementary school and a nonprofit organization called the Seeds of

Living Education to teach kids the basics of gardening. She let the children choose the garden's name ("The Giving Garden") and the vegetables they wanted to plant. In just the project's first two seasons, more than four hundred kindergarten-through-fifth-grade students took part in growing sixty different types of heirloom plants.

Bridget O'Boyle, a mother of two from Minnesota, used her grant to support a nutrition- , cooking- , and gardening-education program at a community center near Minneapolis serving at-risk families and children living in poverty. When she had trouble finding an urban lot that was large and sunny enough to sustain a garden, she and teenagers from the center came up with the idea of having a "mobile garden," planting seeds in containers placed in wagons that could be moved to follow the sun and that would be easy to water. The wheeled gardens produced purple carrots, herbs, lettuce, edamame, tomatoes, and zucchini with great success, and Bridget and her team were invited to display their work at local farmers markets.

It impressed me to see what these relatively small investments in community gardens could accomplish, and I was happy to have contributed some of the educational tools these women needed to develop their plans. I was beginning to see the full potential for community-driven change in the food system, but at the same time, I was becoming more aware of the barriers that stood in the way. In a speech delivered that June in front of her new vegetable garden on the White House lawn, First Lady Michelle Obama voiced support for a number of key initiatives to bring fresh, healthy food to more Americans: improving the nutritional quality of school lunches, strengthening childhood education in nutrition and gardening, and encouraging community gardens in urban areas. But the First Lady, a native of Chicago, also mentioned the persistent problem of "food deserts" in America—large geographic areas with limited or no access to grocery stores and fresh produce. The vast majority of food deserts are low-income city communities that have been dismissed by retailers as unprofitable—leaving residents no option but to buy their meals at gas stations, convenience stores, liquor stores, and fast-food restaurants.

I'd met some of the key people in Illinois who were working to combat the problem—people including Ken Dunn, Harry Rhodes, and Erika Allen, whose efforts in Chicago (as in cities across the country) were having a positive effect: Over a five-year period, the number of Chicagoans living in food deserts dropped by 39 percent. But the large percentage of citizens who were still affected was stunning: Chicago's food deserts currently span no less than fifty-five square miles, an area that is home to nearly four hundred thousand residents, a quarter of whom are children. The more I learned about the food-desert problem, the more I wondered whether the benefits of gardening could be true for anyone if they were not true for everyone.

IN ADDITION TO ITS negative effects on public health, the rise in popularity of fast food in recent decades has had hidden climatic impacts. One fast-food cheeseburger, according to one estimate, generates between seven and fourteen pounds of carbon dioxide, versus roughly half a pound of carbon dioxide per pound of many fresh-grown vegetables. Processed foods take an environmental toll: 16 percent of the total energy currently used in the U.S. food system goes toward food processing. Food miles are also part of the cost: Packaged junk foods and fast foods travel many carbon-intensive miles from where their separate ingredients are grown to where they're processed and then to where they're packaged and consumed.

As the problem of climate change intensifies, and as more people move into urban centers, the need for sources of fresh, organically grown food within and around big cities will only become more urgent. I knew that a large portion of my business would remain in the suburbs: that had been my steadiest source of work, and I enjoyed it. But I also understood that cities could play an ever-larger role in the future of food production—that every urban rooftop, courtyard, schoolyard, and abandoned city lot could become productive farmland in the coming decades. I wanted to do more to participate in that shift.

IV.

HARVEST

Chapter 20

TOWARD THE END OF THE 2009 SEASON, I MET TWO KEY FOOD-AND-nutrition activists in the Chicago area. Kathryn Guylay, a mother of two with an MBA and a degree in nutritional health counseling, asked me to teach a gardening class for her nonprofit, Nurture, which offers low-income Chicago-area families greater access to healthy foods. Nurture holds workshops in public schools, community centers, and food pantries to educate kids and adults about nutrition, cooking, and exercise. Kathryn designed the workshops to address the three main barriers to bringing healthy foods to low-income households: cost, time, and knowledge. Nurture gives each adult participant a one-button device—a rice cooker—and teaches easy, quick ways to prepare six types of low-cost beans and grains: lentils, split peas, brown rice, bulgur wheat, quinoa, and couscous.

The missing link in Kathryn's curriculum was fresh fruits and vegetables. While the beans and grains could be purchased for a dollar or two a pound—making the cost of meals comparable to or even less than the cost of fast food—the fresh fruits, vegetables, and herbs needed to complete those meals would be much more expensive. Kathryn's solution was to help participants grow their own fruits and vegetables. She asked me to teach a class aimed at low-income, primarily Latino families in the Chicago area who would have access to community gardening spaces funded by Nurture.

A second opportunity to participate more in urban growing efforts came through Julie Samuels of Openlands, who was developing a new initiative called HomeGrown Chicago aimed at helping inner-city neighborhoods reclaim vacant lots and turn them into community gardens. Each family would be given its own plot within the garden, and take responsibility for planting, tending, and harvesting it; neighbors could build personal connections and a sense of community as they collaborated on the gardening tasks. My role would be to arm participants with the practical skills they'd need to grow their own food.

I began to prepare a presentation for Nurture and HomeGrown Chicago that focused on the simplicity of gardening, with a new emphasis on cost savings. My own gardening education at the farm had been in growing on the cheap: We'd grown our food at Zendik on a bare-bones budget, usually investing no more than a few hundred dollars total in seeds and supplies to grow an acre or more of vegetables. Many of the money-saving techniques I'd learned there could be adapted to urban growing—techniques such as finding scraps and reclaimed wood for raised beds and fences (there are organizations across the country, including Chicago's Rebuilding Exchange, that offer inexpensive supplies for reuse). We also saved and planted seeds from our most successful crops; got in touch with local agricultural extensions to see what seeds and seedlings were on sale; mixed our own fertilizer, compost tea, and potting soil from ingredients purchased in bulk (*Rodale's Ultimate Encyclopedia of Organic Gardening* has great recipes for these); and made our own compost. Many municipalities give away compost made from yard waste for free to urban growers. It's also relatively easy to build your own composter, which can sit at the edge of a community garden space and incorporate food waste collected from neighborhood households and local restaurants.

In recent years, the grow-your-own-food movement has been expanding rapidly in the United States, in large part because the economic recession has put pressure on families to cut back on their grocery budgets. Roughly seven million more households grew their own fruits and vegetables in 2009 than in 2008. The National Gardening Association estimates that when the average price of produce is taken into account, a basic, no-frills food garden can yield a return, above and beyond its start-up and maintenance costs, of five hundred dollars.

The Internet has played a big role in spreading information and support to novice organic gardeners. Any rookie who encounters a pest he doesn't know how to handle, or who needs advice on assembling her own irrigation system, can get instant answers online. Websites such as *Better Homes and Gardens* (bhg.com) have gardening experts who answer questions for free, and Frugal Gardening (frugalgardening.com), *Mother Earth News* (motherearthnews. com), and others offer a steady supply of tips for low-budget gardening. These sites show how, for instance, a generic plastic milk jug can be used as a trowel, a watering can, or even a mini-greenhouse to protect new plants from frost; how strips of old shirts or tablecloths can be used to tie plants to stakes; how layers of cardboard can be used to line the bottoms of raised beds; how five-gallon buckets can be made into self-watering containers; and how kitchen shears from the dollar store can take the place of fancy pruners.

I learned as much sharing my presentations for Nurture and HomeGrown as I did from researching them. One young Latina mother in a Nurture workshop, speaking through a translator, told me that she and her kids had had success sprouting seeds in their kitchen in egg cartons and yogurt cups; once they'd transferred their seedlings to the garden, they'd place empty tuna cans around the garden to measure rain and sprinkler water and to make sure all areas were getting at least an inch a week. That kind of ingenuity and determination to make a garden work on a tight budget has convinced me, perhaps more than anything else, that the urban-growing movement has tremendous promise.

SHORTLY AFTER I STARTED giving the Nurture and HomeGrown presentations, a suburban client of mine, Kathy Deveny, invited me to
spearhead an inner-city project that has since become one of the
gardens I love most. It was my first opportunity to oversee an urban
growing project from beginning to end—from the first sketches to
the final harvest. In the process, I began to understand myself, and
my past, in unexpected ways.

Kathy, a woman so petite and energetic that at first I mistook
her for ten years younger than her age, had hired me to design a
backyard garden in 2009. Her kids loved it, referring to the harvesting process as "scavenger hunts." On a visit to a homeless shelter for young men ages sixteen to twenty-one that was founded by
a member of her Glencoe church, Kathy noticed a few five-gallon
buckets filled with dirt that were growing watermelon vines in the
corner of the shelter's cement courtyard. She wanted the shelter's
residents to have what she and her family had experienced, and
snapped a few pictures of the barren courtyard on her cellphone,
emailing me that same day with the photo attachments to ask what
would be possible there.

The shelter, Solid Ground Supportive Housing Program, is an
offshoot of La Casa Norte, an organization that offers support and
counseling to homeless youth and families in Chicago's poorest
neighborhoods. Both are located in Humboldt Park, a neighborhood on Chicago's troubled West Side that's known for its heavy
gang presence. All around the neighborhood, plywood covers the
windows of vacant storefronts and apartments; pawnshops and
convenience stores are guarded by metal grates; and cash registers
in liquor stores are encased in bulletproof glass.

I'd traveled through communities like Humboldt Park before,
but never with such an awareness of the ways food-scarcity issues
affect residents. The neighborhood spans roughly five square miles,
and large portions of it are government-designated food deserts.

Among Humboldt Park's 65,500 residents, diabetes and obesity rates are exceptionally high. The average resident's daily budget for food is $2.18 per meal. Fast-food outlets and liquor stores are located on virtually every block, but there's a scant selection of grocery stores. I went inside one of those grocers before my first visit to the shelter and saw that its produce selection consisted of shriveled limes, sprouted onions and potatoes, and some bruised, waxy apples.

One bright spot on the same block caught my eye: a small, neat periwinkle blue house set back about twenty feet from the sidewalk with a pretty black fence bordering the front yard. The grass was worn and pale, but the walkway to the house was lined with dozens of cinder blocks being used as planters, with big bunches of greens and herbs and colorful flowers growing up from rich, dark potting soil. Against the leafless landscape and the dun-colored brick buildings, the growth in those concrete planters seemed surreally vibrant, as though celebrating the universal impulse to garden, and proving that almost anything can grow in the most surprising circumstances.

Solid Ground's leader, Joe Hankey, greeted me at the door to the shelter—a narrow three-story brick building with no signage except for a mural of a winged man above the door. The interior was bright, spare, and clean, with white walls and green trim that looked freshly painted. Joe explained that the shelter had opened its doors in 2006 after renovations supported by government and private funding (including donations from Kathy's church) were completed. It houses sixteen young men, each for up to two years, whereas typically shelters for male youth provide housing for no more than 120 days. Many of the residents come from domestic violence situations or have incarcerated parents and have lost their homes. The primary role of the shelter is to provide the men with a safe, stable place to live where staff can help them learn the behavior and skills needed for continuing education and employment. Joe and other staff members also provide substance abuse and mental health services, tutoring, and career counseling, and help with school and job applications.

A garden, Joe thought, could be a kind of living laboratory where residents could learn the basics of nutrition, agriculture, and food preparation. He also saw it as a potential job-training opportunity, allowing residents to explore careers in gardening, landscaping, green-space care, and urban farming. Even if none of those goals were met, he saw the garden serving as a communal space for the residents that would unite them around a common goal.

Joe took me through the kitchen, a sunny room where the residents drifted in and out as they grazed on snacks, chatting with and ribbing one another. I felt a wave of recognition when I saw the stacks of stainless steel bowls, the extralarge tubs of peanut butter, the apples and winter squash by the crate, and the oversize pots and pans for group cooking.

The courtyard was a stark counterpoint to the cheerful, buzzing kitchen. There was plenty of space—at least 1,800 square feet—but it was neglected and empty except for two fold-out metal chairs, a rusty card table, and a basketball. The area was covered with concrete paver blocks, and thorny weeds pushed through the cracks. The makeshift garden of watermelon vines stood almost shyly in the corner. But there was ample sunlight and a water spigot, which meant there wasn't any reason why a garden couldn't succeed there. It felt to me, in fact, *necessary* for a garden to succeed there, especially when I saw the large mosaic on the courtyard's wall. On ceramic tiles of blue, brown, and green was inscribed a thirteen-word creed in bold capital letters:

OUR MISTAKES ARE

EMPOWERMENT

WISDOM

BROTHERHOOD

LEADERSHIP

KNOWLEDGE

INNER POWER

SOLID INDIVIDUAL

INDEPENDENCE

Joe explained that these were the eight goals that all residents were encouraged to adopt when they entered the shelter; this was their code of nonviolence and personal transformation. Zendik Farm, at its best, had encouraged me to adopt similar goals, and I was still, in my own way, seeking them. I understood that the residents of Solid Ground were trying—just as I had—to know, heal, and rebuild themselves.

I couldn't wait to begin drafting plans. I started by taking a soil test that turned up almost no trace of contaminants—a wonderful surprise because it meant we could plant in-ground apple trees with patches of strawberries around their base, a combination that works well. I wanted to construct the vegetable garden as two large planter boxes with "L" shapes arranged like puzzle pieces fitting together. That would allow the courtyard to be a mixed-use space, leaving room for benches and tables so that residents could use the space for rest and recreation, while also providing room to grow enough food to supplement full weekly meals for twenty.

The challenge would be the cost—the planter boxes, fruit trees, and other supplies would add up. Over the next six months, as we hashed out the plans in a series of meetings with Joe and members of the Glencoe Union Church, we found ways to scale back expenses. Some church members agreed to donate the fruit trees and the wood for the beds and to help clean up the space; another member who was a carpenter offered to build the raised beds we'd designed.

When I went to Solid Ground for the planting that June, nearly half of the residents had assembled to help, along with a dozen members of the Glencoe Union Church. We got to work, and as we began planting I explained some of the techniques we were practicing, such as companion planting—why it works well to place basil

PLANTING DAY, THE SOLID GROUND SUPPORTIVE HOUSING PROGRAM, 2011

plants, for example, next to tomato plants in order to create conditions beneficial to both. One young resident named Josef began asking questions about life on a farm. "What's the average day's work if you want to be a farmer—how much time does it take?"

"It can be a pretty long day," I said, "but it's a seasonal thing. Some seasons you have to work dawn to dusk, seven days a week. Other seasons the days are shorter; life is slower."

"But isn't the air always fresh and clean? And you're not working in a crowded office with a bunch of crazies?"

"True," I said.

"How much land do you need to feed a family?"

"An acre, if you used it efficiently for animals and crops, could feed a family of five."

"But how long would it feed you for?"

"For your whole life."

Josef thought for a moment, and then said, "That sounds like a good life."

At the end of our day of planting, after eight large deep-dish pizzas had been polished off and hip-hop beats had been cranked up on the boom box, first one, then three, then five of the volunteers who'd participated were dancing in the dining area. Outside, a light mist of rain started to fall on their new apple trees and the seedlings they'd just tucked into the soil. It seemed to me a very auspicious beginning for our project.

The enthusiasm I saw among the Solid Ground residents gave me great hope for the many low-income urban gardening programs that had been gaining momentum in Chicago and across the country. Even during the recession, I'd been impressed to see that a number of these programs were growing fast, attracting new funding and motivated participants. In 2011 alone, Will Allen's Milwaukee-based organization Growing Power (growingpower .org) took in more than one million dollars in funding from Walmart and built partnerships with Sysco and Kohl's. The corporate support has enabled Allen to expand his operation and diversify his food production. In 2012, he employed more than one hundred urban farmers, many of them formerly incarcerated, at a rate of $15 an hour, significantly higher pay than the average wage for farm work, which is $10.22 an hour, and he planned to more than double his number of employees in 2013. Growing Power cultivates high-quality and specialty crops to support these wages: In 2011, the organization produced half a million dollars' worth of produce.

The organization Urban Farming (urbanfarming.org), based in Detroit, has also grown dramatically in recent years. It was founded in 2005 and has since spawned more than forty-three thousand urban food gardens around the country, thanks to millions of dollars of funding from Kraft, Coca-Cola, and other companies, and celebrity support from people such as Prince and Snoop Dogg. Urban Farming funds and installs community gardens around the country and provides free workshops and resources to help inner-city families grow their own food. The group also raises awareness about green businesses and provides job training and placement opportunities for people who want to join the urban-farming workforce.

The Oakland, California–based organization Urban Releaf (urbanreleaf.org) is another success story. The nonprofit has planted more than fifteen thousand trees in the most impoverished neighborhoods of Oakland; with the award and grant money this tree-planting effort has generated, the group is working to launch a new program planting urban farms on parcels of land on foreclosed properties throughout the city. Urban Releaf now employs ten full-time staffers and works with dozens of regular volunteers.

These people are all part of a revolution that's taking place within the food system across the country, in the most profound, intimate, and essential of ways, one garden at a time.

A resident at Solid Ground named Amaury Valentin, who had grown up in Puerto Rico and moved to Chicago when he was seven, told me that he remembered in great detail the tropical garden behind the apartment where he'd spent his early childhood: It was filled with mango and banana trees so lush and high that he could pick their fruits from his second-story bedroom window. "My grandmother had a saying," he told me. " 'The closer the garden is to your home, the closer it gets to your heart.' "

Chapter 21

THE 2010 AND 2011 GARDENING SEASONS WERE MY BUSIEST TO DATE, with the number of clients rising from 100 to 145, then to 200 (bumping up our staff to more than a dozen along the way), and I was getting a better sense of the enormous possibilities emerging for urban farming. One new client who lived in a modern townhouse in downtown Chicago's Lincoln Park, Heiji Choy Black, hired us to do what seemed like a fairly simple project—a series of large planter boxes set on the flat roof over her garage—but it turned out to be a crucible of its own.

Planter boxes filled with soil and vegetables can be intensely heavy when the soil is wet, weighing one hundred pounds per cubic foot or more. And yet the average roof is designed to hold only around forty pounds per square foot—anything more can cause a structural collapse. Heiji, a young, chic mother of two and the style editor at *Chicago Magazine,* was already working with an engineer and landscape architect on other aspects of the space. Their design was beautiful—an Asian theme with a green roof area of sedum and grasses and a section of smooth river stones. The engineer did a routine structural assessment of the roof's weight-bearing capacity, and when his results came back they seemed to rule out any hope of growing food successfully. He told me my planters could hold the weight of no more than seven inches of soil.

I had a firm rule of thumb that a depth of at least twelve inches would be essential to give the roots enough room to grow and absorb nutrients, and to guard against the problem of nutrient drainage from the soil. I told Heiji that seven inches could be a deal breaker; I didn't think the food would grow well if the roots couldn't spread and gather nutrients. But she had a clear vision for what she wanted and was game to try it anyway. I suggested we modify our crop list to cut out the more nutrient-greedy vegetables such as eggplants, peppers, and tomatoes, but Heiji felt confident that we should stick with our original plan and happily accepted the risks.

Verd and I strategized accordingly: We doubled the amount of granular fertilizer we typically applied around the plants (twice rather than once per month), and as an additional boost, we fed them extra nutrients through their leaves with foliar feeding (a fish emulsion and seaweed spray). To prevent the thin soil from drying out on the hot rooftop, we planned to irrigate more frequently but with smaller amounts of water. Verd designed a system of micro drip-line tubing at the base of the planter boxes set on a timer that would water for three short intervals, rather than one long interval, every twenty-four hours.

By mid-July, the garden was raging. There was such an abundance of vegetables in those seven inches of soil that Heiji and her family couldn't eat it all and had to give their surplus away to neighbors. When I reached into the soil to find out what had happened, I discovered plant roots that were packed more densely than any that I'd ever seen—an elaborate network of big shoots and smaller, spiderweb-thin side roots that took up every single millimeter of the soil. It was clear that with the nutrient boost we'd added, the plants had adjusted to the constraints and found a way to gather the sustenance they needed. In Heiji's garden, we had adapted to the space, and the plants had, too—they'd found a way to succeed. It made me realize that things were going to seem impossible and things were going to go wrong, but much of the pleasure was in the doing, in analyzing and fixing these wrong turns. It seemed almost a metaphor for life itself. Failures and mistakes are an inevitable part of the gardening process—whether it's faulty fencing, poorly timed planting, runaway weeds, or root competition—all mistakes I've made along the way. But, wonderfully, *that's how it's supposed to be.* Things want to grow, I'd discovered; you just need to learn how to stop getting in the way.

IN THE WINTER OF 2010, I received an email that would lead to a major turning point for our business. Jackie Kotz, a Michigan State–trained landscape architect who had worked for several large firms designing projects for townships, hospitals, schools, and corporations, had heard about the Organic Gardener from her sister, who'd been to one of my gardening presentations. Jackie wrote to ask if I'd ever considered working with a landscape architect who could help to incorporate new elements—trees, edible shrubs, a full range of ornamental plants—into my designs for backyard spaces.

I *had* considered this, because so many of my clients had expressed an interest in sustainable landscaping—clients who were motivated by concerns such as climate change, in addition to their anxieties about the impact of chemicals on their health. They saw planting a vegetable garden as a kind of gateway to a broader effort to reduce the climatic impact of their lifestyle. Kate MacKenzie, for instance, wanted chemical-free lawn care, and I'd pointed her to an Evanston-based company that used electric mowers and organic weed-control products. Other clients had wanted to grow fruit trees, but while Verd and I had incorporated apple trees into a few projects, our expertise was limited in this area.

I emailed Jackie back right away, and we arranged to meet at a coffee shop in Glencoe. Jackie was in her early fifties, with a wide smile and shoulder-length blond hair. She was warm, funny, and personable, and we connected instantly. Her portfolio contained drawing after beautifully rendered drawing that put my scrawled yellow-legal-pad sketches to shame.

Jackie, I could see fairly quickly, had a level of design expertise that I lacked. She had an eye for pattern, balance, and function. Moreover, she had a technical background and knew how to read a property's plat of survey and identify the locations of gas lines and sewage pipes in a city lot. She could analyze the flow of water drainage through a site after rainfall.

She had completed projects on large high school and university campuses and had studied how people move through these kinds of public gardens. She knew how to design gardens for optimal flow—gardens not just with vegetable beds, but beds of native plants, "butterfly gardens" with flowers that attract specific kinds of butterflies, and "rain gardens" with specific plants that help absorb accumulated rainwater into the earth.

The Organic Gardener was operating, as always, on relatively narrow margins, and we didn't have the funds to hire her except as a freelancer on a project-specific basis. Oddly enough, a few hours after I left the coffee shop, a call came in on my cellphone from a Kenilworth resident who had just bought a property on a lake in Wisconsin and wanted to design a garden there, with fruit trees and edible and ornamental shrubs. Minutes later I called Jackie to announce: "I've got us a project."

That project led to many others, and within six months Jackie was creating enough value for our company that we could afford to hire her full-time. In the coming years, Jackie, Verd, and I would take on larger-scale projects, including the food garden for the Westfield Old Orchard Shopping Mall that would offer public demos and workshops, and the half-acre community garden for young-adult residents with disabilities in Lyons Township. These projects required a level of planning, discussion, and plan renditions that we never could have tackled without Jackie's expertise.

In all of these projects, Jackie helped us incorporate "permaculture" aspects into her designs. Permaculture is a concept that arose in the 1970s and was defined by one of its originators, Bill Mollison, as "a philosophy of working with, rather than against, nature;

of protracted and thoughtful observation rather than premature and thoughtless labor; and of looking at plants and animals in all their functions, rather than treating any area as a single project system." In suburban landscape design, that translates in practical terms into incorporating edible shrubs and trees that are native to the local environment, and choosing flowers and ground-cover plants that are water sensible (requiring minimal watering) and low impact (enriching rather than depleting the soil) whenever possible.

On residential projects, Jackie guided us in planting edible shrubs such as serviceberry, currant, gooseberry, and elderberry. With her expertise, we also began to incorporate apple, citrus, pear, and fig trees into our projects, planting some in large pots that could be carried inside in the winter. We removed damaged trees on our clients' properties and replaced them with new varieties. We matched beds of perennial flowers native to the Midwest to existing vegetable gardens.

"The care of the earth," wrote author and permaculture advocate Wendell Berry in *The Art of the Commonplace*, "is our most ancient and most worthy, and, after all, our most pleasing responsibility. To cherish what remains of it, and to foster its renewal, is our only legitimate hope." Our work with Jackie represented, in some ways, a return to where I'd started. It felt, unmistakably, like another circle closing as I watched the jewel-green, chemically enhanced suburban lawns I'd fled from in my teens turn gradually, yard by yard, into landscapes more native and more in balance with their surroundings and the earth.

AT THE END OF JULY 2011, Bryan and I drove together to northern Wisconsin to pick up Thea from her first year at Red Pine Camp for Girls, the summer camp I'd gone to as a child. I spotted her inside the communal dining hall, talking and laughing with a table of cabinmates. She wore shorts, a white T-shirt, and flip-flops, her medium-length brown hair pulled back into a ponytail.

It was strange to realize that at ten, Thea was now the same age I'd been when I'd first started questioning things in the North Shore suburbs. But unlike me, Thea had always been independent minded. Even as a child she felt comfortable standing up for her beliefs. In the moments before she spotted me outside the dining hall, I felt I had a brief glimpse of the young woman she would become—both subtle and strident, funny and passionate, and, more than anything, her own person. And that was what I wanted most for her, that she could know and be herself. It had taken me almost forty years to learn that lesson.

Chapter 22

LATE IN 2010, I RECEIVED AN INTERESTING EMAIL FROM A YOUNG
woman named Lisa Kaehler, who said she was a junior at my old
high school, New Trier, and asked if she could intern at the Organic
Gardener during the upcoming spring semester. She explained that
New Trier had a number of programs allowing students to pursue
off-campus internships for course credit. She wanted to create an
independent study around organic farming, and she'd found us
through a family friend who was a client. Looking at New Trier's
website, I saw a strong and growing bent toward alternative education. For students who want to " 'do school' a little differently,"
read the description of one forward-leaning program, "for students
who want experiential, hands-on learning and who think and act
with a global perspective." Lisa's request made me think back to
my own time in high school and the ways in which I'd become
impatient to experience the real world, when school suddenly
hadn't seemed like enough to me. I asked her to come meet with me
and was so impressed by her can-do attitude and intelligence that I
agreed right away to hire her as an intern.

By the time I met Lisa, New Trier had come back into my life in
several unexpected ways. In 2009, I'd been hired to consult on a
potential garden for the school. And in something of an uncannily
precise closing of a circle, I had started teaching an adult education

course on organic gardening in the very same classrooms where I'd studied as a student. The class was part of New Trier's extension program for district residents, which taught everything from accounting and entrepreneurship to Twitter and Tai Chi. As I walked through the halls, looking at the claustrophobic crush between classes—kids barking sports statistics, texting on cellphones, and cramming for tests—I remembered what I'd felt like in my last year there, isolated and disconnected, estranged from my surroundings and ultimately from myself.

I was surprised and pleased to note the many different ways that it was not the same New Trier I'd left in 1986. Now there were recycling bins throughout the hallways, and posters on the walls sponsored by the student Environmental Club advertising speakers on renewable energy and biodiversity. One poster in particular caught my eye, with the title GAP-YEAR FAIR, an event at which students wanting to take a year off between high school and college could learn about various Peace-Corps-style programs, including building schools in Paraguay, teaching English in Laos, and farming in Namibia.

Though I'd gradually become aware of a deepening commitment to environmental issues in the community through my client relationships, it was the young people I worked with who showed me that a broader and even more profound cultural change was under way. After Lisa Kaehler, I hired a number of local high school students as interns either for course credits or for summer jobs, and all of them wowed me with their combination of idealism, drive, and creativity. One applicant had helped organize a climate-awareness event where hundreds of North Shore students and adults came together at a Wilmette park to spell out in human bodies the number "350," indicating, in parts per million, the safe upper limit of carbon dioxide levels in the atmosphere.

Through Thea and Kisten, I'd also seen indications of just how fully food and environmental issues had been incorporated into early childhood education on the North Shore since my own childhood. Thea's elementary school was equipped with solar panels and rain barrels and had a strong environmental curriculum. After school she'd often share a new fact she'd learned about recycling or renewable energy. Her education was very solutions oriented. In the wake of the Deepwater Horizon oil spill, for instance, the kids experimented with wiping oil residue off the fur of stuffed animals using different cleansing agents in order to better understand the difficulties of the cleanup. Kisten's preschool had a vegetable garden next to the playground, and they started some seedlings in her classroom under grow lights; the teacher told me that when she showed the kids pictures of the vegetables they were growing, she was amused and more than a little surprised when two-and-a-half-year-old Kisten announced the names of each one: "Cawott!" "Zucchini!" "Eggpwant!"

My own work with school gardens was expanding, too. In 2010, I began working with Jaime Zaplatosch on the school garden program she'd developed at Openlands. By 2012, her program had installed and helped maintain gardens in forty impoverished public schools. Many of those schools didn't have gyms or outdoor recess due to budget shortfalls and safety concerns, so the gardens provided students with their only physical activity and the only green spaces within the cramped campus lots.

My role was to teach a team at each school that generally consisted of ten to twenty-five teachers, parents, and staff members how to maintain the gardens. There have been countless examples of public school gardens that have fallen into disuse because the faculty became overwhelmed by the maintenance responsibilities. Jaime hoped to make sure, with proper training and ongoing support, that each school garden would reach its full potential.

Independently of Openlands, I'd worked on another school project in 2010 at Josephinum Academy, a Catholic all-girls school in Wicker Park, where we installed two narrow vegetable beds, each twenty-four feet long, to provide enough room for a full class of students to work side by side. We designed the garden around spring and fall crops because the students would be on break during the prime harvest months for summer crops.

In late 2010, Jackie and I also drew up a plan for a large-scale garden at a junior high school in the North Shore suburb of Northbrook. The project had been inspired in part by First Lady Michelle Obama, who'd encouraged American chefs to partner with schools to help improve food education and school lunches. Chef Sarah Stegner of Prairie Grass Cafe, whom I'd met through Abby Mandel and who had become a close friend, had partnered with Northbrook and brought me on board. The garden area at Northbrook would encompass twelve raised beds with more than two thousand square feet of growing space for vegetables, fruit trees, a composting area, and an outdoor classroom space where twenty-five students could assemble.

EVERY SCHOOL GARDEN I'VE worked on has been rewarding, but a project with particular personal resonance was a design for South School in Glencoe, the K–2 school Thea had graduated from in 2009 and that Kisten would soon be attending. Jill Unger, a highly motivated second-grade teacher, had started the project as an extracurricular garden club, hiring me to help her plan a small garden in a courtyard. Gradually, as her students grew familiar with the garden, Jill integrated it more broadly into the second-grade curriculum. She saw the garden as an opportunity to teach skills in four categories of "social-emotional learning": teamwork and respect, healthy choices, problem solving, and goal setting. As Jill taught her students practical skills in planting, tending, and harvesting, she also brought larger lessons to bear in sharing tools and responsibilities, taking turns, and troubleshooting problems together.

As other teachers came to appreciate the various roles the garden could play, the school expanded the space and integrated it into the entire K–2 curriculum. The same focus on social-emotional learning would be applied in all three grades, with each teacher bringing his or her own twists to their curricula—one might read her students Beatrix Potter books; another would incorporate Smart Board software with interactive programs to teach students to identify botanical parts and learn the nutrient profiles of each plant; another could work with students to chart how many vegetables they ate per day. The possibilities of the project have been so widely embraced by the faculty that many have volunteered to weed, water, and harvest the garden over the summer.

At the end of the school year in 2011, Jill Unger sent me a video of the K–2 school garden, a simple slideshow of kids working in the garden space. Image after image showed a student's face registering the mystery and miracle of a seed. No botany class will ever be able to fully explain how a tiny seed a quarter centimeter long can, in the space of weeks, become a soft, sweet, nutritious fruit a hundred times that size, and adults lose sight of the miracle. But the children captured in Jill's video were recognizing it, and the sense of awe and humility I saw in their faces moved me to tears and made me feel overwhelmingly hopeful.

I understood as I watched the video that the education my daughters would receive as "North Shore girls" would be dramatically different from my own. The rise in childhood gardening education across the nation meant that more and more children would grow up knowing, reflexively, what it had taken me a significant portion of my life to learn. These children were being taught through their own hands-on experience to become responsible stewards of the earth, and they would, in turn, take that knowledge into their families and communities as adults, and as a result into the American mainstream.

IN LATE SEPTEMBER 2011, I returned to the Solid Ground shelter with Verd for the final harvest supper. It was a sunny, warm Sunday afternoon, and the garden was lush with late-summer strawberries and heirloom tomatoes. The autumn greens and root crops had come in, the apple trees were thriving, and the pumpkin patch was full of fat, shiny pumpkins. The beds had been meticulously weeded, the soil was moist, and the garden in its abundance reflected the care and pleasure the residents had taken in it. I was glad to see that a card table holding several decks of cards and a well-worn score sheet had been placed right up next to a garden bed filled with fragrant basil and other herbs—a sign that the garden had become, as I'd hoped, more than a source of food: It was a living space.

Weeks earlier, Joe Hankey had sent me a collection of passages that some of the residents had written about the garden and what it meant to them. "Some would say that the Garden is to save money and eat healthier," wrote seventeen-year-old Dasty, who'd grown up in Ecuador. "To me, the Garden is nature and peace. The Garden brings nature into your head when you look at it. I can feel like I'm back in the beautiful forest like I used to be before I came to the United States." Another resident, Michael, wrote, "I have found it to be very relaxing to sit by the garden on sunny days or even at night and admire the beauty or just daydream. The plants have taught me how nature works so fast."

The kitchen was animated as the young men prepared the meal. Some residents had just harvested onions, tomatoes, potatoes, garlic, and peppers that sat colorfully in large stainless steel bowls on the counter, and others began to mince and chop the vegetables. Verd bantered with the guys as he grated beets and carrots for a salad, while Kathy Deveny and other members of the Glencoe Union Church helped set the table.

Soon a feast was laid out on a big fold-out banquet table that had been set up outside. Platters of ground-beef and potato empanadas, *tostones* (fried plantains), arepas (corn pancakes), and bowls of salads and fresh salsa were spread across a white tablecloth. One resident who'd been a regular caretaker of the garden and who loved to cook had made a pie from the garden's fresh pumpkins and had decorated the top with sugared pecans. He had also used the stringy part of the pumpkins as a "pasta" in a salad mixed with cherry tomatoes, basil, and beans.

Joe started the meal with a moving commentary. "From our hearts to yours, we thank you for this wonderful opportunity. And from our community to yours, we wanted to present a gift—a representation of what we feel this garden has brought to Solid Ground and La Casa Norte." He pulled out from under the table a large canvas painting done in an airbrushed graffiti style by a resident artist. It was a picture of pure abundance in bright, rich colors— a profusion of berries, apples, pumpkins, pea pods, leafy lettuces, and flowers. At the center of it, surrounded by vines, was the word *LIFE.*

I looked around the table and saw that I wasn't the only one wiping away tears. Sitting next to me was Sol Florance, the executive director of La Casa Norte, who over the course of the meal told me that she had plans to make this garden sow the seeds of something bigger. La Casa Norte was working to raise funds for a new shelter modeled after Solid Ground, this one for young women ages sixteen and older who had been homeless or incarcerated. She'd found a location nearby in Humboldt Park that could house up to forty women and had a large, nearly quarter-acre rooftop. She wanted us to help her turn it into a farm.

As Sol and I chatted, Verd was talking with Solid Ground resident Amaury Valentin, who had taken on the responsibility of most of the watering and harvesting of the garden. Amaury was enrolled in community college courses and had heard that Verd was getting a college degree and wanted to go into medicine.

"Do you like the gardening more or the brain science?" Amaury asked.

"I like them both," said Verd. "Working with the earth and plants—there's just as much wonder in this. My favorite are peas: They grow on vines, but those vines don't grow in any random direction, they grow only toward things they can climb. They know how to grab onto things and wrap themselves around them."

"So they're smart, you're saying?"

"It's like they have some sort of awareness, or purpose."

"Purpose—really, you think?"

"Maybe."

"Yeah," Amaury said thoughtfully, "could be."

After the food had been devoured, dishes washed, and the banquet table folded up, Verd and I were reluctant to leave the harvest dinner. Though we were tempted to stick around for a garden-side game of cards with some of the residents, we had to get back to the kids. The night had brought back good memories. My life at Zendik Farm had been a complicated, mixed experience, but I now realized, finally, that I couldn't be doing what I was doing here now if I hadn't done what I did then. One thing had led directly into the other.

After all my travels—in the camper with Mark; in California, then Texas and North Carolina with Zendik Farm; then back home to Chicago—I had learned that an acre, a quarter acre, or a tenth acre of dirt that a person tends with his or her own hands can have an immense impact on that individual and on society at large. I had learned that the meaning and purpose I'd sought in extremity—an authentic way of relating to self, to others, and to the earth—is, in fact, available to us all in our own neighborhoods and yards, in our own suburbs and cities.

And I'd learned something else: Throughout all the years that I'd spent away from Winnetka as a teenager and young adult, changing and growing, the North Shore and other towns and cities across America had been changing and growing as well. It would have been unimaginable to me back in 1987 that Winnetka, Chicago, and the nation at large would, twenty-five years later, be so different—so much more aware of the wider world and open to new ideas about food and the environment. From its inception in scattered farmers markets and offbeat publications, through the efforts of pioneers and writers such as Wendell Berry and Wes Jackson, and after them Michael Pollan, Jamie Oliver, Alice Waters, and others, an awareness of the importance of fresh food and food-related issues was evolving—incredibly, improbably, but also in ways inevitably—to occupy a key place in the American consciousness.

Just as I left home to find meaning, only to find that I could create that meaning at home, all of us today can live out this new awareness—in our towns, suburbs, and cities, in our schools, backyards, urban lots, terraces, and high-rise rooftops—by making both personal and communal choices about food: choices that respect and build our own health and that of our families, our communities, and the earth our children will ultimately inherit. And all that's needed to begin is that most basic, essential human act of digging in the dirt, planting a seed, tending to it, and waiting.

ONE SUNNY, CRISP MORNING IN LATE OCTOBER 2011, I DROVE INTO
the Ravenswood neighborhood on Chicago's North Side to meet
with a potential new client who'd been casually referred by email.
I arrived at a lovely but discreet pale green house with a peaked
roof and a covered front porch, and was more than a little surprised when two uniformed police officers approached me, escorted
me to the door, and rang the bell for me. A pretty, smiling woman
wearing jeans and clogs answered the door and introduced herself
as Amy Rule. "Sorry about that at the door," she said, leading me
into the kitchen. "I . . . I happen to be the mayor's wife." She spoke
in such an understated way that it took me a few moments to register that I was in the home of Mayor Rahm Emanuel.

Amy Rule, I later learned, is a famously private person who has
steered clear of her husband's media spotlight while she raises their
three kids. But in her home that morning and during the many
times we met thereafter, she was not at all reserved—on the con-
trary, she possessed impressive gravitas spiced with a playful irrev-
erence. "It absolutely slays me to pay eight dollars at the grocery
store for five leaves of kale," Amy groused good-naturedly while
pulling a tray of kale chips from the oven. "Good food is worth its
weight in gold these days—we should all be lucky enough to grow
it." As a high schooler during the seventies in a small town in Ohio,
where her dad sold equipment for greenhouses, Amy had planted
and tended a food garden with her sister in their backyard. Now,

decades later, having finally settled her family full-time into their Ravenswood home after years of shuttling between Chicago and Washington, D.C. (where Emanuel had been an adviser to President Clinton, then a congressman, and then chief of staff to President Obama), Amy wanted to introduce her kids to the rhythms and rituals of growing food.

We scheduled the planting for the following spring, May 2012, on Mother's Day. The soil had tested off the charts for lead, so Jackie and I had designed the garden with four long, narrow raised beds that wrapped around the garage. The garden would be highly visible from the Emanuels' central living-dining room area, a warm, open space on the first floor of the house with blond wood floors, abstract art, and floor-to-ceiling windows looking onto the backyard. I worked with Amy and her kids to plant the full gamut of vegetables and herbs, berries, a pear tree, and ornamental flowers. At one point, Mayor Emanuel came out to the garden to check on our progress. Noting my dirt-caked hands, he offered me a fist bump and joked with more than a hint of sarcasm, "Just what I always wanted—a kibbutz in my backyard!"

During the summer of 2012, Verd and I were juggling more than two hundred urban and suburban gardens, many of them larger scale projects than we'd ever worked on before. In early May, Verd graduated cum laude with a bachelor's of science in neuroscience from the University of Illinois at Chicago, receiving the highest departmental distinction. His success was immensely rewarding. Having never gone to college myself, I was wildly proud of him. At the same time, I worried I would never be able to run the business without him. He would now be applying to enroll in medical school for the fall of 2014, and, if accepted, he'd have to commit to it full-time. It would surely be a very *good* problem if Verd had the opportunity to leave our business to pursue his dreams in medicine, but it still added complexity to our already complex lives.

Part of what fueled me throughout the demanding 2012 season

was sharing in the awe, enthusiasm, and humor that the Emanuel family brought to their garden project. "Our vegetables are on steroids," Amy deadpanned when I arrived one afternoon in mid-July. "It's *Little Shop of Horrors* out there—the plants are so shiny and perfect we think they might start talking." She recounted how in the early morning she and her daughters would walk outside in their bare feet and pajamas to get berries for their cereal or herbs and vegetables for their omelets, and they'd be stunned by the beauty of the food amid a sea of zinnias, snapdragons, and cosmos. They would look for changes that had happened overnight—cucumbers that had suddenly emerged under their big green leaves, or tomatoes that were newly ripe for the picking. Her teenage son had also struck up his own relationship to the garden. When he craved privacy, it became his go-to place for cellphone calls. One day while chatting, he filled up a big basket with vegetables and then took them to a friend's house, where her mother cooked them into a feast.

"It has amazed me to discover," Amy told me toward the end of the season, "that our experience of nature can be so up close and personal—that we don't have to go somewhere else, to a park or a beach or a mountain, to find it. It's right here." The garden, she'd also found, brought a dimension of intrigue and excitement to their home. "The first thing everybody says when they come home from their day is '*What happened?*' and then they go investigate the progress in the garden. Except maybe Rahm—he hasn't done much hands-in-the-dirt work, but he's been very happy eating whatever we cook from it."

What Mayor Emanuel wasn't doing in the family garden, he was doing, more broadly, for school gardens throughout Chicago. While the recession had forced the city to shut down Greencorps and other programs that in previous years had supported the installation of edible gardens in about half of Chicago's roughly 650 public schools, the mayor's team had begun collaborating with nonprofits to support new programs for school-garden installation.

In 2012, the city committed one million dollars to the Kitchen Community to install sixty new edible gardens at public schools using prototype raised beds made of high-tech molded plastic. It also worked with the group Openlands to develop the "Chicago 21st Century Schoolyard Initiative," which would help ensure that edible gardens would be installed over the next five years at all schools that didn't yet have them.

BEYOND THESE MUNICIPAL EFFORTS, the grow-your-own trend was also spreading fast throughout Chicago at the grassroots level. In 2010, John Taylor, a grad student at the University of Illinois at Urbana-Champaign, analyzed satellite data to discover that, in total, roughly sixty acres of land within Chicago were being used to grow food—and a majority of that acreage was in private back-yards and vacant urban lots. In 2012, Taylor repeated his analysis using updated satellite imagery and found a *50 percent increase* in food production within the city in just two years. His research helped inspire the Chicago Urban Agriculture Mapping Project, a collaborative effort among researchers at several local universities to track grassroots food production within city limits.

What's particularly fascinating about this trend is that it shows an environmental solution arising *from the people*. These Chicago-ans are growing their own food not as a response to a government directive or restriction, but voluntarily—because they see it as an opportunity to enhance their quality of life. When the Westfield Old Orchard Shopping Mall in Skokie, Illinois, which encompasses more than one hundred chain stores and restaurants, approached me about designing an edible garden for their shopping mall, the representatives said that the concept had arisen from the shoppers themselves. In a customer survey conducted by Old Orchard, peo-ple responded overwhelmingly that they would shop more often if they could get hands-on experience growing food when they came to the mall. I found this stunning—that a mecca of commerce would plant a community garden not as a public service but as a public attraction. It was one of many recent signs that the grow-your-own movement was gaining ground in the mainstream.

As Americans have shown a greater interest in producing their own food, more local businesses have been forming to help them do so. At least sixty businesses have sprung up nationally in recent years that are helping families, restaurants, schools, and nonprofits grow food gardens.

IT'S A STRANGE—OR, PERHAPS, a fitting—irony that just as the grow-your-own trend was experiencing its first big wave of popular support, Zendik Farm was meeting its demise. In June 2012, Arol died after a long battle with cancer. By the time of her death, the commune had dwindled to twenty members. Within a few months of her passing, half of those members had left. The adults and children who remained—Fawn (the thirty-six-year-old daughter of Arol and Wulf) and her inner circle—shut down the farm's website and stayed only long enough to clean up the property and sell it. By the end of 2012 I had heard that Zendik Farm had effectively been dissolved.

When Verd and Bryan heard about Zendik's closing, they cheered the news. We'd predicted that the farm would disband without Arol at the helm—it had been inevitable—but my own feelings about it were strangely mixed. I was profoundly relieved to put the memory of Zendik to rest once and for all, but I also felt a stab of grief as I accepted the now conclusive evidence that the community to which I'd committed seventeen years of my life— a community with many good intentions, for all its faults—had utterly failed to fulfill its ideals. Verd said what I knew to be true— that we were now finally getting the chance to fulfill our *own* ideals, and that doing so would be the best way to honor all that had been good about our experience on the commune.

His comment reminded me of the kibbutz joke Mayor Emanuel

had made on planting day. Kibbutzim are Israeli farming communes that began in the early twentieth century as utopian communities. There are still more than 250 in operation today that collectively provide nearly half of Israel's agricultural output (though in recent decades many kibbutzim have struggled, both financially and with their social structure). The mayor's quip had been unintentionally, but unmistakably, apropos given my own commune experience, and it now struck me as a profound insight into the motives behind my work.

During the 2012 planting season, Verd and I moved more than a hundred tons of soil and compost, thousands of seedlings, and truckload after truckload of fertilizer bags and tomato cages, cedar timbers and fencing materials. Our schedule had grown more demanding and our process more systematized. But our goal was still, as it had been from the beginning, to help people find a closer relationship with the earth—and perhaps, as the mayor implied, to offer them a slice of communal life, the *best* part of that life, without the baggage and the heartache. The fact that we'd been able to do this on a large scale felt gratifying, as if we'd begun, in a way, to resuscitate the failed dream of Zendik Farm. And by sharing it with more and more people, it was perhaps no longer just a dream but the beginning of a reality. As the French novelist Victor Hugo wrote, "There is nothing like a dream to create the future. Utopia today, flesh and blood tomorrow."

ACKNOWLEDGMENTS

THIS BOOK WAS TRULY A TEAM EFFORT AND I HAVE BEEN PRIVILEGED
to work with a team of women who had a shared vision for what
it could be, and who understood, guided, and encouraged me
throughout the writing process. Amanda Little and Deborah Murphy found the words to convey my story. I am deeply appreciative
of their talent, insight, dedication, and friendship. I am grateful to
my agent, Kimberly Witherspoon, for taking me on and guiding me
throughout the book's publication, and to Cindy Spiegel, my editor; I am forever glad that our initial recognition of each other was
mutual, and I am grateful for your editorial smarts. Thanks to Jennifer Cayea, for calling me in 2009 to suggest that I write a book,
and to Alice Waters for insisting that I do it and for generously
writing the Foreword. To Penny Mesic, Anthony Walton, Sophie
Robinson, Katharine Kinkel, and Hana Landes, for your hard work
and contributions to the project. To Martha and Steve Rosenblatt
for an early read and honest feedback when I needed it most. To
Arol and Wulf and those whom I worked alongside at Zendik
Farm, for daring to try. To the board of Green City Market, for
supporting the Edible Gardens in Lincoln Park Zoo and for valuing
my contribution to the Market's mission. To the families that I garden with, heartfelt thanks for your continued support and shared
love of growing food. To Amy Rule, for the fun of knowing you
and gardening together. To the team at the Organic Gardener, for
putting up with my time away working on the book, and for keep-

ing the gardens running smoothly. To my colleagues in Chicago and around the country, for creating the movement that inspires me every day. To all of those whose stories are part of this book, I thank you for helping me tell this story. To my in-laws, Phil and Annette Nolan, for your calm reassurance. To my beloved daughters, Thea and Kisten, for sharing me throughout the book process. To Bryan, for supporting Thea and me in so many ways. To my parents and Hallie, for your love and encouragement of this project. To Verd, my Love—although I don't believe in reincarnation, you must have lived past lives to have stored up the wisdom you have about how to handle and enjoy life's challenges.

TEN LISTS OF TEN ESSENTIALS
FOR EVERY ASPIRING GARDENER

TEN REASONS TO GROW A FOOD GARDEN

1. HEALTH

More nutrient-dense than conventional produce, homegrown fruits and vegetables can improve the eating habits of adults and children and help prevent diabetes, obesity, and some cancers. The *Journal of the American Dietetic Association* found that children more than doubled their overall fruit and vegetable consumption after their parents grew a food garden in their yard.

2. TASTE

Homegrown, fresh-picked vegetables, herbs, and fruit offer an unparalleled taste experience: juicy, crisp, with a great depth of flavor and intensity.

3. SAFETY

Foodborne illnesses such as salmonella and E. coli are routinely found on produce grown on industrial farms. In 2006, spinach tainted with E. coli from cow manure on industrial farms in California sickened hundreds of Americans and took five lives. There is no safer source of food than your own backyard.

4. EXERCISE

Working in a garden is an antidote to the sedentary, indoor lifestyles that are becoming increasingly prevalent in a technology-driven world. The joy of physical activity in a natural setting to produce something tangible is not only good for your body but fulfilling to the spirit.

5. FOCUS

Gardening helps overstimulated and hyperactive kids focus and perform better academically. A 2004 report from the University of Illinois at Urbana-Champaign found that green outdoor settings, including gardening, reduced symptoms of ADHD in the more than four hundred kids in the study.

6. CLIMATE

The equivalent of about four hundred gallons of oil is used annually to feed each American. This accounts for the energy that flows into petrochemical pesticides and fertilizers as well as fuel for farming machinery, irrigation, food processing, and distribution. By comparison, an organic food garden can have a zero-carbon footprint or even a positive climate impact, due to the absorption of carbon dioxide by its leafy plants.

7. BUDGET

Gardens can considerably reduce grocery bills. A recent National Gardening Association study found that the average family with a vegetable garden spends just seventy dollars a year on it and grows an estimated six hundred dollars' worth of vegetables.

8. COMMUNITY

Growing food brings families together in the garden and at the table. The tending and harvesting rituals slow down one's lifestyle and encourage more home-cooked meals. Gardens can also be social magnets that get neighbors talking over the fence, connecting families to their communities.

9. HAPPINESS

Dirt makes you feel good. A 2007 study from the University of Bristol in England showed that when injected in mice, a specific soil bacterium, *Mycobacterium vaccae,* targets immune cells that release chemicals, which, in turn, stimulate the serotonin-releasing neurons in the brain—the very same neurons activated by Prozac and other antidepressants.

10. NATURE

Growing food offers an accessible way to connect with the natural world. The basic lesson that when we take care of the earth, the earth takes care of us is learned hands on. I certainly want my kids to be computer literate, but I also want them to be exposed to the wonders of plant growth and natural ecosystems.

HOW TO GROW A FOOD GARDEN, IN TEN STEPS

1. GOALS

Articulate your goals: Why do you want to grow a garden? How much food do you want to grow? An average-size garden for a family of four would be roughly eight feet by sixteen feet if planted in a raised bed and ten feet by twenty feet if planted in the ground.

2. SUNLIGHT

Most fruits and vegetables require loads of sun, so pick a spot for your garden that gets at least six to eight hours of sun per day (you can measure the amount of sun you get with an affordable device like a SunCalc). If your location has limited sun (five to six hours), choose crops that can tolerate less sun, such as leafy greens, cucumbers, beans, and herbs. (See pages 142–43, 149–51.)

3. SOIL

Nothing is more important to the success of your garden than soil health. Whether you are working in the ground or in a raised bed, you ideally want to plant in twelve to eighteen inches of well-aerated, nutrient-dense soil. Use a generous amount of compost. You really can't use too much, though if you want help determining how much to add, Gardener's Supply Company (gardeners.com) has a helpful online soil calculator. Follow the directions that come with your granulated organic fertilizer. Be sure to aerate your soil and add compost and fertilizer annually. If you are planning to garden near an old house or in the city, test your soil for lead or other toxins. (See pages 15, 20, 98–100, 137–38, 151.)

4. PATHS

Without paths, the soil in a garden can get compacted, which makes it hard for roots to spread and chokes off the oxygen that's essential to plant growth. Be sure to clearly demarcate the paths around your rows with straw, wood chips, stone, or another medium. (See pages 15, 152–53.)

5. FENCING

Rabbit-proof fencing extends two and a half to three and a half feet high and at least four inches belowground; the holes in the mesh should be no bigger than one inch by two inches. Deer-proof fencing can range from five to eight feet high depending on the size of the deer population and the amount of open space around the garden (the more space the deer have to run and jump, the higher the fence should be). (See pages 151–52.)

6. IRRIGATION

Some gardeners enjoy the task of hand watering. But if you have only an hour a week to spend in your garden, use that time to tend your plants and install a watering system on an automatic timer. (There are affordable timers with sensors that measure soil moisture and then prompt your system to irrigate as needed.) I particularly like drip-line tubing because it delivers water to plants at their roots.

An ordinary sprinkler connected to your garden hose can work as well, particularly when attached to an automatic timer. (Be sure to time the sprinkler to irrigate in the early morning or evening so that wet plants are not scorched by the midday sun.) (See pages 152–53.) For information, equipment, and other resources, go to dripworks.com.

7. PLAN

On paper, map out where you want to put paths and rows and the rough location of each crop; be sure to account for companion planting and put tall plants on the north side of the space so that they don't shade the others. If a row has paths on both sides, the row should be no wider than four feet so that plants can be reached and tended from both sides. If a row can be reached from only one side, make it roughly two feet wide.

The single most common problem I encounter in gardens is overplanting—try to use restraint in the planting process! Read the information on the back of your seed packet closely or reference the online Kitchen Garden Planner at gardeners.com, which has great advice about planting density and garden layouts.

When you are planning your garden after the first year, keep in mind that it is best to rotate your crops, as soil can get depleted and plants are more prone to problems when you grow the same crop in the same place every year. I pay particular attention to rotating where I plant my tomatoes, as they are susceptible to soilborne disease.

8. SUPPLIES

All your supplies—fertilizer, compost, seeds, labels, plant supports, trowels, round-nose shovels, hard rakes, and broadforks—can be purchased online or from a local nursery. Organic seedlings can also often be purchased from local farmers at your farmers market. All types of compost from your local nursery or home improvement store work well—just go as organic as you can. Seed catalogs are a fantastic resource for seeds, tools, plants, and advice. A few of my favorites are johnnyseeds.com, seedsavers .org, and highmowingseeds.com.

9. PLANTING

There are two basic ways to plant—by placing seeds directly in the ground or by putting plants (seedlings) in the ground (transplanting). The seedlings get you a head start on the season, as they're grown in a greenhouse, cold frame, or indoors during the late winter or early spring. I always plant tomatoes, peppers, eggplant, and other large fruiting crops as seedlings. Vegetables including carrots, beans, and radishes I always plant from seeds. (See pages 20, 110.)

You can think of crops in two basic categories—cold-tolerant crops that can be planted in early spring and will germinate and grow in cool soil and air temperatures (such as spinach, broccoli, and peas) and heat-loving crops (such as tomatoes, peppers, and cucumbers) that must be planted in the late spring or early summer after the threat of a frost has passed. (See pages 21, 205–206.)

Find out which USDA Hardiness Zone you live in (go to the National Gardening Association's website: garden.org/zipzone). This will help you determine what to plant when in your region and will also give you an idea of the timing of the first and last frosts.

10. TENDING AND HARVESTING

Critical tending activities include thinning your plants so that they don't crowd each other, staking plants to support vertical growth, and weeding regularly by hand. Fertilizing to give your plants a boost is optional but does wonders for plant health and productivity. I like to use a liquid organic fish emulsion and seaweed spray every other week, and side dressing with granulated organic fertilizer once a month during the peak growing season. (See pages 49–50.)

I also like to walk through my gardens at least once a week, doing "rounds" to observe their needs—taking the time to notice if any plants are leaning over that need staking; if any leaves are discolored, indicating that the plants may need nutrients; or if any pests have arrived that need troubleshooting.

My harvesting advice is simple: Don't wait too long and don't be shy—if something looks and smells ripe to you, pick it and taste it. The best way to become a good harvester is to learn by doing.

TEN WAYS TO TACKLE WEEDS AND PESTS WITHOUT CHEMICALS

1. HEALTHY SOIL

The soil acts as the immune system of your plants. If plants are getting what they need from nutrient-dense, well-aerated soil, they will be much more resistant to disease, and fewer pests will prey on them. A generous layer of compost spread annually has the added benefit of helping to reduce weeds.

2. BENEFICIAL INSECTS

Use companion planting, crop diversity, and interplanted flowers to attract beneficial insects to your garden that will deter or attack harmful insects. Basil planted among tomato plants, for instance, will draw insects that prey on tomato hornworms. (See page 47.)

3. PROTECTIVE LAYER

Deter weed growth with a protective layer of alfalfa hay or straw around your plants; the layer can starve potential weeds of sun and prevent their growth. An added benefit is that this layer helps retain moisture and provides nutrients to the soil as it decays. (See page 152.)

4. WEED BY HAND

Far and away the most effective method for keeping out weeds is to pull them up at the root by hand or hoe. (If snapped off above the root they will grow back quickly.) The key is consistency—pull the weeds out when they're still young and never let them get established. If you stay on top of it, weeding won't take more than thirty minutes a week in most gardens. Never let the weeds go to seed, or produce seed.

5. HANDPICK BUGS

If you have Japanese beetles, squash bugs, or cabbage worms, arm your kids or your neighbors' kids with cups of soapy water and tell them to pick off the bugs and drop them in their cups. This may be the least appealing task in an organic food garden, but kids love it.

6. GARLIC BARRIER

A natural insect repellent, Garlic Barrier (garlicbarrier.com) is a preventive measure, so apply it before bugs arrive to deter them. You can also make your own garlic spray at home with a simple recipe that's easily found online. I routinely mix it with Neptune's Harvest (neptunesharvest.com) fertilizer spray and apply it every other week to plant leaves, so that the vegetables and fruits get nourished with a protective scent of garlic that most bugs don't like.

7. BT

The certified organic insecticide *Bacillus thuringiensis* (Bt for short) is derived from a bacterium that is common in soil and benign to humans. It's especially effective at killing caterpillars as well as beetles, flies, and mosquito larvae.

8. SAFER SOAP

The best way to handle aphids is to first remove them from plant leaves with a hard spray of water from the garden hose and then spray them with a layer of Safer Brand Insect-Killing Soap (saferbrand.com) to finish them off. Safer Soap can also tackle mealybugs and whiteflies.

9. SAFERGRO MILDEW CURE

This organic spray (safergro.com) helps prevent "powdery mildew," a common disease that afflicts pumpkins, squash, and melons in particular.

10. SLUGGO

A barrier of Sluggo scattered around a plant or bordering the entire garden is the best way to deter snails and slugs. The granulated pellets made with iron phosphate are pet- and wildlife-friendly (www.montereylawngarden .com/products/organic/#Molluscicides).

TEN EASY-TO-GROW VEGETABLES
FOR THE NOVICE GARDENER

1. ARUGULA AND LETTUCE

Don't wait too long to harvest these greens—they grow fast. If you start from seed, they should be ready just thirty to forty-five days after planting. Young arugula and lettuce are tender and sweet, but they get tougher and ultimately bitter as they grow.

2. BEANS (GREEN, PURPLE, YELLOW, HARICOT VERT, EDAMAME)

Start harvesting beans when they are young and tender. Harvest frequently to ensure that the plant keeps producing more. With edamame, especially, it's very easy to miss the harvesting window; as soon as pods are slightly plump, open them up and taste them.

3. BEETS

After the greens have emerged from the soil and are about one inch tall, thin the plants (pulling out the extra baby plants) so they're a fist's length apart, then mound soil around each plant. (Don't hesitate to eat the thinned-out sprouts—they're delicious!) Harvest roughly sixty days after planting—pull and see if the bulb is roughly one and a half inches in diameter. If you want bigger beets, wait.

4. BROCCOLI

Don't wait too long to harvest—florets will open, get yellowish, and ultimately flower. Harvest time depends on variety, fifty-five to seventy-five days from planting. Judge readiness by the texture of the head, not the size (it's ready when the florets look tight and green). After you've harvested the main head, look for side shoots to harvest throughout the season.

5. CARROTS

Thin your young carrots aggressively: When the tops are about two inches tall, pull out the weakest-looking plants so that you have roughly two inches between those left in the ground. Carrots are sweetest when planted in the summer for fall or early winter harvest.

6. CUCUMBERS

These plants are very prolific. If you plant six to eight seeds, leave only the healthiest, largest one-to-three-inch seedlings in the ground or you will be overwhelmed by too much fruit. Cucumbers are well camouflaged—look closely as they could be hiding from you! They may be harvested young—or you can wait for bigger fruit.

7. GREENS (SWISS CHARD, KALE, AND COLLARD GREENS)

Thin aggressively so that plants are eight to twelve inches apart—you will be rewarded with more growth. Eat the thinned-out greens along the way. Harvest the leaves from the bottom up, starting with the outside of the plant, and keep some leaves in place so that the plants will continue to regenerate.

8. PEAS

Pods are most succulent when they are young and tender. Once they are ripe, harvest frequently. The taste is best if you eat them immediately after harvesting. You can grow three types of peas: sugar snap (eat the whole puffy pod), English or garden type (eat only the peas inside the pod), and snow or Asian (flat, edible pod).

9. POTATOES

When the potato plant is six to eight inches aboveground, mound soil or compost in a hill to cover two-thirds of the plant. When you bury the stem, it grows more potatoes. The best time to harvest the first new spuds is right after the flowers bloom. Once the foliage starts to yellow and die back, the tubers are fully grown. If the weather is not too warm or wet, they will keep in the ground for at least several weeks. Have fun growing blue, red, or gold potatoes and all types of fingerlings.

10. TOMATOES

Tomatoes are tall vining plants that benefit from growing in a cage that offers them support. Be sure to gently train the stems to grow vertically within the cage. Foliar feed tomato plants with a fish emulsion and seaweed liquid fertilizer sprayed on the leaves every other week. If squirrels or chipmunks are munching on your tomatoes, harvest them on the early side of ripe and put them on your windowsill to finish ripening.

TEN FAVORITE GARDENING PRODUCTS

1. HO-MI OR KOREAN HAND PLOW

This sickle-shaped hand plow designed like an ancient Korean gardening tool is great for weeding, digging, mounding, and leveling. It's weighted so that if your soil is heavy or rocky, it slices right through clumps.

2. SELF-WATERING CONTAINERS

If you are planting on a rooftop, terrace, porch, or fire escape, gardeners .com has great self-watering planters, window boxes, and containers. I also like the EarthBox Organic Ready-to-Grow Kit, which you can find at earthbox.com. You can also make your own self-watering container from five-gallon buckets, following DIY instructions online.

3. TRADITIONAL GERMAN VEGETABLE HARVEST BASKET

You can wash and drain vegetables directly in these baskets made of galvanized wire mesh. The wooden handles are comfortable so you can really load them up. You can find them at kinsmangarden.com.

4. BLUNDSTONE BOOTS

These leather Australian slip-on boots are my everyday work shoes—they are incredibly comfortable and durable, and they clean easily. To my eye, they're also great looking. Find them at blundstoneus.com. (On hot summer days, I go for Keen sandals—the closed toe is great for garden work: www.keenfootwear.com/us/en/.)

5. TEXAS TOMATO CAGE

My favorite way to grow tomatoes is in a Texas tomato cage (tomatocages .com) and with tomato trellis clips from johnnyseeds.com. (Gardeners' Supply Company also has lots of great vertical plant supports; go to gardeners.com.)

6. SUNDAY AFTERNOONS HAT

I rarely go into a garden without a wide-brim hat. Sunday Afternoons has a great selection of lightweight, full-coverage hats. (Go to Sundayafternoons.com.)

7. SOLO TWO-LITER PRESSURE SPRAYER

This bottle sprays a fine mist that's great for applying liquid fertilizer to plant leaves, as well as organic solutions that kill insects and prevent disease (www.solousa.com/store/browse/handheld_sprayers.html).

8. RAISED BED KITS

If you don't have the time or skill to build a raised bed from scratch, gardeners.com has great, affordable, easy-to-assemble kits. For the folks who want to splurge, Williams-Sonoma (williams-sonoma.com) also sells high-end raised-bed kits in their Agrarian line.

9. BROADFORK

The five-tine broadfork from Johnny's Selected Seeds (johnnyseeds.com) deeply aerates while preserving soil structure and bringing minimal weed seeds to the surface.

10. IPHONE APPS

I'm no technophile, but I love these apps for the iPhone and iPad: iGarden USA has encyclopedic but accessible information on vegetables, fruits, and herbs, and offers planting and harvesting dates for your particular geographic zone (the planting and tending directions it offers are not exclusively organic, but the app is useful anyway); Herbs+ has excellent information and images on every herb you'd ever want to plant, complete with tips on cooking with herbs and recipes for herbal remedies. The Organic Gardening Planting Planner app by Rodale is a condensed version of my favorite indispensable gardening book with a location-specific planning/weather component. It even includes moon phases for all those biodynamic gardeners out there.

TEN TIPS AND RESOURCES FOR GARDENING WITH KIDS

1. MAKE IT FUN!

Don't make gardening an unpleasant chore. It's just as important for kids to relax and explore in this space as it is for them to master specific skills. The more time children spend enjoying a garden, the more they will absorb its best benefits—learning to slow down, focus, engage their senses, and strengthen their powers of observation.

2. OWNERSHIP

Let kids have an area of the garden where they can decide what they want to grow. Here they should have the freedom to do all the steps. Suggest some fun, interesting crops such as baby gherkin cucumbers or fun-shaped gourds.

3. PARTICIPATION

Kids will follow your lead in the garden. Slow down your own life for an hour or two a week and work with children on all garden tasks: weeding, planting, harvesting. You can guide toddlers and even babies as soon as they can crawl in simple pleasures such as patting the soil and munching on the harvest.

4. COLOR

Grow vegetables of unusual color: rainbow carrots, Easter egg radishes, blue and red potatoes, purple asparagus, tricolor beans. Spend time looking at seed catalogs with color photos to help kids choose what they want to grow; Baker Creek Heirloom Seeds has a fun catalog. (Go to rareseeds .com.)

5. LABELS

Let kids who can write make the plant labels. I like to get the large wooden plant labels at johnnyseeds.com, which have plenty of space for kids to write the name of each plant and decorate.

6. PATHS

Clearly marked paths are crucial when gardening with kids so you don't have to constantly remind them not to step on the plants or compress the soil you've worked so hard to aerate.

7. KIDSGARDENING.ORG

This is a great online resource from the National Gardening Association, with information and tips on family and school gardening. NGA has delivered to date more than four million dollars in funding for youth gardens, and applications for their grants and awards can be found on the website.

8. *How Groundhog's Garden Grew* by Lynne Cherry

Lynne Cherry has written a beautifully illustrated children's book that captures the miracle of plant growth and shows how everything from peas to pumpkins matures from seeds to foods.

9. *A Seed Grows: My First Look at a Plant's Life Cycle* by Pamela Hickman

I used to give a copy of this illustrated picture book with flaps to every client with kids. It contains everything a child needs to know about the life cycles of vegetables and fruits and is great to read to children as young as three or four. It is a favorite of both of my daughters.

10. EDIBLESCHOOLYARD.ORG

The website for Alice Waters's Edible Schoolyard Project is hands down the best online resource for school gardening curricula and ideas.

TEN HEROES TO FOLLOW

1. ALICE WATERS

Chef, writer, and activist Alice Waters has been at the helm of the sustainable foods movement since 1971, when she founded her seasonal, organic restaurant Chez Panisse in Berkeley, California. The Edible Schoolyard Project she created in 1995 at Berkeley's Martin Luther King, Jr., Middle School has since inspired a nationwide trend in school gardening.

2. MICHAEL POLLAN

Perhaps no one has educated more Americans on the problems of our industrialized food system than Michael Pollan, author of the bestselling books *The Omnivore's Dilemma* and *Food Rules*. Pollan has criticized in particular the prevalence of corn-derived ingredients in the American diet that are fueling the obesity epidemic and are grown with heavy petroleum inputs.

3. WES JACKSON

The president of the Land Institute, which he founded in 1976, Wes Jackson sees farming as the root of all problems we face as a civilization. As he sees it, fossil fuel dependency, environmental pollution, overpopulation, and global warming stem from the moment when humans first started tilling the soil. He advocates small-scale "natural-systems agriculture" that nourishes the soil rather than depletes it.

4. MARK BITTMAN

A longtime weekly food columnist for *The New York Times,* Bittman has been on a mission for decades to help Americans understand how to cook and eat healthy, whole foods simply and affordably. Recently he has been exposing the links between meat consumption, obesity, and global warming, and has been advocating vegetarianism.

5. MARION NESTLE

New York University professor Marion Nestle is an indispensable voice working to reform the agricultural policies in the United States that are supporting the industrialized food system and putting small organic farmers at a disadvantage.

6. MICHELLE OBAMA

First Lady Michelle Obama's "Let's Move!" campaign has pushed the food issue into the public consciousness, showing how America's fast-food diet fuels childhood obesity. She planted the first vegetable garden at the White House since Eleanor Roosevelt's victory garden during World War II.

7. WILL ALLEN

At his three-acre Growing Power farm in Milwaukee, Will Allen has demonstrated that urban agriculture can bring not only good food to the inner city but good jobs as well. Allen now employs more than one hundred urban farmers, most of them formerly homeless or incarcerated, and has brought the essential goal of social justice to the food movement.

8. WENDELL BERRY

Farmer, activist, and author Wendell Berry has published more than twenty-five books, none more influential than his 1977 masterpiece *The Unsettling of America: Culture and Agriculture,* which arguably touched off the movement to reform the American food system. His writing is grounded in the notion that your work must be rooted in the land and the place you inhabit.

9. JAMIE OLIVER

The provocateur formerly known as "the Naked Chef," Jamie Oliver has brought an edgy but passionate voice to the sustainable food movement through his hit TV show *Food Revolution,* in which he teaches middle- and low-income Americans, many struggling with obesity, to cook healthy food from scratch.

10. ELIOT COLEMAN

Farmer, author, researcher, and educator Eliot Coleman has helped define and push the limits of organic farming. On his Four Season Farm in Maine, Coleman produces year-round food crops under extreme winter conditions, using highly efficient and minimally heated greenhouse structures.

TEN BOOKS, MAGAZINES, AND WEBSITES TO READ

1. *Silent Spring* by Rachel Carson

An impassioned exposé about the human and ecological impact of pesticides first published in 1962, *Silent Spring* is widely credited with helping to launch the environmental movement. Its publication led to the 1972 ban of the pesticide DDT and the book has since sold millions of copies.

2. *Rodale's Ultimate Encyclopedia of Organic Gardening:*
   The Indispensable Green Resource for Every Gardener

This canonical book taught me how to garden. You'll find it has virtually everything you need to know about growing organically, from apples to zinnias.

3. *The Vegetable Gardener's Bible* by Edward C. Smith

This book has an easy-to-use format for the novice or more experienced gardener, with great photos and simple instructions for soil preparation, composting, organic methods of weed and pest control, and information on specific crops. Smith is also the author of another great book, *The Vegetable Gardener's Container Bible*, on growing vegetables in self-watering containers.

4. *American Grown: The Story of the White House Kitchen Garden and*
   Gardens Across America by Michelle Obama

The First Lady offers a behind-the-scenes peek at how the White House garden was designed and how it has evolved as a part of White House life. Hopeful and inspiring, the book includes stories of garden projects nationwide and their positive impacts on children.

5. *Food Rules: An Eater's Manual* by Michael Pollan

This "eater's manifesto" lays out a set of simple rules for eating wisely, and shows how different cultures through the ages have arrived at the same enduring wisdom about food.

6. *Living Downstream: An Ecologist's Personal Investigation of Cancer*
   and the Environment by Sandra Steingraber

Living Downstream is the closest thing we have to a modern *Silent Spring* by a preeminent ecologist and cancer survivor who investigates the impacts of synthetic fertilizers and pesticides on human health in America. (Go to livingdownstream.com.)

7. *The Elements of Organic Gardening* by HRH The Prince of Wales

A beautiful and inspiring book full of photos from several royal estates, Prince Charles's *Elements of Organic Gardening* demonstrates organic gardening with style. There are many decades of experience and wisdom within these pages.

8. *Organic Gardening* Magazine

Organic Gardening (organicgardening.com) is an accessible monthly magazine that often has great gardening tips, products, essays, recipes, and photos.

9. FOODPOLITICS.COM

This indispensable blog of food activist Marion Nestle meticulously tracks problems and progress in the legislation that governs our food system. It is named after Nestle's excellent book *Food Politics: How the Food Industry Influences Nutrition and Health.*

10. GRIST.ORG

This hip and humorous website of environmental news and opinion tracks the sustainable food movement with writing that's as smart and serious as it is entertaining.

TEN ORGANIZATIONS TO SUPPORT

1. SLOW FOOD USA

This organization has become a nerve center of the international slow-food movement. Now millions strong, the movement celebrates the cultural and biological diversity of homegrown, local food traditions, and advocates policies that will protect them. (Go to slowfoodusa.org.)

2. URBANFARMING.ORG

Founded in 2005, this organization has since spawned more than forty-three thousand urban food gardens all around the world thanks to millions of dollars of funding from Kraft, Coca-Cola, and other companies, and celebrity support from the likes of Prince and Snoop Dogg. (Go to urban farming.org.)

3. ENVIRONMENTAL WORKING GROUP

This Washington, D.C.–based group has campaigned tirelessly to overhaul federal farm policy to support sound public health and environmental goals. The group's website (ewg.org) has an excellent "Eat Smart" section and a Meat Eater's Guide to Climate Change and Health that can help you calculate the carbon footprint of your diet.

4. NATIONAL SUSTAINABLE AGRICULTURE COALITION

NSAC (sustainableagriculture.net) is an alliance of grassroots organizations that's on the front lines of the battle for federal policy reform to support local and organic farms.

5. THE NATURAL RESOURCES DEFENSE COUNCIL

NRDC (nrdc.org) sponsors the Growing Green Awards, which offer annual cash prizes to food producers, business leaders, and food justice leaders.

6. KITCHEN GARDENERS INTERNATIONAL

KGI (kgi.org) is a community of more than twenty thousand people from one hundred countries who are helping low-income communities grow their own vegetables and achieve higher levels of food self-reliance.

7. SCHOOL LUNCH INITIATIVE

Alice Waters protégé Ann Cooper has founded the first comprehensive program in the nation advocating school lunch reform in public schools and promoting student learning in school gardens and nutrition education in classrooms. (Go to schoollunchinitiative.org.)

8. LOCAL HARVEST

Local Harvest (localharvest.org) is the definitive nationwide directory of small farms, farmers markets, and other local food sources.

9. THE KITCHEN COMMUNITY

An ambitious young organization that works to connect kids to real food by creating learning gardens in schools and community organizations across America, the Kitchen Community (thekitchencommunity.org) developed an easy-to-install, affordable, and scalable school garden system.

10. OPENLANDS

One of the most dynamic and effective Chicago-based environmental groups I know of, Openlands (openlands.org) creates greenways, protects open spaces, and funds and facilitates community and school gardens in Illinois.

I'M ALSO INSPIRED by the work of many other Chicago-based groups: Green City Market, the Chicago Botanic Garden, Growing Home, the Gary Comer Youth Center, the Resource Center, Nurture, and Purple Asparagus, to name a few.

TEN WAYS TO BE A PART OF
THE SUSTAINABLE FOOD MOVEMENT

---

1. PLANT

Grow your own garden at home or at an allotment or community garden. If you don't have a front yard, a backyard, or a rooftop, plant in containers on your fire escape or even in window boxes. Virtually everyone, everywhere can grow their own food.

2. COMPOST

Turn your kitchen waste into fertilizer. Some of my favorite plastic-tumbler compost units include the Tumbleweed, the ComposT-Twin, and the Envirocycle. For the apartment dweller, consider a worm bin or tower.

3. COOK

Fresh, ripe homegrown fruits and vegetables can make a master chef of anyone. Alice Waters has said that the perfect dessert is a bowl of ripe peaches. Homegrown food is the tastiest food on earth and makes cooking incredibly simple.

4. CONNECT

Use social media to connect with your community: Create and publicize events on Facebook and "like" sustainable agriculture pages. Use Meetup .com to create and attend events such as local-food potluck dinners, sustainable agriculture book clubs, or outings to farmers markets. Use Twitter to circulate recipes featuring local products; follow the tweets and blogs of activists such as Bill McKibben, Mark Bittman, Jamie Oliver, and Tom Philpott. Create a blog about your garden, your lifestyle, and your recipes.

5. CSA

Community supported agriculture has become a popular way for consumers to buy local, seasonal food directly from a farmer. Through a CSA, a farmer offers a certain number of "shares" of the harvest to the public, and regularly delivers boxes of seasonal fruits and veggies to the homes of its members. Find a CSA in your area through localharvest.org.

6. FARMERS MARKET

Your local farmers market is a great place to meet like-minded people in your community and also connect to local farmers. Don't hesitate to introduce yourself to the farmers, learn from them, and ask if they have organic seedlings you can purchase for your own garden.

7. MEATLESS MONDAY

The quickest way to reduce the carbon footprint of your diet is to eat less red meat and more local vegetables. Give up meat one day a week and challenge yourself to try a new vegetarian recipe instead. (Go to meatless monday.com.)

8. FOOD DESERTS

Volunteer to help create an allotment or community garden in a food desert. Or create a "giving garden" in your local community where you can grow fruits and vegetables that can be donated to a local food pantry.

9. RESTAURANTS

The green-restaurant movement is growing fast. Support local restaurants that feature local and organic foods, and encourage your favorite restaurants to expand their sustainable offerings.

10. GET POLITICAL!

Exhort your senators and representatives to support federal legislation that can reform the American food system—removing subsidies from industrial farms and incentivizing small and midsize farms. Ask your local elected officials to support legislation that helps remediate food deserts and fund school gardens.

NOTES

INTRODUCTION: FAITH IN A SEED

xvi "growing plants without using synthetic": Frances Tenenbaum, *Taylor's Dictionary for Gardeners* (Boston: Houghton Mifflin, 1997), 221.

CHAPTER 2

15 ten pounds of pressure per square inch: Edward C. Smith, *The Vegetable Gardener's Bible: Discover Ed's High-Yield W-O-R-D System for All North American Gardening Regions* (North Adams, Mass.: Storey Publishing, 2000), 6.

17 eighty million pounds of pesticides: Environment and Human Health, Inc., "Risks from Lawn Care Pesticides," http://www.ehhi.org/reports/lcpesticides/summary.shtml#top.

17 forty million acres of lawn grass: Thomas Hayden, "Could the Grass Be Greener?" *U.S. News and World Report,* May 8, 2005.

17 carbaryl, pendimethalin, and malathion: Arthur Grube et al., "Pesticides Industry Sales and Usage: 2006 and 2007 Market Estimates," U.S. Environmental Protection Agency, February 2011, http://www.epa.gov/opp00001/pestsales/. See also "Chemicals Evaluated for Carcinogenic Potential," Office of Pesticide Programs, U.S. Environmental Protection Agency, August 2010.

17 While lawns evolved relatively late: Michael Pollan, *Second Nature: A Gardener's Education* (New York: Grove Press, 1991), 58.

17 80 percent of households: S. R. Templeton, D. Zilberman, and S. J. Yoo, "An Economic Perspective on Pesticide Use," *Environmental Science and Technology,* September 1998, 416A–423A.

17 238 gallons of water per person: Hayden, "Could the Grass Be Greener?"

CHAPTER 3

31 "Rather than love": Henry David Thoreau, *Walden, Civil Disobedience, and Other Writings: Authoritative Texts, Journal, Reviews and Posthumous Assessments, Criticism,* 3rd ed. (New York: W. W. Norton, 2008), 222.

33 "Our life is frittered away": Ibid., 65.

37 wealth of chemicals became widely available: Center for Integrated Pest Management, "Pesticide Usage in the United States: Trends During the 20th Cen-

tury," North Carolina State University, 2003. See also Stephanie Ogburn, "The Dark Side of Nitrogen," Grist.org, February 5, 2010, http://grist.org/article/2009-11-11-the-dark-side-of-nitrogen/.

37 damaged the underlying balance and biodiversity: David Tilman et al., "Agricultural Sustainability and Intensive Production Practices," *Nature* 418 (2002), 671–77.

37 more vulnerable to insects and disease: Hope Shand, *Human Nature: Agricultural Biodiversity and Farm-Based Food Security* (Pittsboro, N.C.: Rural Advancement Foundation International, 1997), 21.

37 more than two hundred new chemicals: Rachel Carson, *Silent Spring* (Boston: Houghton Mifflin, 1962), 7.

37 from 124,259,000 pounds: Ibid., 17.

38 60 percent of all food: U.S. Environmental Protection Agency, "Pesticide Residues in Food," Report on the Environment, http://cfpub.epa.gov/eroe/index.cfm?fuseaction=detail.viewInd&lv=list.listBySubTopic&r=224028&subtop=312&ch=48.

CHAPTER 4

41 Harmony Society: Robert Paul Sutton, *Communal Utopias and the American Experience: Religious Communities* (Westport, Conn.: Praeger, 2003).

42 Brook Farm: Richard Francis, *Transcendental Utopias: Individual and Community at Brook Farm, Fruitlands, and Walden* (Ithaca, N.Y.: Cornell University Press, 2007).

42 Oneida Community: Spencer Klaw, *Without Sin: The Life and Death of the Oneida Community* (New York: Allen Lane, 1993).

CHAPTER 6

78 invented only two generations earlier: Paul Ellickson, "The Evolution of the Supermarket Industry: From A&P to Wal-Mart," Simon School Working Paper Series No. FR 11-17, April 1, 2011.

78 industrial-scale farms began to swallow: James Risser and George Anthan, "Why They Love Earl Butz," *The New York Times,* June 13, 1976.

78 all forms of transportation: Ellickson, "Evolution of the Supermarket Industry."

82 The original Edible Schoolyard: Tamir Elterman, "For Schoolyard Gardens, a Global Network," NYTimes.com, March 26, 2012, http://green.blogs.nytimes.com/2012/03/26/a-global-network-for-schoolyard-gardens/. See also the Edible Schoolyard Project, "Explore the Network," http://edibleschoolyard.org/network.

83 huge quantities of compost: David Zivan, "Somebody Give This Guy a Genius Grant," *Chicago Magazine,* September 2004, http://www.chicagomag.com/Chicago-Magazine/September-2004/Somebody-Give-This-Guy-a-Genius-Grant/.

83 three to five times more productive: Author conversations with Ken Dunn.

83 had been savvy about navigating: Zivan, "Somebody Give This Guy a Genius Grant."

84 no less than twenty-five thousand pounds: Resource Center Chicago, "Resource Center's City Farm," http://www.resourcecenterchicago.org /70thfarm.html.

84   **when people take responsibility:** Growing Home, "History," http://growing
homeinc.org/learn-more/history/.

85   **Growing Power's Milwaukee-area programs:** City of Milwaukee, Wisconsin, Year 2011 Draft Consolidated Annual Performance and Evaluation
Report, https://docs.google.com/viewer?a=v&q=cache:ANHwWmDc1kQJ:
city.milwaukee.gov/ImageLibrary/User/jsteve/2011CAPER-WEBSITE-FEB
22-2012.pdf+milwaukee+%22year+2011+draft%22&hl=en&gl=us&pid=
bl&srcid=ADGEESg4UxwGINT0N8Cxs3OGdYR4ur95_qf_8trsWf91cQX
dk52rt8NS1ZycXffqhTSjhNWytnF1lbMwP5JkThP-AaDPuk94-Eh5IFpgd
N2TRdtd5ac7eLOqzJ1e3azvsFUgQPQdiIJW&sig=AHIEtbTIi9kavjEqy
HBLAfaiHMOL_B9_jA.

CHAPTER 8

100   **as high as 160 degrees:** Fern Marshall Bradley, Barbara W. Ellis, and Ellen
Phillips, eds., *Rodale's Ultimate Encyclopedia of Organic Gardening: The
Indispensable Green Resource for Every Gardener* (New York: Rodale,
2009), 160.

103   **more than eighty thousand of them:** Mount Sinai Hospital Children's Environmental Health Center, "Children and Toxic Chemicals," http://www
.mountsinai.org/patient-care/service-areas/children/areas-of-care/childrens
-environmental-health-center/childrens-disease-and-the-environment/children
-and-toxic-chemicals.

103   *only 2 percent:* Sandra Steingraber, *Living Downstream: An Ecologist's Personal Investigation of Cancer and the Environment* (New York: Da Capo
Press, 2010), 102.

103   **237 chemicals from the environment:** Centers for Disease Control and Prevention, "Fourth National Report on Human Exposure to Environmental
Chemicals," 2012, http://www.cdc.gov/exposurereport/.

103   **1,400 different kinds of pesticides:** U.S. Department of Health and Human
Services and National Institutes of Heath, "Reducing Environmental Cancer
Risk: What We Can Do Now," President's Cancer Panel 2008–2009 Annual
Report, http://www.nih.gov/.

103   **"linked to brain/central nervous system":** Ibid.

104   **roughly forty** *known* **carcinogens:** Ibid.

104   **eighteen new pesticides:** Ibid.

104   **thirteen different insecticides:** Richard Wiles, Kert Davies, Chris Campbell,
"Overexposed: Organophosphate Insecticides in Children's Food," Environmental Working Group, January 1998, http://www.ewg.org/report/overex
posed-organophosphate-insecticides-childrens-food.

104   **The EPA later tightened:** Environmental Working Group, "Prenatal Pesticide
Exposure Linked to Diminished IQ," press release, April 21, 2011, http://
www.ewg.org/release/prenatal-pesticide-exposure-linked-diminished-iq.

104   **All three studies found:** Maryse F. Bouchard et al., "Prenatal Exposure to
Organophosphate Pesticides and IQ in 7-Year-Old Children," *Environmental
Health Perspectives* 119, no. 8 (August 2011): 1189–95; Stephanie M. Engel
et al., "Prenatal Exposure to Organophosphates, Paraoxonase 1, and Cognitive Development in Childhood," *Environmental Health Perspectives* 119 no.
8 (August 2011): 1182–88; Virginia Rauh et al., "Seven-Year Neurodevelopmental Scores and Prenatal Exposure to Chlorpyrifos, a Common Agricul-

tural Pesticide," *Environmental Health Perspectives* 119, no. 8 (August 2011): 1196–1201.

104   increase of 55 to 72 percent: M. F. Bouchard et al., "Attention-Deficit/Hyperactivity Disorder and Urinary Metabolites of Organophosphate Pesticides," *Pediatrics*, June 2010, e1270–e1277.

105   highest measurable levels of pesticide: Environmental Working Group, "Shopper's Guide to Pesticides in Produce," 2012, http://www.ewg.org/foodnews.

105   A 2008 Emory University study: Chensheng Lu et al., "Organic Diets Significantly Lower Children's Dietary Exposure to Organophosphorus Pesticides," *Environmental Health Perspectives* 114, no. 2 (February 2006), 260–63.

105   concentration of eleven essential nutrients: Charles Benbrook et al., "New Evidence Confirms the Nutritional Superiority of Plant-Based Organic Foods," Organic Center, March 2008, http://www.organic-center.org/science.nutri.php?action=view&report_id=126.

105   58.5 percent higher: D. K. Asami et al., "Comparison of the Total Phenolic and Ascorbic Content of Freeze-Dried and Air-Dried Marionberry, Strawberry, and Corn Grown Using Conventional, Organic, and Sustainable Agricultural Practices," *Journal of Agricultural and Food Chemistry* 51, no. 5 (February 2003), 1237–41.

CHAPTER 10

127   study by the University of Illinois at Urbana-Champaign: Frances E. Kuo and Andrea Faber Taylor, "A Potential Natural Treatment for Attention-Deficit/Hyperactivity Disorder," *American Journal of Public Health* 94, no. 9 (September 2004), 1580–86.

128   attention restoration theory: Eric Jaffe, "This Side of Paradise: Discovering Why the Human Mind Needs Nature," *Association for Psychological Science Observer* 23, no. 5 (May/June 2010), http://www.psychologicalscience.org/index.php/publications/observer/2010/may-june-10/this-side-of-paradise.html.

128   "a way to help manage ADHD": University of Illinois, "Children with ADHD Benefit from Time Outdoors Enjoying Nature," press release, August 27, 2004, http://news.illinois.edu/news/04/0827adhd.html.

CHAPTER 11

137   Lead can be found anywhere: Kate Murphy, "For Urban Gardeners, Lead Is a Concern," *The New York Times,* May 13, 2009.

137   a serious human health concern: Ibid.

138   millions of metric tons: U.S. Environmental Protection Agency, "Lead-Safe Yards: Developing and Implementing a Monitoring, Assessment, and Outreach Program for Your Community," January 2001, http://www.epa.gov/region1/leadsafe/pdf/entire_document.pdf.

138   history of waste incineration: Christopher Thale, "Waste Disposal," *The Electronic Encyclopedia of Chicago,* Chicago Historical Society, 2005, http://www.encyclopedia.chicagohistory.org/pages/1322.html.

CHAPTER 12

150   more than one billion pounds: Mark Bittman, "The True Cost of Tomatoes," NYTimes.com, June 14, 2011, http://opinionator.blogs.nytimes.com/2011/06/14/the-true-cost-of-tomatoes/.
150   chemically ripened in warehouses: Ibid.

CHAPTER 13

157   An Inconvenient Truth, directed by Davis Guggenheim and starring Al Gore (2006, Paramount).
158   70 percent more carbon dioxide: Environment News Service, "Study: City Living Helps Limit CO2 Emissions," June 24, 2009, http://www.ens-news wire.com/ens/jun2009/2009-06-24-091.asp.
159   The three critical factors: Christopher L. Weber and H. Scott Matthews, "Food-Miles and the Relative Climate Impacts of Food Choices in the United States," Environmental Science and Technology 42, no. 10 (May 15, 2008), 3508–13.
159   Food alone accounts for about 20 percent: M. M. Kling and I. J. Hough, "The American Carbon Foodprint: Understanding Your Food's Impact on Climate Change," 2010, Brighter Planet, Inc., http://brighterplanet.com/.
159   release around four and a half metric tons: Weber and Matthews, "Food-Miles and the Relative Climate Impacts of Food Choices in the United States."
159   travels 1,500 miles: Rich Pirog, "Checking the Food Odometer: Comparing Food Miles for Local Versus Conventional Produce," Leopold Letter, Leopold Center for Sustainable Agriculture, Iowa State University, July 2003.
159   twenty or more pounds of carbon dioxide: Cars emit roughly twenty pounds of carbon dioxide per gallon of gasoline burned: Daniel Engber, "How Gasoline Becomes CO2," Slate.com, November 1, 2006, http://www.slate.com/articles/news_and_politics/explainer/2006/11/how_gasoline_becomes_co2 .html. The Department of Energy estimates carbon dioxide emissions for diesel trucks to be 22.38 pounds per gallon; for bunker fuel burned by ships, the figure is 26.03 pounds; for jet fuel, the figure is 21.09. John Talberth, "Carbon Footprint Analysis for Kaiser Permanente Food Procurement Alternatives in Northern California," Center for Sustainable Economy, August 2006, http://www.community-wealth.org/content/carbon-footprint-analysis-kaiser -permanente-food-procurement-alternatives-northern.
159   about 85 percent: Weber and Matthews, "Food-Miles and the Relative Climate Impacts of Food Choices in the United States."
159   roughly 6.2 billion pounds: From the International Fertilizer Industry Association, http://www.fertilizer.org: The United States uses 3.13 million tons of nitrogen as ammonia for direction application per year, which equals 6.2 billion pounds.
160   three hundred times the global warming impact: Kari Hammerschlag, Environmental Working Group's Meat Eaters Guide, 2011, http://ewg.org/meateatersguide/eat-smart/.
160   When PepsiCo launched a study: Bryan Walsh, "Tropicana: Trying to Make a Greener Orange Juice," Time.com, March 11, 2010, http://www.time.com/time/magazine/article/0,9171,1978783,00.html. See also Andrew Winston, "Greening Pepsi, from Fertilizer to Bottles," HarvardBusinessReview

.org, May 2010, http://blogs.hbr.org/winston/2010/05/greening-pepsi-from -fertilizer.html.

160 Beef generates 14.8 pounds of carbon dioxide: Elizabeth Weise, "Eating Can Be Energy-Efficient, Too," *USA Today,* April 21, 2009, http://www.usa today.com/news/nation/environment/2009-04-21-carbon-diet_N.htm.

160 1,160 fewer miles: Weber and Matthews, "Food-Miles and the Relative Climate Impacts of Food Choices in the United States."

160 Organic soils capture and store: Paul Hepperly, "Organic Farming Sequesters Atmospheric Carbon and Nutrients in Soils," Rodale Institute, October 15, 2003, http://newfarm.rodaleinstitute.org/depts/NFfield_trials/1003/ carbonwhitepaper.shtml.

160 storing roughly a third: Bradley, Ellis, and Phillips, *Rodale's Ultimate Encyclopedia of Organic Gardening,* 10.

160 thirty-year study of farming practices: Rodale Institute, "The Farming Systems Trial," 2011, http://www.rodaleinstitute.org/fst30years.

160 "puts agriculture into a lead role": Rodale Institute, "Organic Agriculture Yields New Weapon Against Global Warming," press release, 2003, http:// www.strauscom.com/rodale-release/.

160 160 million acres of U.S. farmland: Paul Hepperly, "Organic Farming Sequesters Atmospheric Carbon and Nutrients in Soils."

CHAPTER 14

172 article in *Discover Magazine*: Josie Glausiusz, "Is Dirt the New Prozac: Injections of Soil Bacteria Produce Serotonin—and Happiness—in Mice," *Discover Magazine,* July 2007, http://discovermagazine.com/2007/jul/raw-data -is-dirt-the-new-prozac.

172 "regulation of emotional behavior": Christopher Lowry, "Identification of an Immune-Responsive Mesolimbocortical Serotonergic System: Potential Role in Regulation of Emotional Behavior," *Neuroscience,* May 11, 2007, 756–72.

172 Therapeutic gardening has been practiced: American Horticultural Therapy Association, "The History and Practice of Horticultural Therapy," http:// www.ahta.org/content.cfm?id=history.

172 therapeutic gardening in hospitals: Kim Painter, "Planting the Seeds of Healing: Nature 'Makes You Feel Better,'" *USA Today,* April 16, 2007.

CHAPTER 15

177 "mother of slow food": Tara Parker-Pope, "The Mother of Slow Food," NYTimes.com, March 16, 2009, http://well.blogs.nytimes.com/2009/03/16/ the-mother-of-slow-food/.

177 "single-handedly changed the American palate": Marian Burros, "Alice Waters: Food Revolutionary," *The New York Times,* August 14, 1996.

177 "the one central thing": Alice Waters, "A Delicious Revolution," Center for Ecoliteracy, http://www.ecoliteracy.org/essays/delicious-revolution.

181 "nature deficit disorder": Richard Louv, *Last Child in the Woods* (Chapel Hill, N.C.: Algonquin Books, 2005).

182 rates of depression among adults: Stephen Ilardi, "A Path Out of Depression," *Experience Life Magazine,* May 2011, http://experiencelife.com/ article/a-path-out-of-depression/.

182 16 percent of American adults: Centers for Disease Control and Prevention,

Morbidity and Mortality Weekly Report, "Mental Illness Surveillance Among Adults in the United States," Supplement/vol. 60, September 2, 2011, http://www.cdc.gov/mmwr/preview/mmwrhtml/su6003a1.htm?s_cid=su6003 a1_w.

182   "Human beings," writes Dr. Andrew Weil: Dr. Andrew Weil, "Don't Let Chaos Get You Down: You Aren't Depressed: Our Brains Just Aren't Equipped for Twenty-First-Century Life," *Newsweek*, November 14, 2011, 9.

182   *Environmental Science and Technology* showed: Jo Barton and Jules Pretty, "What Is the Best Dose of Nature and Green Exercise for Improving Mental Health?" *Environmental Science and Technology* 44, no. 10 (March 25, 2010), 3947–55.

182   a sizable majority of Americans: Federal Highway Administration, 2000 Census, http://www.fhwa.dot.gov/planning/census_issues/archives /metropolitan_planning/cps2k.cfm.

183   twenty thousand vacant acres: Author conversations with Ken Dunn.

183   eighteen tons of produce per year: Tracie McMillan, "An Urban Farming Pioneer Sows His Own Legacy," *The New York Times*, May 18, 2010.

183   six thousand pounds of organic food: Urban Homestead, "The Urban Homestead at a Glance," http://urbanhomestead.org/urban-homestead.

183   twenty-eight city lots: Patrick Crouch, "New Agtivist: Edith Floyd Is Making a Detroit Urban Farm, Empty Lot by Empty Lot," Grist.org, December 8, 2011, http://grist.org/urban-agriculture/2011-12-08-new-agtivist-edith-floyd -is-making-an-urban-farm-lot-by-lot/.

183   nearly five thousand acres of land: Michigan State University, "Urban Farms Could Provide a Majority of Produce for Detroiters," press release, November 16, 2010, http://news.msu.edu/story/8600/.

183   Will Allen of Milwaukee's Growing Power: Tom Philpott, "The History of Urban Agriculture Should Inspire Its Future," Grist.org, August 4, 2010, http://grist.org/article/food-the-history-of-urban-agriculture-should-inspire -its-future/full/.

183   using only 6 percent: Eliot Coleman, *The Winter Harvest Handbook: Year-Round Vegetable Production Using Deep Organic Techniques and Unheated Greenhouses* (White River Junction, Vt.: Chelsea Green, 2009), 15.

184   five thousand new food gardens: City of New York Parks and Recreation Department, "Not Just For Kids," http://www.nycgovparks.org/about/ history/community-gardens/not-just-for-kids.

184   five million in 1918: Charles Lathrop Pack, *The War Garden Victorious* (Philadelphia: J.B. Lippincott, 1919), 3. See also "Sidewalk Sprouts," *Sprouts in the Sidewalk,* http://sidewalksprouts.wordpress.com/history/.

184   half a billion pounds: Pack, *War Garden Victorious*, 17.

184   more than *twenty million* gardens: Sam Bass Warner, Jr., *To Dwell Is to Garden: A History of Boston's Community Gardens* (Boston: Northeastern University Press, 1987), 19. See also "Sidewalk Sprouts."

184   70 percent of the world's people: "Vertical Farming: Does It Really Stack Up?" *The Economist*, December 11, 2010, 15–16.

184   production will have to jump: Ibid.

184   The concept of rooftop gardens: Elisabeth Ginsburg, "The History of the Roof Garden," Garden Guides, http://www.gardenguides.com/131046 -history-roof-garden.html.

185   Chicago's Gary Comer Youth Center: Greenroofs.com, "Gary Comer Youth Center," http://www.greenroofs.com/projects/pview.php?id=998.

185   The Brooklyn Grange farm: Brooklyn Grange, "About the Farm," http://www.brooklyngrangefarm.com/aboutthegrange/.

185   *fourteen thousand* acres of rooftop space: Glenn Rifkin, "Cash Crops Under Glass and Upon the Roof," *The New York Times,* May 19, 2011.

185   the heating and cooling needs: Chicago Department of Environment, "A Guide to Rooftop Gardening," http://www.greenroofs.com/Greenroofs101/how-tos.htm#2001.

CHAPTER 17

198   The three teachers who founded Polaris: Polaris Charter Academy, "History," http://www.pcachicago.org/about/history/.

198   six thousand school gardens: Lester Brown, "The Local Food Movement: Farmers Markets, School Gardens and Urban Gardens," Earth Policy Institute and *Mother Earth News,* December 29, 2009. See also Mary MacVean, "Maria Shriver Says Edible Garden Will Be Planted in Capitol Park Flower Bed," *Los Angeles Times,* March 27, 2009.

198   "to attain fully his destiny": Friedrich Froebel, "Man Is a Creative Being!" http://Froebelweb.org.

199   seventy-five thousand school gardens: Erika Christakis, "Michelle Obama's Garden and the Problem with Growing Your Own Food," Time.com, May 30, 2012, http://ideas.time.com/2012/05/30/the-problem-with-growing-your-own-food/.

199   California, Oregon, and Alaska: In 2006, the California Legislature passed Assembly Bill 1535, the California School Instructional Garden Act, which provides $15 million for new and ongoing garden efforts; see Rose Hayden-Smith, "California Says 'No' to Trans Fats," Victory Grower, http://ucanr.org/blogs/blogcore/postdetail.cfm?postnum=532. In March 2009, Alaska passed legislation for a Farm to School program that supports school gardens and farms; see Alaska State House of Representatives, "Sponsor Statement: House Bill 70," http://housemajority.org/spon.php?id=26hb70. The Oregon State Legislature passed House Bill 2800, the Farm to School and School Garden Bill, in June 2011, and it was later signed into law; see Ecotrust, "Farm to School," http://www.ecotrust.org/farmtoschool.

199   Chicago, Boston, and Denver: Boston has more than two hundred active school and community gardens; see Boston Natural Areas Network, "Finding a Community Garden," http://Bostonnatural.org/cgFind.htm. The Denver School Garden Coalition has helped install gardens in dozens of public elementary schools; see Denver Urban Gardens, "Denver School Garden Coalition," http://dug.org/dsgc.

199   former mayor Richard M. Daley: Author's interview with Jaime Zaplatosch, education director for Openlands.

200   scored higher on science tests: C. D. Klemmer, T. M. Waliczek, and J. M. Zajicek, "Growing Minds: The Effect of a School Gardening Program on the Science Achievement of Elementary Students," *HortTechnology Journal* 15, no. 3 (July–September 2005), 448–52.

200   their fruit and vegetable consumption: Jessica McAleese and Linda L. Rankin, "Garden-Based Nutrition Education Affects Fruit and Vegetable Consumption in Sixth-Grade Adolescents," *Journal of American Dietetic Association* 107, no. 4 (April 2007), 662–65.

CHAPTER 18

207 **biggest purchasers of locally grown:** "Walmart Switches to Local Fruits, Veggies," Associated Press, April 17, 2009. See also Corby Kummer, "The Great Grocery Smackdown," *The Atlantic*, March 2010, http://www.theatlantic.com/magazine/archive/2010/03/the-great-grocery-smackdown/307904/.

207 **sourcing one billion dollars' worth:** Stephanie Clifford, "Wal-Mart to Buy More Local Produce," *The New York Times*, October 14, 2010.

207 **biggest organic foods distributor:** Scarboro Research, "Wal-Mart Supercenter and Costco Are the Top Grocery Stores Among Organics Consumers," press release, October 10, 2007, http://www.scarborough.com/press-release.php?press_id=Organic-Food-Consumers&q_string=start_set=55&s_string=/press-results.php. See also Tom Philpott, "Is Walmart Really Going Organic and Local?" *Mother Jones*, March/April 2012, http://www.motherjones.com/environment/2012/03/walmart-groceries-organic-local-food-deserts.

CHAPTER 19

213 **40,000 in the 2007 season:** Green City Market, "Mission and Background," http://www.greencitymarket.org/about/.

215 **Chicagoans living in food deserts:** Barbara Abrajano et al., "Food Deserts in Chicago," Illinois Advisory Committee to the U.S. Commission on Civil Rights, October 2011, http://www.usccr.gov/pubs/IL-FoodDeserts-2011.pdf.

215 **no less than fifty-five square miles:** Mari Gallagher Research and Consulting Group, "The Chicago Food Desert Progress Report," June 2011, http://www.marigallagher.com/site_media/dynamic/project_files/FoodDesert2011.pdf.

215 **nearly four hundred thousand residents:** Ibid.

215 **One fast-food cheeseburger:** Michael Bloch, "Carbon Emissions and Our Food," Green Living Tips, September 10, 2009, http://www.greenlivingtips.com/articles/The-carbon-footprint-of-food-.html.

215 **16 percent of the total energy:** David Pimentel et al., "Reducing Energy Inputs in the U.S. Food System," *Human Ecology* 36, no. 4 (August 2008), 459–71.

CHAPTER 20

221 **Roughly seven million more households:** Bruce Butterfield, "The Impact of Home and Community Gardening in America," National Gardening Association, 2009, http://www.garden.org/articles/articles.php?q=show&id=3126.

221 **The National Gardening Association estimates:** Ibid.

222 **government-designated food deserts:** LaSalle Bank and Mari Gallagher Research and Consulting Group, "Examining the Impact of Food Deserts on Public Health in Chicago," 2006, http://www.marigallagher.com/projects/4/. See also Alisha Coleman-Jensen, "Household Food Security in the United States," U.S. Department of Agriculture, September 2011, http://www.ers.usda.gov/publications/err-economic-research-report/err125.aspx.

223 **diabetes and obesity rates:** Monifa Thomas, "Taking Diabetes Fight to the Streets," *Chicago Sun-Times*, April 27, 2010. See also Puerto Rican Cultural Center and Sinai Urban Health Institute, "The Community Survey in Humboldt Park: Preventing Obesity and Improving Our Health," April 2006, http://www.ghpcommunityofwellness.org/uploads/communityofwellness/documents/obesity_study_hp.pdf.

223   **$2.18 per meal:** Dr. Julie Hwang, "Spatial Representation of Humboldt Park Community and Nutritional Assets," DePaul University and Puerto Rican Cultural Center, November 16, 2010, http://prcc-chgo.org/.

227   **Will Allen's Milwaukee-based organization:** Christine Grillo, "The Will Allen Index: Growing Power to the People," Center for a Livable Future, March 9, 2012, http://www.livablefutureblog.com/2012/03/the-will-allen-index.

227   **Urban Farming (urbanfarming.org):** Michael Sigman, "Urban Farming's Detroit Roots Blossom into Global Vision," HuffingtonPost.com, July 25, 2011, http://www.huffingtonpost.com/michael-sigman/urban-farmings-detroit-ro_ b_907670.html.

228   **The Oakland, California–based organization Urban Releaf:** "From Concrete Jungle to Urban Oasis," *NBC Nightly News,* April 15, 2012, http://video .msnbc.msn.com/nightly-news/47181533#47181533.

CHAPTER 21

229   **forty pounds per square foot:** Chicago Department of Environment, "Guide to Rooftop Gardening."

232   **"a philosophy of working with":** Bill Mollison, *Permaculture: A Designers' Manual* (Tyalgum, Australia: Tagari, 1988), 2.

233   **"The care of the earth":** Wendell Berry, *The Art of the Commonplace: The Agrarian Essays of Wendell Berry* (Berkeley, Calif.: Counterpoint, 2002), 46.

CHAPTER 22

235   **students who want to " 'do school' ":** Integrated Global Studies School, "Frequently Asked Questions," http://org.newtrier.k12.il.us/academics/igss/faq .htm.

AFTERWORD

248   **50 percent increase in food production:** Sarah Zielinski, "How Google Earth Revealed Chicago's Hidden Farms," NPR's *The Salt,* January 9, 2013, http:// www.npr.org/blogs/thesalt/2013/01/08/168895084/finding-chicago-s-hidden -farms.

APPENDIX

253   **sickened hundreds of Americans:** Elizabeth Weise and Julie Schmit, "Spinach Recall: 5 Faces. 5 Agonizing Deaths. 1 Year Later," *USA Today,* September 24, 2007.

254   **four hundred gallons of oil:** David Pimentel and Mario Giampietro, "Food, Land, Population, and the U.S. Economy," Cornell University and Istituto di Nazionale della Nutrizione, Carrying Capacity Network, November 21, 1994, http://www.farmlandinfo.org/index.cfm?function=article_view&article ID=37350.

254   **National Gardening Association study:** Butterfield, "Impact of Home and Community Gardening in America."

ABOUT THE AUTHOR

JEANNE NOLAN has been growing food organically for over twenty years. She is a well-known educator and consultant and is the founder of the Organic Gardener Ltd., which works with families to develop gardens that are beautiful, productive, and uniquely suited to their homes and lifestyles. She also works extensively with schools, restaurants, not-for-profit organizations, and other institutions. In partnership with Green City Market, she designed, installed, and maintains the Edible Gardens, a five-thousand-square-foot vegetable garden for children in Chicago's Lincoln Park Zoo. She has been featured in *Food & Wine, Woman's Day, Shape, Chicago Tribune, Parade,* and other national publications. She lives with her husband and two daughters in Glencoe, Illinois.